M A MESSENGER'S EMOIRS

A MESSENGER'S MEMOIRS

Sixty-One SOUTHERN BAPTIST CONVENTION Meetings

Robert E. Naylor

Foreword by Duke K. McCall

PROVIDENCE HOUSE PUBLISHERS
Franklin, Tennessee

Printed in the United States of America

99 98 97 96 95   6 5 4 3 2 1

Library of Congress Catalog Card Number: 95-69284

ISBN 1-8881576-46-9
ISBN 1-881576-48-5 (deluxe)

Front cover: The Southern Baptist Convention, One Hundred Ninth Session, One Hundred Twenty-First Year, Detroit, Michigan, May 24-27, 1966. Photo by Carl H. Jones. Courtesy—Southern Baptist Historical Library and Archives.

Published by
PROVIDENCE HOUSE PUBLISHERS
P.O. Box 158 • 238 Seaboard Lane
Franklin, Tennessee 37064
800-321-5692

To Goldia

My love and life, who missed only one of these sixty-one Conventions, and who taught me that Convention is a family affair.

Contents

Foreword

THE MAN IS THE MESSAGE. ROBERT NAYLOR DOES NOT CRITIQUE THE PAST SIXTY-ONE SOUTHERN BAPTIST CONVENTION MEETINGS. HE RESONATES TO WHAT HE saw and heard. The result is focused biography that begins relaxed, but winds the reader tighter and tighter into the changing Southern Baptist Convention.

Exposing the thoughts and values of this Southern Baptist statesman suggests how this branch of Baptists became the largest Evangelical denomination in the land. A participant with a passion comes to life—not a political leader with a program. He cares about everything Baptist churches are doing through their united efforts. Nothing is unimportant. Central, however, is world outreach in the name of Christ and the training of God-called ministers, especially at Southwestern Baptist Theological Seminary.

Bob Naylor could run with horses and win. Disciplined and logical, he was faster than a calculator. Literally, he could cover a page with penciled numbers and get the answer to a complicated math problem before other seminary presidents could finish the job with calculators. Stubborn, he never modified his principles or changed his position. That is different from negotiating the settlement of a conflict.

There was a reason. Naylor operated on what he believed the Bible taught. Even so, everyone has the right to be wrong; so each must be heard. That sounds arrogant, but it is softened by diligence in listening to the opinions expressed to the contrary and willingness to accept the fresh insights provided.

Careful with his words, he spoke precisely on any subject. The nuanced distinctions he made required careful listening. His opinions were worth the attention because they were rooted in a knowledge of the history of Baptists and kept the long future in focus. He would trade present advantage for future progress.

9

Reading this volume, one is made aware that Bob Naylor was never timid in exercising responsibility nor eager to grasp power. Early as a minister he moved among denominational leaders as one of them. They were friends whom he knew well, honored, and respected. This book does not have a snide remark about any of them; yet, he knew their human side all too well. No wonder that they trusted him! He was a statesman who is now an Elder Statesman.

His memories of past Conventions are measured against the biblical principles that controlled his life. As changes in the way things are done in the Southern Baptist Convention take place, they are highlighted over against these principles. Thus, movement within the Convention which was so gradual that it went unnoticed by those present becomes visible in these *Memoirs*.

An even more important lesson highlighted is how good intentions of good leaders designed to ride a squall set in motion destructive waves that grow larger with the years. Without any deliberate intention to diagnose the current ills of the Southern Baptist Convention, these *Memoirs* note from time to time innovations that have altered the very character of Baptist connectional life. Now "not all our piety nor wit can cancel half a line of it." (I apologize to the author for the changes to make the quotation fit here.)

Naylor is consistently angry with the messengers to conventions who vote in the presidential election and then disappear. To him the Convention is called to carry out the will of God. Each individual has the divine gift of participation in what God is doing. There is nothing so small as to be beneath our concern.

A Messenger's Memoirs reminds us that as Christians we must continue to give voice and vote to the truth as God has revealed it to us. Sixty-one Conventions is a long time, but God called us for life.

—Duke K. McCall
President (1951-1982) and Chancellor (1982-1992)
The Southern Baptist Theological Seminary, Louisville, Kentucky

Preface

FROM THE TIME THAT I BECAME PASTOR OF A SOUTHERN BAPTIST CHURCH, I KNEW THAT THE ANNUAL MEETING OF THE SOUTHERN BAPTIST CONVENTION HELD UNUSUAL significance. Of course, I had opportunity to learn that in the home in which I grew up. My mother and father attended Southern Baptist Convention meetings. They had farmed out the children to faithful members, and I somehow understood that this was very special.

As a matter of historical fact, "Convention" means more to Southern Baptists than to most Christians in America. The word was first used to describe a denomination in 1845 when the Southern Baptist Convention was organized in Augusta, Georgia. The title was discussed and was meant to describe the unusual genius of this new Baptist organization. Most of those in attendance were there with sacrifice. While the meeting did reflect tension between North and South, there was also an underlying urgency about preaching the gospel in all the world. And that became the wellspring of the Convention.

The meeting in actual session is important for several reasons. First of all, it is the best fellowship in the world. More importantly, the meeting represents the authority of the Convention. We make much of our autonomy, but the Southern Baptist Convention is in charge of the Southern Baptist enterprise.

Enough of that, all of these things that follow are suddenly the reflection of a lifetime. God has given me such health that I have not missed a Southern Baptist Convention meeting since 1933. I think that such participation is important, both to the Convention and to the preacher.

It is my hope that something said will encourage one of you to say, "I must go to the Convention," and suddenly realize that you have chosen one of the ministry's great joys.

PART ONE

Municipal Auditorium • Memphis, Tennessee

Robert Naylor (signature)

MAY 9-12
1929

THIS CONVENTION VOLUME WAS MEANT TO BEGIN WITH 1933, IN THAT I HAVE NOT MISSED A SINGLE SOUTHERN Baptist Convention meeting since. Yet, my first Southern Baptist Convention was this one in Memphis. This was my first year at Southwestern Baptist Theological Seminary. Much to my surprise, at the close of the year, Dr. T. B. Maston of the faculty told me that he was driving to the Convention, and invited me and two others to accompany him. I was flattered that my professor would give me such a wonderful opportunity.

The trip itself was a delight. Among those present was Irving Prince, my personal friend and one of the older students at the seminary. He was pastor of a fine church and very particular in everything that he did. I loved him as a friend. We spent that first night at Bastrop, Louisiana. There were not many motels in those days, so we chose a tourist's home. Prince insisted on turning down the sheets just to be sure the room was as clean as he thought that it ought to be. On the return trip we drove onto the campus of Ouachita University. Little did I realize that in a not too distant future, I would be pastor in Arkadelphia.

As to the Convention itself, it was pure inspiration. Dr. George W. Truett was the president of the Convention, and his president's address was worth the trip.

The minutes of the meeting report 2,678 messengers attending. Dr. Truett was reelected without opposition. Four vice-presidents were elected by acclamation. Six messengers from Arizona were recognized, an early year for messengers from that state.

In my notes I recorded that my good friend E. E. Lee, whom we called "Hotdog Lee," was critically ill. He was greatly beloved in the Convention.

The mission boards made presentations. Notable in Baptist history was an address by John A. Broadus on "Baptists." The Relief and Annuity Board presented recommendations that were one after the other rejected.

The Second Annual Report of the Executive Committee included a report on a special crisis at the Home Mission Board, noting "the disappearance of its Treasurer" and the embezzlement by C. S. Carnes. Three million dollars in traveler's checks were found on Carnes' person when he was eventually arrested. That was a sad day for us. A special offering was authorized by the Promotion Commission of the Southern Baptist Convention for Sunday, November 11, 1928.

I noticed that the minutes record that there were eleven lynchings in the United States that year. For many years following, this was one of the regular reports at the Convention.

The Convention closed on Sunday afternoon. I had been pastor of Oak Avenue Baptist Church in Ada, Oklahoma, for less than two months, and the 1929 Convention changed my life and helped to fix directions for my immediate and long-range future.

Washington Auditorium • Washington, D. C.

MAY 19-22

1933

IT SEEMED AS NATURAL AS ANY ACT OF MINISTRY TO BE GETTING READY TO GO TO THE SOUTHERN BAPTIST Convention in the spring of 1933. Like other acts of ministry, there were no real thoughts of the ultimate dimensions of our attendance at the Convention. After all, I had been reared in a preacher's home where Mother and Dad thought it important to attend the Conventions. Sixty-one conventions later, I realize that you can write the biography of a Southern Baptist preacher in terms of his relationship to the Southern Baptist Convention.

True, the country was in a terrible financial depression. Every bank in the country had been closed in March. As the pastor of the First Baptist Church in a county seat town, Nashville, Arkansas, there was not really much salary. There was a new car, however, and a new son, for that matter—who was ten months old—as we prepared to go to Washington, D. C. It would be our first trip to the nation's capital.

A neighboring pastor, J. F. Queen, pastor at Dequeen, Arkansas, indicated that he would like to go along. He was an older pastor who had been a wonderful friend that first year in Arkansas. We were delighted.

On Sunday afternoon, May 14, he came over from Dequeen. I preached at our evening service, and we left immediately after church for the Convention. We drove all night and all the next day to Beckley, West Virginia, where my wife Goldia's sister lived. It was some trip. Much of the road in those days was gravel. I remember just outside Nashville, Tennessee, I had been pushing the car along when we ran into a terrible rainstorm. It must have lasted thirty minutes; and I am sure, in retrospect, that it was a harrowing experience. As we emerged from the storm, my friend said, "That was a terrible

17

storm. I noticed you slowed down to fifty miles an hour." For a generation, we would recall that particular moment.

At Beckley, we left our ten-month-old son, and drove on the next day to Washington. Rooms had been found for the messengers, and we stayed in a two-story boarding house. It was a beautiful brick home. Actually, the Convention began on Friday morning at 9:30, as Dr. M. E. Dodd of Shreveport, Louisiana, called the Convention to order. As vice-president of the Convention, he was presiding in the absence of Dr. F. F. Brown of Knoxville, Tennessee, who was ill. The Convention acted on a motion authorizing a message of sympathy to Dr. Brown.

The Convention was meeting in Washington in order to have fellowship with the Northern Baptist Convention, meeting the next week in Washington.

Nothing impressed me more than the noon period of worship that had been scheduled. Promptly at twelve o'clock, the doors to the Convention hall were closed. No one was admitted, and the Convention entered into an hour of worship in which Dr. George W. Truett was to preach. Heaven alone will reveal the moving experience that was mine. On Friday at noon, the record says, "We sang 'Rock of Ages,' and Dr. Truett preached on the text 'Thy Will Be Done in Earth as in Heaven.'"

On Saturday at the same hour, we sang "What a Friend We Have in Jesus." Then Dr. Truett spoke on "Intercessory Prayer." On Monday the theme of the message was "Fear Not, I Am He That Liveth." No convention would have a more serious world in which to meet, but the hour of worship seemed to lift us above the storm.

By order of the Convention, a committee consisting of one from each cooperating state of the Convention was appointed to bear to the White House the greetings of the Convention. Among those appointed was H. L. Winburn of Arkansas, whom I was to follow in a pastorate; Dr. John R. Sampey of Kentucky, who had preached the commencement sermon that year previously, when I graduated from the seminary; and J. W. Storer of Oklahoma, whom I had known slightly and who was to be a lifetime friend. Later, the Convention was to instruct this committee to protest strongly to the new President (Franklin D. Roosevelt) his encouragement of the repeal of Prohibition.

This was to be the Debt Convention. The cloud of debt was simply paralyzing. Even in that first year of ministry, there had been three debt-raising special offerings to which our church had responded. The report of the Program Committee underlines this fact. During the

Dr. Naylor at work in
presidential office of
Southwestern Baptist
Theological Seminary, with
Dr. Robert A. Baker in fore-
ground and a portrait of Dr.
George W. Truett in back-
ground. Courtesy—
Southern Baptist Historical
Library and Archives.

year, a "Special Emergency Mission Relief Campaign" had been conducted. The goal of the offering was $300,000. It was announced that
$203,908.51 had been raised. The report said, "It saved the day for
Home Missions and Foreign Missions." There had also been
employed an organization, "Crucible Service," to conduct a campaign. They reported raising $16,297.73, of which twenty percent was
to go to the organization for expenses. The Convention authorized an
annual debt-paying offering on January 15 through March 1 of each
year. The receipts were to be divided fifty-fifty between state and
south-wide indebtedness. I sat there thankful that there had not been
a single instance where I had hesitated to lead churches to reach out
to the extra need, even though they also were struggling to stay alive
financially.

The "Debt Paying Campaign" was made a special order of business
Saturday night at 9:30 P.M. J. E. Dillard presented the recommendations
of the Executive Committee as to the indebtedness of the agencies. The

details of the Baptist Hundred Thousand Dollar Club were presented by Frank Tripp. The names of many brethren were called who discussed the proposal. The name was due to the appeal to find one hundred thousand Southern Baptists who would give as much as one dollar a month over and above their tithe to retire the indebtedness that was choking our denomination. Finally, the program was adopted, and the beginning structure set in place. Immediately, we committed ourselves personally to that program. From then until its conclusion, "Debt Free in '43," we were members of the Baptist Hundred Thousand Dollar Club. It seemed so little, but it actually represented one percent of our monthly income.

There was great emphasis on the "Every Member Canvas," which was new terminology and a new promotion. B. L. Bridges of Arkansas reported for his state, "If it had not been for the "Every Member Canvas," I do not know that we could have gone on this year."

The Committee on Time, Place, and Preacher recommended that the Convention meet in Fort Worth in 1934, at a time that became May 16, 1934. T. L. Holcomb was to be the preacher.

The Virginia Baptist General Association presented a memorial to the Convention urging elimination and consolidation of agencies and structure. The Executive Committee reported to the Convention this response:

> We feel it would be unwise to disturb the minds of Southern Baptists by upsetting in any way the machinery of our denominational agencies. No agencies or boards will be consolidated or eliminated at this time. It would be unwise to undertake to combvine our Foreign and Home Mission Boards.

The Convention sermon was preached on Sunday afternoon by J. L. White of Florida. I was impressed, even then, by the fact that his two preacher sons assisted in the service.

The Committee on Social Service made a major report. They reported that the number of lynchings during the year was only eight. A great deal of attention was given in the report to the awful crime of the repeal of Prohibition. The world has heard very little of the other side of the Prohibition story and the good that it introduced. The Congress, by more than a two-thirds vote, had passed a constitutional amendment to be given to the states for ratification to repeal the Eighteenth Amendment. Every pastor there knew that the battle lines were drawn. Our struggle in Arkansas could make another complete account.

Finally, a committee of five from the Southern Baptist Convention was appointed to meet with a committee from the Northern Baptist Convention to study ways the two conventions could cooperate.

A footnote to the report of this first Convention would be that this was to be the low point of the Cooperative Program; the year just completed my first year in the pastorate after the seminary. Total receipts through the Cooperative Program amounted to $1,198,679.96. In the report of the Executive Committee, the Southern Baptist Foundation was established.

Arkansas had thirty-three messengers officially listed at the Convention. The total reported at the opening session was 1,850 messengers.

My preacher father had said, "Always go to the meetings. God has something for you there." The first Convention made it a lifelong truism. That a preacher brother accompanied us only underlined the fact that the Convention spoke to New Testament fellowship.

The Coliseum • Fort Worth, Texas

Robert Naylor

MAY 16-20
1934

THIS WAS TO BE SUCH A PERSONAL CONVENTION BECAUSE WE WERE GOING BACK TO FORT WORTH. WE HAD not been to the seminary since graduation two years before. Our love for the institution that had so greatly enriched us added much to our anticipation. We had met at the seminary, fallen in love, married, and shared the deepest appreciation for Southwestern.

It seemed that we had been getting ready to go to the Convention all spring. Our second son arrived on January 18. The Arkansas State Baptist Convention, which had historically met in the fall, had been moved to January. Since we were awaiting this arrival day-by-day, I missed the Convention, the only state convention missed in these years. Instead of going to El Dorado, I went some three weeks later to a Bible conference at the First Baptist Church in Shreveport which was personally hosted by Dr. M. E. Dodd. This was to have bearing on the Fort Worth Southern Baptist Convention, because he was the president.

We had also made our annual pilgrimage to Virginia in late March, since the Convention was meeting in another direction. Mother was to keep the children for us. Most preachers' families owe a debt of gratitude to someone for keeping children in order that we might attend denominational meetings. To leave them with Goldia's mother was something else again. She loved those children, and they loved her. It was as though they had moved into a better dimension when we left town to go to the meeting.

The Convention convened in the Old Northside Coliseum on Wednesday morning at 9:00 with the theme, "O Lord, revive thy work in the midst of the years." Even now, the coliseum is an historical reminder that we are a city of the West. Dr. Dodd was presiding and was using the historic gavel brought by Dr. John A. Broadus from the banks of the Jordan. It was announced that 2,277 messengers had enrolled at the time of the opening of the Convention. This was almost five hundred more than the previous Convention in Washington. Our Arkansas had almost two hundred enrolled at the opening compared to thirty the year before.

The pastor of my home church, Dr. C. C. Morris, whose ministry had been so formative in my college years, led in prayer.

Then followed the important reading of messages from various conventions and people around the world. There were fraternal greetings from the Northern Baptist Convention and its president; from the Columbia Association of Baptist Churches in Washington, D. C.; from the President of the United States; and others as the Convention proceeded. It still seems important that Southern Baptists remember that we are a part of a total world and in fellowship with people who serve our Lord.

It is here that I want to remember very personal, lifetime memories from the Convention. They centered in the fact of fellowship. First, there were those of my own past and circle of friends. I remember a particular pastor, my seminary classmate, whom we saw with his bride we had not yet met. An hour spent together was to seal a friendship that was to cover much of a lifetime. I also had discovered a new circle of friends. My pastorate was in the midst of churches pastored by men from the other seminary. In our meetings together, in good spirit, we used to debate the merits of the two institutions. At this Convention, I found myself introduced by them to a new circle of friends that became very much a part of my life. When I think of the Fort Worth Convention, therefore, I remember some moments sitting down together with others to be blessed by their friendship and to be enriched by an understanding of their ministries.

I suggest now that the seminary was very much a part of the Convention. Dr. L. R. Scarborough chaired the committee on local arrangements. In every movement of the Convention, as it struggled to lift itself out of debt, his name always appeared. His report to the Convention will get a special note in this document. He was to be elected the first vice-president of the Convention, and his prayer was to conclude its sessions. A visit to "the hill" was to remember, "I will lift mine eyes unto the hills from whence cometh my help."

When the time came for the election of officers, there was not a single case of contest. The president, vice-presidents, and secretary were all elected unopposed. A bylaw of the Convention required that all votes must be by ballot. The motion that became familiar to me was "I make a motion that the bylaw of the Convention be suspended and that someone be instructed to cast the unanimous ballot of the Convention to the election of this man." It seemed perfectly normal to me, the young preacher, that we should be of one mind. This may have been the only Convention where there was no contest anywhere. If so, it could stand as a shining example for us in a new day and a new fellowship.

The financial problems seemed to have deepened with the year. The Hundred Thousand Dollar Club had gotten off to a good beginning as reflected in the report of Frank Tripp. The organization had been structured in every state. I noticed that Southwestern Seminary received just in excess of $12,000 from the Hundred Thousand Dollar Club that year. The stipulation was that every dollar was to go to the payment of principal of debt. In some of our institutions, it was a life-and-death matter.

In the case of our seminary, the report by Dr. George W. Truett used the phrase, "the most difficult times of our history." He followed this with a report of the financial affairs and needs, and it was concluded with "A Statement and a Request." This reflected the drop in individual donations that had been a source of life and strength. It made a plea for a change in the percentages by the Southern Baptist Convention in the distribution of the Cooperative Program funds. It reflected the salary crisis at the seminary in which salaries had been cut in half, and then paid in amounts of thirty and forty percent only. It was a plea for help from the Convention.

The report of the Social Service Commission of the Southern Baptist Convention was given large attention. Even then it was growing in its organization and its emphasis. There were the paragraphs about lynchings in the United States. There were twenty-eight during 1933, compared to eight the year previously. I have no memory of being particularly shocked at these statistics. I guess I thought many of them were well-deserved. The annual report of violence seemed to be an accepted part of the scene. There was a call to observe the Sabbath, the Christian Sabbath, to rally our forces against the liquor traffic, and a statement on the repeal of the Eighteenth Amendment. Then until now, there was to be an upward curve of deaths directly attributable to this enemy.

Early on in the Convention, Dr. Truett had been requested to deliver his Spurgeon Centenary Address which he had delivered in

Great Britain on the one hundreth anniversary of the birth of Charles Spurgeon. This was made a special order of business. In the light of this request, Dr. R. G. Lee, was asked to deliver the closing address on Sunday afternoon. What magnificent preaching that was an encouragement to everyone of us so called.

On reflection, there was another significant, emergent fact. From my own state of Arkansas, it was apparent that certain brethren were in the ascendancy. In a kind way, they "ran" our Convention affairs. They were on the committees, on the boards, and in leadership. I remember no resentment at that fact. I came to know them early and was blessed by their leadership. Our present struggles for place seem oddly out of place.

The music deserves a place. I noted that the young preacher from Arkansas, Dr. Perry Webb, had been asked to preach on spiritual revival. It was said that at his request, the Golden Girls Quartet from Simmons University sang "How Tedious and Tasteless the Hours" and "Jesus, Lover of My Soul."

This second Convention simply deepened the impact on our lives of the gathering of the fellowship. It never was a chore for me to follow my preacher father's advice, "Always go to the meetings." Dad was a messenger at this Fort Worth Convention. For us both to appear on the list of messengers is a lingering touch of grace.

Ellis Auditorium • Memphis, Tennessee

Robert Naylor

MAY 15-18
1935

MEMPHIS WAS MUCH MORE THAN AN
AVERAGE CONVENTION CITY TO ME.
HERE, FOR THE FIRST TIME, I HAD SEEN
the "Father of Waters" in 1926. All of my years I have known that I
was west of the River and vaguely understood that there must be
something east of the River. Set in the middle of the Southern Baptist
Convention that year, it was indeed fitting that we should meet there.

There were two personal considerations for us. I had attended
my first Southern Baptist Convention there in 1929. At the time, I
was a student at Southwestern Baptist Theological Seminary, toward
the end of my first year. Just a month previous to the Convention, I
had been called to my first pastorate, the Oak Avenue Baptist Church
in Ada, Oklahoma, and had been ordained. None of this would have
made it likely that I would attend the Convention. Dr. T. B. Maston,
professor at the seminary, had invited me to go with him to the
Convention. There were two other students that he invited, and the
memorable journey and sessions are recorded in my 1929 account.
Memphis would remain different.

In our family, the year 1934 through 1935 after the Fort Worth
Convention could have been called the "Memphis year." Just two
weeks after returning from the Convention in Fort Worth, Goldia
was involved in a car accident and broke her leg. From that time
until the meeting in Memphis, she had not been able to stand unsup-
ported. In November we had at last gone to a world-famous surgeon
in Memphis, whose extensive surgery made her able to walk again.
Each month we had returned for a checkup. When we arrived at the
Convention in Memphis, we stayed at the old Hotel Tennessee. There
on the first evening, for the first time in a year, she stood up without

26

crutches, brace, or special shoes, on the new leg that God had given her. The emotion of it was so intense that the 1935 Convention will remain ever personal.

As always, the Convention is larger than these personal considerations. On Wednesday afternoon, May 15, the Convention opened with Dr. M. E. Dodd presiding. We sang "All Hail the Power of Jesus' Name." The Southwestern Seminary Girls' Quartet sang "He Died of a Broken Heart." The tone of the Convention was set.

At the close of the Wednesday evening session, a reception was held on the platform of the auditorium. The messengers had an opportunity to greet the officers of the Convention and the special guests, and enjoy a period of fellowship. This was unique to this Convention.

Six men were nominated for the office of president including L. R. Scarborough, Pat M. Neff, F. F. Brown, Ellis A. Fuller, and John R. Sampey. Scarborough, Neff, Brown, and Fuller having withdrawn, Sampey was elected president. Frank Tripp and J. R. Hobbs were elected vice-presidents.

Already the Executive Committee had achieved formidable stature. Their report came early in the Convention. They showed receipts through the Cooperative Program having gained over the previous year. In 1933 the receipts were $880,488.62. In 1934 they were $1,135,870.04. In the division of denominational funds, as approved by the states, it was noteworthy that Kentucky, Mississippi, and Maryland were all on a fifty-fifty basis.

The report of the One Hundred Thousand Club, of ever-increasing interest to us, was brought by the Executive Committee. The expenses had been paid by the Sunday School Board, and for that year amounted to $11,000. They had received $180,074.36, all applied directly to debt. There was a lengthy proposal from the state secretaries that the One Hundred Thousand Club program be enlarged and that the states share in its distribution. It does seem that we cannot stand prosperity. Everybody wants in on that which offers hope.

Southwestern Seminary said, "We have had a very successful year in the great matters of teaching, cooperating, missionary passion, and soul-winning." For those of us who love the seminary, the words and their order were significant.

By heritage, by training, and by pastoral practice, the Foreign Mission Board report was always primary. The best part of the program was the presentation of missionaries present. They came to the microphone and called their names and the names of their fields. Sometimes it would be husband, wife, and children. It was an emotion difficult to contain.

In this Convention, George W. Truett delivered addresses on the Baptist World Alliance and the outlook of the Baptist Sunday School Board.

The report of the Social Service Commission occupied many pages. There were regular references to lynchings. A decrease was noted in the fifteen persons lynched in 1934. The opposition to the liquor traffic was steadfast.

The reports revealed a continual growth of the denominational structure. The boards themselves presented a picture of burgeoning strength. This was evidence that from then until now, we have had no greater struggle than to adjust to prosperity, however limited.

It should be noted that 3,300 messengers had enrolled at the start of the Convention sessions. This stood over against a 2,800 number that had been present in 1929 in the same auditorium.

We returned to our home in Nashville, Arkansas, to report to a New Testament church that God was blessing Southern Baptists. We must be steadfast. We must pay our debts and address the whole world. Then we offered special thanks to God for new health.

Municipal Auditorium • St. Louis, Missouri

Robert Naylor

MAY 14-18
1936

WE MOVED TO A NEW PASTORATE, THAT OF THE FIRST BAPTIST CHURCH OF MALVERN, ARKANSAS, IN OCTOBER 1935. When Convention time came in 1936, it was from a new church, a new work, and an even keener understanding of our Convention.

Like other Conventions, this one was to have a very personal identity. When Convention time came, we had no one with whom to leave the children. Goldia's mother, upon whom we had so constantly relied, was not with us at that particular time. Goldia decided that she could not go, the only Convention that she was to miss in these years. I learned something that I thought I already knew. Conventions are made for husbands and wives, if at all possible. I surely lost something when she did not go.

We lived on the Missouri-Pacific Railroad now, a direct line to St. Louis. A pastor friend in Little Rock had former members living in St. Louis in an apartment complex not far from the Convention auditorium. He and I went together and stayed with these friends. The hospitality was lovely, but I found out firsthand about apartment living. They hardly knew the people who lived next door to them. The anonymity of apartment complexes, later to be underscored in our modern life, became a first-time reality.

The Convention opened with the theme, "The Uplifted Christ," on May 14, at 9:30 A.M., with Dr. John R. Sampey presiding. Dr. Scarborough led the opening prayer, and the announcement was made that 2,887 messengers had enrolled at the time of the Convention.

On that first morning, with Vice-President Frank Tripp presiding, Dr. Sampey's address was "The Faith of a Southern Baptist."

Early in the Convention, the report of the Social Service Commission loomed ever larger. Titled "Twenty-Eighth Annual Report," it technically could have been the twenty-second. "The Convention had created a standing committee on social service at the 1913 session, but had heard a report on civic righteousness at a Sunday afternoon meeting in Hot Springs, Arkansas, in 1908.

The report brought us the lynching statistics, twenty in 1935. The commission recommended that its work be enlarged. There was a minority report "that the work of the Social Service Commission of the Southern Baptist Convention be not enlarged." Both reports were laid on the table by the Convention.

The report of Southwestern Seminary indicated receipts through the Cooperative Program of $23,078.76. The total received from the Hundred Thousand Dollar Club since its beginning was $60,396.48. Forty-five graduates were reported.

I noticed that the Education Commission recommended the employment of a full-time secretary.

A note of historical interest was that Frank Norris offered two resolutions which were referred to the Resolutions Committee. A later item in the minutes said, "A statement was made by Frank Norris of Texas correcting a report that he was not treated fairly by the Convention yesterday and expressing appreciation for the courtesy extended him."

The report of the Executive Committee said, "Distribution of funds was adopted without discussion." How typical! Concerning the future of the Hundred Thousand Dollar Club, Dr. Frank Tripp was thanked for his leadership. He had not been a paid director. The 35,964 names received from the states were declared members of the Hundred Thousand Dollar Club. Election of a director of promotion was recommended.

The officers of the Convention were elected unanimously.

The plan of the Home Mission Board to reestablish a department of evangelism was approved. In the afternoon Dr. Dodd preached a message entitled "The Magnetic Master." In the closing moments of the Convention on Monday morning, B. B. McKinney and William Hall Preston sang a duet entitled, "He Lifted Me."

A carry-over resolution—be sure to take your wife to the Convention. Mutual support makes the meetings more enjoyable.

Municipal Auditorium • New Orleans, Louisiana

Robert Naylor (signature)

MAY 13-16

1937

THE SOUTHERN BAPTIST CONVENTION MET IN NEW ORLEANS, LOUISIANA, THURSDAY THROUGH SUNDAY, MAY 13-16, with the theme, "The Work of the Holy Spirit." This was our second year at the church in Malvern, Arkansas. Mrs. W. G. Hodges, wife of our family doctor, and president of our Woman's Missionary Union, accompanied us on the trip. This was a bit unusual for us, but she was an unusual person and friend. In addition, Goldia and I were totally committed to Woman's Missionary Union. As pastor, I knew the value of this organization both to our church and to the total Baptist cause. Goldia was heart and soul a part of it. If anyone was to accompany us, surely this would be reason enough.

There was a personal experience to underscore this Convention. On the way, in Alexandria, Louisiana, I had stopped the car at a stop light. When the light changed to green, the car in front of us began to move and so did I. About that time someone said something about an event taking place to our right, in the heart of the city. When I looked back, it was too late, I had plowed into the car that had suddenly stopped in front of us. It was indeed embarrassing. Fortunately, it did little damage to the car in front of us, but it really marked up the front end of our car. We were, however, able to proceed. Goldia reminds me that Mrs. Hodges later quietly insisted on paying for the damage. I do not remember that, but it could well be.

This was our first trip to New Orleans. The Baptist Bible Institute of Southern Baptists, located in New Orleans, had been a missionary thrust for the whole Convention. We found the city delightful in every way. In the years that were to follow, that trip to New Orleans always remained special. I was intrigued by the cemeteries which had the burial places above ground. It seemed to me one "advanced step to glory."

The Convention opened on Thursday at 9:30 A.M. with Dr. Sampey presiding. It was reported that there were 3,631 messengers by the time of the opening of the Convention.

Here it might be said that with the election of Dr. Sampey as president of the Convention, an unusual cycle began. In succession, the presidents of the three theological institutions were elected president of the Convention in recognition of their leadership. Sampey served for three terms; Scarborough for two terms; and W. W. Hamilton of the Institute, for two terms.

Among the highlights of the Convention, Dr. J. W. Storer of Tulsa, Oklahoma, preached the Convention sermon. An effort was made to move the date of the meeting of the Convention in succeeding years from May to June. Upon motion of Frank Tripp, the Executive Committee was instructed to include the Baptist Brotherhood among other agencies in the allocation of Cooperative Program receipts.

The reports of the Foreign Mission Board and Home Mission Board were always highlights in the Convention. The Foreign Mission Board reported 415 missionaries. At the time of the reports, each agency presented the missionaries present at the Convention. My preacher father had always been total in his support of mission causes and enterprises. The whole world was basic to his calling.

Though I did not realize it, it was of personal significance that the death of H. L. Winburn, pastor of Arkadelphia, Arkansas, was announced at the Convention.

The Convention expressed its desire that theological institutions now be required to present to the Convention a classified report of the number of enrolled students, distinctly the "number of men definitely pursuing studies in preparation for the ministry of the Gospel." Even then, as now, one of the best-kept secrets in the world is the exact enrollment of an educational institution.

The Social Service Committee reported nine lynchings. They also deplored child marriages. There was even a resolution calling attention to the prevalence of smoking and its perils, especially among preachers.

When Dr. Dodd brought the word of the Committee on Resolutions, there was a strong protest on his part, and on the part of the committee, against interdenominational alliances. How well I remember the ecumenical wave that was even then cresting in our churches. Our leadership steadfastly maintained our Baptist distinctive.

A committee for "Coordination and Correlation" of programs and activities was established. This was a thrust that was to bear fuller fruit in later Conventions.

Notable in the report of Southwestern Seminary was an "asking increase of Southwestern Seminary percentage in the Cooperative Program." "This is absolutely necessary for us," said Dr. Scarborough.

On Sunday evening, Dr. George W. Truett, president of the Baptist World Alliance, preached on the text "We Preach Christ—The Power of God" (1 Cor. 1). With the singing of the "Hallelujah Chorus" by the combined choirs of the city, the Convention adjourned, and messengers returned to their homes.

The Mosque • Richmond, Virginia

Robert Naylor [signature]

MAY 12-15
1938

HOW EXCITED WE WERE THAT THE CONVENTION WAS MEETING IN VIRGINIA. FROM THE FIRST TIME THAT I HAD SEEN her mountains, when I went out there for our wedding in 1930, I had loved Virginia as my own. Now the Convention was to meet in historic Richmond, and we were eagerly anticipating going back again.

During the year, we had moved again. On the first of December 1937, I became pastor of the First Baptist Church in Arkadelphia, Arkansas. Ouachita Baptist University and Henderson State Teachers' College were both schools in Arkadelphia. The church had a great history. The significance of the church and community in our own lives and ministry would be another chapter.

It seems that every Convention had its special significance. Woman's Missionary Union, which is auxiliary to the Southern Baptist Convention, had been organized in Richmond, May 14, 1888. The Fiftieth Anniversary of that organization was to be a part of the Richmond experience. With our commitment to Woman's Missionary Union, this was a special part of our anticipation.

President Sampey called the Convention to order at 9:30 A.M. on Thursday, May 12. It was reported that 4,356 messengers had registered by the beginning of the session. One of the first items of business was always the formal approval of the report of the Committee on Order of Business. This time there were two innovations in the order. Thursday evening was to be the evening of the Home Mission Board report. In addition, there was to be an alternative service at the Grove Avenue Baptist Church, which was also under the direction of the Home Mission Board.

On Friday evening, the Foreign Mission Board hour also had its duplicate service at the same place under the direction of the Foreign

Mission Board. Both of these items spoke to the crowded facilities of the Convention.

E. P. J. Garrett, pastor of the First Baptist of Conway, who would become a close friend, was to preach the Convention sermon.

Early on, Dr. Scarborough asked the Convention to appoint a special committee to examine the Articles of Faith of the Southwestern Baptist Theological Seminary, and make a report at this session. The committee appointed had Dr. E. D. Head as the chairman. On the committee was J. D. Grey, my classmate of seminary days. The report later brought to the Convention stated that the charter of the seminary called for the approval of the articles of faith and the bylaws by the Convention itself. The documents presented showed the articles of faith to be rooted in the New Hampshire Confession, plus certain additional articles that had been approved by the Southern Baptist Convention in 1925. There was also an article concerning "the origin of man" that had been approved by the Convention in 1926. The bylaws of the seminary, previously approved by Dr. B. H. Carroll and the Baptist General Convention of Texas, were also submitted for approval. Finally, all of the official documents of the seminary were made the commitment of the Southern Baptist Convention.

Interdenominational relationships and the ecumenical thrust continued to be the headlines. The Convention refused to appoint a committee to confer with other denominational bodies. The motion calling for the committee said "to study the proposals of this fellowship of churches." Looking back, I can be humbly grateful for the strength of our Baptist commitment. Coordination and correlation of programs and activities continued to be a key concern of the Convention.

On Thursday evening, the report of the Woman's Missionary Union was presented by Mrs. W. J. Cox of Memphis. Since its organization in historic Richmond on May 14, 1888, the Woman's Missionary Union had observed the Jubilate in 1913, celebrating twenty-five years, and the Ruby Anniversary in 1928, celebrating forty years. Women were introduced to the Convention who had been present at the organization in 1888. On Saturday, May 14, we attended services commemorating the organization in the very church where it had taken place.

There was personal involvement in my notes that read, "By request, B. B. McKinney sang his composition, 'I Shall Live in Vain.'" Four months later, he was to be a guest in our home, leading the singing in a revival meeting in our church.

The Baptist One Hundred Thousand Dollar Club reported its best year. A section in the annual for this Convention read, "Southern Baptists are Paying Their Debts." It was reported that $394,619.97 had been received in the past year and all of it was paid on the principal of the debts. In 1932, the debts of the agencies of the Convention had amounted to $5,880,351.63. Now that total was $3,465,274.06. What a thrill! The report hoped for a "debtless denomination in 1945."

Plans were laid for a south-wide evangelistic campaign in 1939 under the leadership of Roland Q. Leavell, secretary of evangelism for the Southern Baptist Convention. My own calendar notes for 1939 revealed how deeply I was involved in this south-wide campaign.

For the first time, the Convention adopted a Business and Financial Plan for the Executive Committee to enforce. Later on, I would deal with this plan for twenty years in the leadership of an agency of the Convention.

For the first time, there was a call for a "Ridgecrest" west of the Mississippi River. This was referred to a committee for a report the next year.

The Time, Place, and Preacher Committee recommended Oklahoma City for our next meeting, on May 17-21, 1939, with Dr. Perry Webb as our preacher.

Dr. Scarborough was elected President of the Convention. It was noteworthy to me that Ellis Fuller was nominated, but Dr. Scarborough was elected.

In summaries of other years, I have indicated that Foreign Mission Night was always a highlight. This was a must on my personal calendar of attendance. This time there was a host of missionaries to be recognized as being at home and present at the Convention. I was particularly struck by the large group from China.

The reports of the seminaries and the Bible Institute were optimistic. The easing of the debt burden had reflected itself in every part of the program.

The Social Service Commission had its lengthy report. I should have previously mentioned the name of Arthur J. Barton. Dr. Barton always emerged as a crusader. He was before the Convention in behalf of so many causes that I am afraid the right attention was not given. He was an able and dedicated man. Later, I was a guest in the home of a brother, a deacon in the First Baptist Church of Jonesboro,

Arkansas. For the first time in the report, there was no reference to lynchings.

We came to the final session of the Convention on Sunday evening. It was to be "Young People's Night." B. B. McKinney led the singing. The closing address of the Convention was given by J. Clyde Turner of North Carolina on "Church Loyalty."

The last item in the report of the Convention said, "After singing the hymn 'The Son of God Goes Forth to War,' the Convention finally adjourned with prayer by Dr. J. H. Rushbrooke of London, England." He would be elected president of the Baptist World Alliance in 1939.

Municipal Auditorium • Oklahoma City, Oklahoma

MAY 17-21
1939

VIRGINIA IN 1938, AND OKLAHOMA IN 1939. IT WAS TRULY A CASE OF GOLDIA AND ME BEING AT HOME FOR two years. My father was a pastor in Oklahoma. I had brought Goldia to Oklahoma as a bride when my student pastorate was in Ada, Oklahoma, so it was in truth a sentimental journey.

In addition, my good friend, Enoch Brown, pastor of the First Baptist Church, Benton, accompanied us. Enoch and Evelyn were living nearby when he came to that church in 1935. We had become the closest of friends. Evelyn stayed at home with her newborn, Don. They had just learned that there would be another baby before the end of the year. You can imagine that this news was a bit of a crisis for them, but I have often reflected on what fine sons these two boys turned out to be.

It also seemed to me that it was going to be a Southwestern Seminary convention. Dr. Scarborough was president and Dr. I. E. Reynolds, who had founded the School of Church Music at Southwestern, was leading the music. President Scarborough called the Convention to order with the theme, "He that winneth souls is wise" (Prov. 11:30), on Wednesday, May 17, at 2:00 P.M. It was reported that 3,537 messengers had registered at that time.

Dr. Reynolds led the congregation in singing "How Firm a Foundation." In my seminary years, we must have sung this song hundreds of times. The music all bore the flavor of the Southwest and of the seminary. Hymns such as "All Hail the Power of Jesus' Name," "My Jesus, I Love Thee," "Rescue the Perishing," and "Amazing Grace" were in the mainstream. Special music included the "Hallelujah Chorus," "Unfold, Ye Portals" by Gounod, "The

Heavens Are Telling" by Haydn, and selections from "The Messiah."
B. B. McKinney provided special music throughout the Convention.

There was the announcement of the Committee on Committees.
W. F. Powell of Tennessee was chairman, and Arkansas was represented by Dr. L. M. Sipes, who was also our Arkansas representative on the Southwestern Board of Trustees.

The Committee on Time, Place, and Preacher included Dr. E. D. Head of Texas.

The president's address on Wednesday afternoon was a highlight on the subject, "Vital Essentials Worth Preserving and Perpetuating." The Executive Committee Report, then, as now, was a primary order of business. They were affirming "Debtless Denomination by 1945." There was a growing response to the Hundred Thousand Dollar Club. The new Social Security Act was dealt with in the report. The appropriation to the seminary was a vital personal concern. In the report of the Executive Committee, there was approval given to the action of the Southwestern Seminary Board of Trustees to give to the Baptist Foundation of Texas of the Baptist General Convention of Texas the power of attorney to handle endowment funds and the investments of the seminary. What a long blessed shadow this was to cast for the seminary! It was specifically understood that nothing was to nullify or supersede any instruction of the Southern Baptist Convention.

Dr. J. B. Lawrence of the Home Mission Board concluded the Thursday morning session with an address, "Baptist Denominational Integrity." Later on, my seminary roommate, Robert Hughes, was to offer a motion that the address be printed in full.

Virgil Mott, a seminary classmate, sang "Hallelujah for the Cross."

The officers of the Convention were elected unanimously with not more than one nomination to an office.

Significantly, the Committee on Time, Place, and Preacher recommended that the 1940 Convention be in Baltimore, Maryland. It was to meet, however, in June on Wednesday after the second Sunday. For four years, there had been sentiment to move the meeting time to June so that the children would be out of school and families could go to the Convention together.

Thursday evening was Foreign Mission Board Night. I have always been blessed by the presentation of new missionaries. It was to be a moment when it was as deep a personal experience in our lives as we could have had. At this Convention, among the new missionaries

Dr. Lee Rutland Scarborough, president of Southwestern Baptist Theological Seminary (1915-1942) and of the Southern Baptist Convention (1938-1940). Courtesy—Southern Baptist Historical Library and Archives.

presented were Josephine Skaggs and Dr. and Mrs. B. J. Cauthen. Josephine was a missionary for Africa, and the Cauthens were missionaries to China.

The seminary reports all reflected increased enrollments. President Scarborough said he had received a communication from the newly organized World Council of Churches, inviting the Southern Baptist Convention to join. How should the invitation be dealt with? On motion, a committee of twelve was appointed to make a courteous and suitable response. The response was to be considered at next year's convention. An amendment required that Dr. Scarborough be included as a member of the committee. When named, the committee included such names as George W. Truett of Dallas as chairman, L. R. Scarborough, John R. Sampey, Charles E. Maddry, Ellis A. Fuller, M. E. Dodd, and W. R. White. There were "giants in the land" in those days.

A special sermon on "Christ and Youth" was preached by Chester Swor. Friday evening was Home Mission Night, and among the missionaries presented was Jacob Gartenhaus, missionary to the Jews; the Hancocks, missionaries to the Indians; and Paul Bell, missionary to the Spanish.

On Saturday morning, President Scarborough announced the Committee on Boards who would report to the Convention next year.

Dr. Louie Newton was chairman. Suddenly, the Arkansas member of that committee was Robert Naylor. This was to be my first Southern Baptist Convention denominational assignment. No one asked me if I would serve or if I wanted to serve. From the first, I had believed that the Convention was mine. My attendance bespoke my concern and involvement. It did not occur to me that I was an outsider. I had come to know many of the people who were our leaders in denominational life, but it was a bit overwhelming to suddenly be a part of the structure in terms of assigned responsibility. I am sure it was not all that important to the Convention, but for me, it was a matter of real humility and joy.

In 1939 the South-Wide Evangelistic Campaign was in full swing, and there were glorious reports. I discovered from my own records that while pastor of a church, I was also involved in five evangelistic meetings elsewhere, and also preached one in my own church.

Coordination and correlation were still headline considerations.

On Saturday afternoon, the Committee on Centennial Session of the Southern Baptist Convention recommended that the session be held in Augusta, Georgia, in 1945. There were the usual detailed resolutions. It was noted that six persons were lynched in 1938. There were resolutions concerning accidental death, crime, and the freedom of religion.

Evidently, we returned to Arkadelphia later Saturday evening. My records show that on Sunday morning, I reported to the church about the Southern Baptist Convention. I had done this every year and continued to do so in all of my years of pastorate. I felt it was of supreme importance in carrying out the commission. I noted also that Wallace Rogers, pastor of the First Baptist Church of Vicksburg, Mississippi, my neighboring pastor, and a very personal friend in our first pastorate at Nashville, preached in my pulpit on that Sunday evening. This meant that on the way home from the Convention, he must have stopped by to visit with us.

How quickly this circle of friendships, this sense of belonging to each other, this awareness of our need for one another had grown. It was a fellowship to be enjoyed, to be protected, and to be paid for.

Fifth Regiment Armory • Baltimore, Maryland

Robert Naylor [signature]

JUNE 12-16

1940

GOING TO THE CONVENTION CAN BE ALMOST AS EXCITING AS ATTENDING THE CONVENTION. SINCE THE CONVENTION was meeting in the East, we would be able to combine the Convention and a few days with our family in Virginia. We would not forget the year 1940. As we approached Bristol, Tennessee/Virginia, I topped a hill and found a man parked right in the middle of the highway. At sixty miles an hour, my decision had to be instantaneous. With ditches on either side, I did as well as I could by braking the car, then decided to hit him directly. The impact was not major but it was enough to disable both cars, and cause Goldia some scratched knees. As we got out of the car, a crowd was beginning to gather. We began to question each other, "Why were you standing still?" Why were you going so fast?" It became apparent that the older man driving the other car was a resident of the nearby community. Almost immediately someone came up to me from the crowd and said, "I am a representative of GMAC. I just figured this wreck was mine." He seemed to know that I was making my payments to GMAC.

At this point, a local resident slipped up to me and whispered in my ear, "Sir, I wouldn't settle anything until the police arrive." Here was a friend indeed. Presently, Sergeant Buckles, of the Tennessee Department of Safety, appeared. No one could have been kinder. He went back to where Goldia and the children were standing and said to her, "How fast was your husband driving?" She responded, "Sixty-five miles an hour." He said, "Just a good cruising speed." We all need experiences in which the stranger befriends us.

My first impression of Baltimore included two things. I have a picture of the row houses where women are scouring those front marble steps, and the spotlessly clean windows of the houses. Baltimore also gave me that historical impression of "Oh say, can you see."

Later, I based my report to my church on the subject, "Christian Totalitarianism." The emphasis was on the voluntary principle in Christianity.

My first denominational assignment bore fruit here when the Committee on Boards reported. At that time, it was the customary guiding principle of the committee that the representative from a particular state would suggest the names that were needed for the full report. It seemed eminently fair to me then, and eminently desirable even now. I nominated my close friend, E. C. Brown, as a trustee of the Southern Baptist Hospital in New Orleans. I did not ask him if he wanted to serve. I simply proceeded on the basis of the knowledge that was mine as a faithful servant of the denomination. He made a good trustee.

President Scarborough called the Convention to order on Wednesday morning under the authority of the Great Commission, read by Secretary Hight C Moore. Dr. I. E. Reynolds of Southwestern Seminary was in charge of the music of the Convention. It was reported that at the time of beginning, there were registered 2,230 messengers. I noted later that the final figure was 3,776.

Among the items of that first morning, C. E. Matthews presented the report of the Committee on Order of Business. The president's address by Dr. Scarborough was "God's Call and Challenge to Southern Baptists." The Convention sermon was preached by W. R. White on the subject of "Apostolic Distinctiveness."

In the afternoon, the rules of the Convention were suspended in order that a resolution might be offered and adopted protesting the action of the President of the United States in his appointment of a representative to the Vatican with rank of Ambassador. The vote, which was unanimous, began a chapter that was to last to this very hour.

The Foreign Missionary Society of British Baptists requested aid in carrying on their mission work in the midst of the great war. It was a war that, even then, seemed very close.

Wednesday evening was Home Mission Night at the Convention.

The next day, the Executive Committee reported. J. E. Dillard presented the report of the Hundred Thousand Dollar Club. The tempo had quickened, and the club featured positive growth. The debt of $6 million in 1933 was now $2,843,000. The slogan "Debtless

Denomination by '45" was still in place. The report of the Foreign
Mission Board reflected our emergence from the awful paralysis of
our debts. There were new appointees, the missionaries on furlough
were recognized, and we had 455 active missionaries under appointment.

At the next session the report of the Committee on Time, Place,
and Preacher set May 14-18, 1941, at Birmingham, Alabama, as the
place of our next meeting.

The report of the Social Service Commission noted that lynchings
had almost disappeared. After a long and involved discussion, the
Convention refused membership in the World Council of Churches.
It seems to me that this represented the cresting of the tide of the ecumenical movement as it affected Southern Baptists.

The final session of the Convention on Sunday afternoon featured a sermon by R. G. Lee on "Unsmothered Fires."

The distance involved in going to Baltimore was underlined by
the fact that Arkansas was represented by only eighty-six messengers. In the midst of these messengers, Goldia and I were surrounded
by close friends who were given to us by the denomination.

Municipal Auditorium • Birmingham, Alabama

MAY 14-18

1941

THE 1941 CONVENTION MEETING IN BIRMINGHAM IS EASY FOR ME TO REMEMBER FOR TWO VERY PERSONAL reasons. It was my second trip to Birmingham for a convention. In my college year of 1926, I had gone to Birmingham to attend the first Southwide Baptist Student Union Convention under the leadership of Dr. Frank Leavell. It was a memorable experience that could occupy a chapter. At that time, however, it never occurred to me that I would one day be going back to Birmingham as a pastor of a Southern Baptist church to attend the Annual Convention. I heard things, saw things, and met people, but on that first journey, I would always remember that it never occurred to me that Birmingham would have anything to do with my later ministry. I remember Birmingham.

The second personal reason is of far greater significance in my ministry. The Convention met in the Municipal Auditorium in downtown Birmingham. The attendance was almost twice that of the year before in Baltimore. There was no air conditioning such as we have now, and we depended upon fans. There were loudspeaker amplifiers that allowed us to sit outside in the afternoon session, on a parklike bench, and listen to the proceedings from within. On Friday afternoon I was sitting there among some friends, and suddenly it was announced that we would hear the report of the Committee on Boards. When the report was read, there was the name of Robert Naylor given a five-year term as a trustee of Southwestern Baptist Theological Seminary.

To say that I was surprised is to understate the case. I was certainly delighted. Not only was it my first trustee assignment in the

Convention as a pastor, but more than that, it was a choice assignment.
I loved the seminary. For a lifetime, since I first knew about the seminary in 1928, I have considered myself a debtor to the institution
because of that which God did for me there as a student. I considered
the seminary God's basic strategy in an effective ministry among
Southern Baptists. I have never ceased to believe that these are the
basic qualifications for a good trustee.

I had been a faithful alumnus of the institution. I attended the
alumni luncheons and our state conventions. In every communication
from the seminary, I sought to faithfully discharge my debt. I held the
men of the faculty, and certainly Dr. Scarborough himself, in the highest esteem. Suddenly God had provided me with an open door
through which I eagerly walked. There will be more about this later.

The Convention was called to order on Wednesday afternoon, at
2:00 P.M., by President W. W. Hamilton, and began with singing
"How Firm a Foundation." The registration at the hour of opening
was 4,696. This was almost a record. In the course of the afternoon,
E. L. Carnett sang "Holy Spirit, Breathe on Me," and we heard the
Convention sermon by J. Clyde Turner of North Carolina.

The Wednesday evening session was opened with prayer and
Scripture reading by T. B. Maston of Texas. It was to be Foreign
Mission Night. We never missed those nights. It seemed as though
all of our missionaries were out of China. Ten new missionaries were
introduced to the Convention and set apart for their work abroad.
Among those were Katherine Cozzens of Texas, whose family I was
to pastor at Travis Avenue.

The highlight of the Thursday morning session was a heartbreaking letter from Dr. J. H. Rushbrooke, president of the Baptist
World Alliance, reflecting the terrible hour that had come upon
Great Britain. In the letter he said, "As a British Baptist, I write from
the very heart and center of the titanic struggle. The war has
exacted a heavy toll in material possessions, historical and cultural
monuments, the homes of the people, and above all, the lives of
men, women, and children. We have learned in a stirring school
that a man's life consisteth not in the abundance of the things he
possesses." It was a moving moment and it made us realize that the
war was ever closer.

The report of the Executive Committee reflected the financial
changes that were being brought about by the One Hundred

Thousand Dollar Club. Almost half of the recommendations had to do with the refinancing of agencies' indebtedness, including that of the seminary, which would have resulted in material savings in interest for the institutions.

The recommendation for the centennial session of the Convention to meet in Augusta, Georgia, in May 1945 was adopted.

With reference to the war, the Convention took official action with reference to the registration of conscientious objectors. It was required that these men and women be spared the draft and the war. Instead of active military service, the government placed them in positions of civilian service. The report indicated that 125 objectors had officially signed cards for action by the Convention.

Theological education was discussed by Jeff D. Ray of Southwestern Seminary, our honored teacher.

To suggest that we Southern Baptists have not changed much, on Friday afternoon there was a discussion about a proposed change in the bylaw that would have required the members and trustees of the boards and agencies to be limited to two terms of service. The minutes read: "An extension of time to thirty minutes, each speaker limited to four minutes was granted." The arguments could have been ten years before or twenty years later. The upshot was this, "The motion to postpone was lost; the motion to table was lost; and the recommendation was not adopted."

The resolutions focused on the war abroad, its immediate effects here, a national draft in which we were already engaged, the wreckage wrought by the liquor traffic, and even on the embezzlement of power—meaning that the government was not listening to the people.

For the first time, the Convention concluded with a Young People's Night sponsored by the Baptist Training Union Department of the Baptist Sunday School Board under the direction of J. E. Lambdin. The conclusion of the Convention was a sermon by M. E. Dodd of Louisiana on "Following the Living Christ."

By the time the Convention would meet the next year in San Antonio, our nation would be at war.

Municipal Auditorium • San Antonio, Texas

Robert Naylor

MAY 16-20

1942

WITH THE NATION AT WAR, SOUTHERN BAPTISTS GATHERED IN SAN ANTONIO, TEXAS, ON MAY 16, 1942, FOR THEIR annual Convention. A new format had been adopted with the special indication that it was to be tried for one year only. The Convention was to open on Saturday morning and close Wednesday at noon.

It was a family affair for us. Goldia and I, along with our two sons, Bob and Dick, attended the Convention and stayed at the lovely Hotel St. Anthony. Truly significant for us was that the Convention's annual listing of messengers included the name Robert E. Naylor, Jr., First Baptist Church, Arkadelphia, Arkansas. The war conditions and the added difficulty of travel limited the attendance. The number having registered at the beginning was 3,271. More than two hundred of these were from Arkansas, and our widening circle was indicated by the fact that of these two hundred, sixty percent were personally known by us.

When we had gone home from the Birmingham Convention, I was full of anticipation for the privilege of serving as a trustee of Southwestern. My first communication indicated that there would be an appreciation dinner at the Hotel Texas in Fort Worth, in appreciation for the faculty and administration as they emerged from the dark ages of the Depression. The invitation specified that it would be formal. I borrowed a tuxedo and we went to Fort Worth. As far as I know, this was a one-time affair in the history of the seminary. Dr. Truett, president of the trustees, presided at the dinner. Goldia and I sat across the table from him and Dr. Scarborough, two men whom we held in the most reverential awe. It was a great occasion.

After the dinner, Dr. Scarborough announced his resignation, due to ill health. This was a blow. When the committee appointed by Dr.

48

Truett to find his successor was named, there was my name as a member of the committee. To say I was shocked would be putting it mildly. As we set out for San Antonio, I knew that the committee would meet and that a successor would be named.

It is just as well that the rest of it be told here. The chairman of the committee was Dr. J. B. Tidwell of Baylor. Dr. Truett was a member of the committee. M. E. Dodd of Shreveport was on the committee and others of his stature, as well as myself. You know that I had nothing to say. My memory is that I had nothing but approval in my heart when they suggested the name of E. D. Head, whom I did not know. He was pastor of the First Baptist Church in Houston. At the Saturday afternoon session of the Convention, Dr. Truett announced that Head had been elected president of Southwestern Baptist Theological Seminary.

In the notes about the Convention which recorded my report to my church in Arkadelphia, I noted that San Antonio was a fine convention city. It was the home of the Alamo. Almost all of my life I had known, "Thermopoli had its messenger of defeat. The Alamo had none." Even now when I go to San Antonio, I go to the Alamo.

Dr. W. W. Hamilton was the retiring president. The auditorium was commodious, and the hospitality the best. The morning session on Saturday concluded with the Convention sermon, preached by Ellis Fuller. Saturday afternoon was given to the report of the seminaries. Southwestern reported the largest number of preachers we had ever enrolled in the seminary. Saturday evening was the time for the report of the Brotherhood.

Sunday morning was taken up with the appointments in the churches. Sunday afternoon was a great hour for foreign missions. There was such a host of missionaries that were home. There was special prayer for beleaguered missionaries going through trials that were heartbreaking. Five new missionaries were appointed at the Convention. This was followed by a special home mission presentation. The business of the Convention began on Monday morning.

The place of the war had to be primary in all of the sessions. There was a recognition in which forty chaplains marched into the auditorium and onto the platform. You can imagine the emotional response that was ours. There was a report from a special committee called "Call to Prayer for a Just and Righteous Peace." There was a listing of conscientious objectors by number; in fact, there were 147. I think it is to our credit that when the report of the Social Service

Commission was given, there was a sentence removed from the report that read, "All our religious, educational, commercial, and political gatherings should have now but one program and that program should be, 'Win the War and establish peace.'"

In response to a motion made by H. H. Hargrove, a committee was appointed to bring recommendations for a great missionary thrust following the conclusion of the war. There were periods of silent prayer in the city every day. These silences were also observed by the Convention.

The California churches were recognized as a Convention by the Southern Baptist Convention. This was the beginning of the great period of convention expansion. Officers were elected unanimously, including Pat Neff of Texas as president and J. Dean Crain of South Carolina and Robert Emmet Guy of Tennessee as vice-president.

In the report of the Executive Committee, a major emphasis was given to the success of the One Hundred Thousand Dollar Club and the retirement of our debts. For the first time, it was said, "Debt Free in '45." Soon the catchword was "Debt Free in '43." I sent in a little verse of my own composition on the theme that was published in our periodicals.

The Convention was asked to rule on the status of education and music directors. The Convention affirmed that they had no authority to determine the official status of Baptists for any governmental agency.

At the close of the Convention, there was an address by Pat Neff of Texas on "America in the Present World Situation," after which we sang "The Star-Spangled Banner." The last note was that "the Convention finally adjourned until the time of its next meeting in Memphis, Tennessee, on May 12, 1943.

Notes in my report to my church included:

It is not the business of the church to wage war.

We believe in the responsibility of every Christian to offer his life to secure freedom for any man of any color to worship God according to his conscience.

Two hundred trained and equipped missionaries ready to send out with the advent of peace.

We must turn from our wicked ways.

The text of the report read, "The light shineth in the darkness and the darkness comprehendeth it not." It was a life-and-death matter.

Municipal Auditorium • Atlanta, Georgia

MAY 16-18
1944

NO CONVENTION IN 1943! FOR THE FIRST TIME SINCE THE CIVIL WAR, THE SOUTHERN BAPTIST CONVENTION failed to meet in 1943. Through the dark days of the Reconstruction, through national panics, through two wars, including that which we call the Great World War, the Convention had met every year. In fact, my one childhood memory of Southern Baptist Convention meetings is that of Mother and Dad going to the Convention in Hot Springs, Arkansas, in 1918. What was different in 1943? The Executive Committee of the Southern Baptist Convention met in February and underlined two things which made it necessary to postpone the Convention. It was to have met in Memphis. Months before, the city had determined that it could not entertain the Convention or make good on its commitment. In addition, there had come a request from our government, not a command, that all meetings of Conventions be postponed and that the whole focus of our country be upon our war effort.

Certainly, we needed no convincing as a nation. The tide had begun to turn in the long, bloody, costly way back from Pearl Harbor. Never had a nation seen such a mighty industrial effort, such total commitment of national personnel that now possessed us. Even now, the shadows of the war in that year linger. The death messages were multiplying. Our national transportation system was bogged down with the moving of military men and supplies.

The 1943 Southern Baptist Convention *Annual* was printed but omitted, of course, the order of business. There was the preliminary statement of postponement and the actions taken by the Executive Committee in the interim. It was determined that all committee assignments and their responsibilities should be extended in the work of the agencies. Reports of the agencies were received and print-ed in the *Annual*. Among these reports was a message from Augusta, Georgia, that they would be unable to entertain the Centennial Convention in 1945. The Executive Committee voted, therefore, that the centennial meeting, upon which our eyes had been focused for five years, would meet in Atlanta, Georgia. So, we came to the Convention in 1944 in Atlanta, Georgia, as previously determined. There was a sense among us at one of the most critical moments of the war that as Southern Baptists we needed to get together.

Aside from the war context of the Convention, there were impor-tant personal developments. If I were simply writing a history of the Naylor family, I would have to devote a chapter to 1944. On January 3, 1944, Rebekah Ann Naylor was born. While it was not a sensation throughout the Southern Baptist Convention, I assure you it was nearly that in the community where we lived, and certainly in the parsonage that was ours. She was a girl, our first and only. Our two wonderful boys were already ten years of age. The church had not had a baby in the parsonage for a decade. Whatever I was to say about 1944 had to relate to her.

She very conveniently arrived at no Convention season. By the time May had come, Goldia was ready to attend the Convention, since her mother would be able to keep the children. I had already learned about Goldia that she had an undaunted spirit. Whatever crisis, she simply moved on to the next thing that waited for us, and to the next Convention to which we were going. Somehow, I had scheduled engagements for 1944 beyond most other years. Though I did not know it at the time of the Convention meeting, I was to change pas-torates and states in the fall. I think, as I reviewed the calendar of the year, if I had not moved to another pastorate, the church would have asked me to leave, due to the fact that I was gone all of the time. Churches are sometimes sensitive about that, and properly so.

We went to Atlanta to attend to Kingdom business, but you can understand that the war and the struggle were always a priority in our programs. We had been to Atlanta once before for convention, for the meeting of the Baptist World Alliance in 1939. We were delighted with the city then, and in this Convention and others that were to follow, we always found Atlanta to be a wonderful Convention city for Southern Baptists.

In the report that I made to our church in Arkadelphia concern-ing the Convention, I noted that I first told them about attending the Pastor's Conference. I was not always faithful in these years to that meeting. The program, however, contained two subjects of vital interest to me. The first was "How to Have a Great Wednesday Night Service," and the second was "How to Have a Great Sunday Night Service." I remember hearing Dr. Ellis Fuller, pastor of the First Baptist Church of Atlanta, discuss the second subject. He said he was faithful in keeping the time contract which he had with his congregation. He spoke of one of his teenage members telling him on a Sunday evening, "Dr. Fuller, you went over three minutes tonight." Dr. Fuller responded, "I will give it back to you next Sunday night." And, he did. He also said he felt he owed his congregation a fresh preacher on Sunday evenings. There came a time when he determined that there would be no Sunday afternoon committee meetings, no activities; but there would be a period of total rest to prepare himself physically for the Sunday evening service. I was so impressed that I made it a cardinal principle of ministry, and even now acknowledge that both principles have blessed me and future congregations also.

In my notes I also saw a line that spoke of the inspiration derived from the crowd. I must not digress only with this Convention, but I bear testimony that there is a spiritual adrenalin, a quickening pulse, to look around at the crowd of people and saying to yourself, "We are Baptists and we serve the Lord Jesus."

The program itself, focusing on the theme, "My Church (Matt. 16:18)," opened on Tuesday afternoon with the president of the Convention, Dr. Pat Neff, president of Baylor University, presiding. We opened the Convention singing "America." Never before or since have we done this. We followed with "How Firm a Foundation." The Convention was ultimately to enroll 4,301; but at this opening session, they reported that a few less than two thousand had registered and become the Convention in session. Reflecting the national atmosphere, our Convention president spoke on "Manhood on the March," after which we all stood and sang "Onward Christian Soldiers." The Convention sermon by Dr. John H. Buchanan of Birmingham, Alabama, was "The Debt We Still Owe." He used as his text, "I am debtor to the Greeks and to the barbarians; both to the wise and to the unwise. So as much as in me is, I am ready to preach the Gospel to you that are in Rome also" (Rom. 1:14-15).

The action of the Executive Committee in choosing Atlanta for our Centennial Convention was approved with recognition of the circumstances in Augusta. Our eyes were still focused on the fact that we were soon to be one hundred years old. A great evangelistic emphasis for 1945 had been planned. The report of the Foreign Mission Board was given in the afternoon, and the official Foreign Mission Night was on Tuesday night. First, they reported that all debts were paid March 12, 1943, and that there were 484 missionaries under appointment. Dr. Maddry reported to a somber Convention the news of the death of Rufus Grey. Rufus and Mrs. Grey had been appointed April 10, 1940, and went to Peking to study language. They then were transferred to the Philippines in 1941. They were taken into custody following Pearl Harbor. Between January and March of 1942, Rufus died in the hands of the Japanese military. Mrs. Grey and their son, Billy, had chosen to remain in the Philippines, and were there as the Convention met. Later on in my ministry, I was to be their pastor.

I think I have never seen as many missionaries home on furlough and seated on the platform at the Convention as on this particular evening. There must have been over two hundred of the great missionary force present. As difficult as conditions were, there were missionaries appointed during the year.

It was personally moving to me that the Convention sent two wires of sympathy and encouragement to Dr. Truett and Dr. Scarborough, both of whom were ill. The 1943 *Annual* included their pictures in the report of the Relief and Annuity Board. Dr. Scarborough had been president of the board since 1941, and Dr. Truett had been chairman of the executive committee of the board since 1941. I can look at their pictures now and think what mighty men God had raised up for Southern Baptists.

The Convention adopted a recommendation concerning a "Centennial Crusade: A Program for World Redemption." As I heard it, I mentally made my own resolutions for participation.

An interesting action of the Committee that cast a long shadow was a recommendation that the Convention establish a certain type of reserve fund. We needed reserves we thought. Yet, a minority of the board brought in a report saying that it would be in violation of the Convention's own business and financial plan to set up such a reserve. They also dealt with matters like the operating budget for the Convention itself, and the percentages of distribution. I mention this mostly because the report of the minority prevailed and the Convention adopted the report as amended.

It was an emotional moment in the Convention when Dr. J. E. Dillard reported that we had become debt free in '43. There was even a balance of $38,000 in the debt-free fund. There was a formal conclusion to the Baptist One Hundred Thousand Dollar Club. It stands as a symbol in our own lives that we were members from the first. We had never passed up a special debt-paying offering called for by the Convention. I had faithfully presented to our churches the opportunity to be a part of such a motion.

The following describes the nature of this Atlanta Convention: "The Executive Committee requested all banquets, lunches, and special breakfasts be discontinued at this Convention on account of the food situation." We just might try that again. There was a reference to gifts for Russia. As a trustee of Southwestern Seminary, there was an interesting note in their report: "One of the highest hours in the eventful history of the seminary came on Friday, November 12, 1943, when we celebrated our freedom from debt. It was so very fitting that Dr. and Mrs. L. R. Scarborough could be with us. Dr. Scarborough struck the match with which he set fire to the note bondage." It was a triumphant conclusion to an ordeal. There had been periods when the faculty had been provided food from a common storehouse. Salaries, painfully low, had been deferred. Now those had been cared for and a new age had begun.

Also, the report said, "We, the faculty and students of Southwestern Seminary, are moved to affirm our confidence in the organizational set up of the seminary as expressed in its three schools: The School of Theology, The School of Religious Education, and The School of Sacred Music." This was to combat a long running discussion that to have three schools was to be only divisive.

There was a sermon by Dr. Lynn G. Broughton on "The Christian and His Country." Recognition was given to the service of the chaplains. I found in my notes: "Pacifism is not Christian. No place for isolationism." I think I have not changed my position on this point.

Though we did not know it, D-Day was only weeks away. The frightful cost would be underlined. A sort of spiritual separation was provided by the Convention for this day.

Finally, in my notes reporting the Convention to the church, a paragraph is headed: "The Values of the Southern Baptist Convention." They read, "First, acceptance of responsibility in transaction of business; second, unity which it breeds in discussion; third, an appeal for democracy; and fourth, it focuses the eyes of the world on the Baptist Message." Number two would still call for some debate.

City Auditorium • Miami, Florida

[signature: Robert Naylor]

MAY 15-19
1946

MIAMI IN 1946 WAS ONE OF AMERICA'S GREATEST CONVENTION CITIES. THERE WAS AN AURA OF PROMISE AND brightness about the city in that year that seemed to prophecy the blessings of the Lord!

Where was our centennial year? A committee of the Convention had been planning its centennial session for five years. They had brought their reports to the Convention yearly. Even in the 1943 *Annual*, the year of the missed Convention, there was a reference to the centennial. Suddenly the formal meeting, which had long been anticipated, never came to pass.

In absentia in the 1945 Convention *Annual*, and then in the 1946 *Annual* there was an explanation. In 1945, the government issued an order that there was to be no gatherings larger than fifty people. The Executive Committee of the Convention called an emergency meeting and planned compliance, but treated it as a thing delayed. By 1946, however, it had become simply one session of the 1946 Convention recognizing the centennial that had passed. I am sure that there was some personal lesson in that for me in that the thing we sometimes major on assumes another dimension.

However, God seemed to have provided some celebration on the centennial for us. On July 7, 1944, Dr. George W. Truett had died. The glory of his ministry through much of the Convention's first century tarried. Then on April 10, 1945, on the very eve of the actual hour of the centennial, Dr. Lee Rutland Scarborough was called home. I could not think of the next Convention without the dominating presence of these two giants of God. In my lifetime that has followed, there have been none to replace either of them. We went to Miami, therefore, with these two absent, but present.

There were personal changes, too, that were important to us which had occurred during the interim. Shortly after the 1944 Convention, I preached for a week at the Kiamichi Baptist Assembly in Oklahoma. Out of it came an urgent invitation to be pastor of the First Baptist Church of Enid, Oklahoma. On October 15, 1944, when Rebekah was nine months old, we moved to Enid to a new chapter and a new denominational fellowship, in terms of state relationship. We were to be messengers from an Oklahoma church and thereby began a new chapter.

Our friends, the Robert Barkers, who were in North Little Rock, Arkansas, at that time, agreed to go to the Convention with us. Goldia and I drove to Little Rock and left our car, and in the Barker's new car, set out for the Convention. Cars were still scarce after the war, and in a sense they were dedicating this new automobile. Three of us had been reared in Oklahoma, and when we first sighted the Gulf with the beautiful white sands of the beach, we stopped the car, took off our shoes, and ran down to the water. That picture still remains vivid in our memory.

When we arrived in Miami about noon, I was driving the car. They had already marveled at the city as we entered, noting big, long bridges. Suddenly, in the noon traffic on one of these main bridges, the car stalled and quit running. It was surely embarrassing for the owner of the new car. Bob got out of the car in the midst of the awful traffic, and trudged across the bridge to find help. A policeman waved to me and said, "Move it on!" To which I replied, "You'll have to do it yourself, Sir." All the time we were getting a fine commentary from the wives.

Our hotel was just across from the Bay Front Park where the Convention auditorium and the open air sessions were to be held. In pre-air conditioned days, our room was a corner room with breezes blowing through the room from one side to the other. To me, it was ultimate luxury. Baptist conventions do have personal dimensions, as I have insisted all along.

The Convention opened on Wednesday morning in the City Auditorium with Vice-President Louie D. Newton presiding. After the regular motion that constituted the Convention, the Committee on Order of Business reported the theme of the Convention to be "Widening Reach and Heightened Power." At the conclusion of the items of the program this quotation was attached:

> And may the men be always ready, as the years come
> and go, to carry on, with widening reach and height-
> ened power, the work we sought to do and did begin! .
>
> —Dr. John A Broadus
> (Closing sentence in his *Memoir of James P. Boyce*)

I was not to see the like of that again.

Convention committees were appointed by President Neff in this first session. The Convention sermon was preached by J. W. Storer of Oklahoma. In the first session, the Southern Baptist Foundation was officially approved. Duke McCall had become the secretary of the Executive Committee and was presented to the Convention.

My special memory is of the evening sessions held in Bay Front Park on the Biscayne Bay. The Miami weather was at its best and there was some of the atmosphere of an "old time camp meeting." The report of the Committee on Centennial Session was given on this first evening. It consisted of a report of the cancellation of the Centennial Session, and the addresses by Louie D. Newton of Georgia and W. R. White of Texas. This was followed by a film, "The Romance of a Century," which concluded the program.

Memorial resolutions concerning George Washington Truett and Lee Rutland Scarborough are worth a much larger space than a simple paragraph. They were printed in the 1945 *Annual* that was distributed to the pastors. Beautifully written and capably expressed, they could not fail to fall short of their subjects. Dr. Scarborough was so personal to me. I have often said that Southern Baptists have never fully understood how much they owe to the remarkable leadership, the dynamic commitment of this man of God. I think that Dr. Truett had perhaps a larger acquaintance, and a certain awe in his leadership. There never could have been any suggestion of ambition on the part of either or anything but joy in the strength of the other. I do want to quote the opening sentence about Dr. Scarborough: "From cowboy on the range to Christian statesmanship in realms of religion is the romantic, miraculous story of Dr. Lee Rutland Scarborough's life."

On Thursday morning there was a report from the Committee on Statement of Baptist Principles presented by Chairman Ellis A. Fuller of Kentucky. It seems that from time to time, Southern Baptists are seized by necessity to create a framework within which they walk together. We always say at the beginning that Baptists have no creed, only the Word of God. That is not a platitude, but it is a simple truth. This statement of principles was in truth like the others we have adopted in the years since. I think the world understands that Southern Baptists are a Bible people. Our problem is not a difference about the Scriptures, our problems are political. So, I read again this statement of principles and the names of those who served on the committee and remembered that there is a strong line of conviction which binds us with yesterday and tomorrow.

Foreign Mission Night on Thursday was another highlight. There were a great number of missionaries still home on furlough who had not been able to return to the fields since the war. In addition, there had been more than fifty new appointments during the year, and the whole pulse of the meeting was one of hope.

The major moment in the Convention was the recognition of the work of chaplains. The roll call of Southern Baptist preachers who had served in the chaplaincy during the war was read at the Convention, and these men were recognized. Also, there was a memorial for chaplains killed in the war.

The Convention was also marked by a revision of the constitution and bylaws. This is always a recurring necessity among us.

I was interested in the nomination of officers since there were six nominations for president. In a final ballot that included Louie D. Newton and Robert G. Lee, Newton was elected president of the Convention. A personal note would include that when the Committee on Boards made its report, I had been named as an Oklahoma trustee for Southwestern Seminary. The shadow was lengthening. A Committee on Church Organizations made its report saying, "It is obvious that there have developed duplications within the same groups doing the same work."

This, my first Miami Convention, remains a significant part of the Convention experience. The city itself was a delight on my first visit, and Florida became a special place for all the following years of ministry. The willingness of the Convention, with the wounds of war still fresh, to turn to our shattered world with witness and with hope became an accelerating force in ministry.

It should be noted that the attendance was 7,973, the largest since the 1920 meeting in Washington, D. C.

Kiel Auditorium • St. Louis, Missouri

MAY 7-11
1947

THIS WAS MY SECOND ST. LOUIS SOUTHERN BAPTIST CONVENTION. THERE WAS THE USUAL ANTICIPATION, being elected as messengers, the determination about the children; but there was one other factor. The Baptist World Alliance was to meet in Copenhagen, Denmark, in July. Our church had already determined that they would send us to that gathering. It would be our first trip abroad. The excitement that this thought generated certainly was ever present as we prepared to go to St. Louis. I was to go this time as a trustee of Southwestern Seminary from Oklahoma. A vacancy had occurred just as I moved from Arkansas, and I was chosen as an Oklahoma trustee.

The meeting was in Kiel Auditorium. It is a little unusual to remember an auditorium, but I remember this one because of its balconies. It seemed to me that they were the steepest balconies I had ever occupied. Those balconies felt like they would pitch you into the arena, if you were not extremely careful. It was certainly a strange sensation. The Convention opened on Wednesday morning, May 7, with President Louie D. Newton presiding. My friend of seminary days, Ira Prosser, was director of music for the Convention. We began by singing "My Country 'Tis of Thee." There were 5,392 messengers registered for the opening session. The Committee on Order of Business presented its report, which was accepted. I noted that "The Battle Hymn of the Republic" was presented by the Southwestern Singers under the direction of Campbell Wray.

This Convention actually became the birthplace of the new seminaries of 1950. Golden Gate was the chief subject, having been accepted as an agency of the Convention. The principle of "rotation in membership on the various boards" was underlined by the Convention.

Early in the Convention, a petition was presented from the Kansas churches asking that Kansas be recognized as a state in the Southern Baptist Convention and that it have membership on Southern Baptist Convention boards. A committee was appointed to present a report to the next session of the Convention. As pastor of a church close to Kansas, I think I was asked to be a member of the committee.

The Executive Committee recommended that a committee of nine be named by the Convention to meet with a similar committee from the Northern Baptist Convention to study the problem of "boundaries." This recommendation was tabled indefinitely.

James E. Dillard was recognized for his wonderful work in leading our Convention into being debt free in 1943.

Dr. E. D. Head presented the report of the Southwestern Baptist Theological Seminary on Thursday morning. There were 1,076 enrolled in the seminary for the previous session, and there was almost enough money on hand to build the Truett Memorial Building. Gifts to the seminary were recorded. Yet, the keynote to the report was in this sentence, "Imperative, clamant, inescapable are our needs." I think I had never known Dr. Head to so insistently and passionately outline the overwhelming needs of the institution.

In personal dimensions, the report of the Committee on Church Organizations, which was presented on Thursday afternoon by Dr. G. S. Dobbins of Kentucky, had special significance. In other Convention reports I have mentioned the desire to eliminate overlapping and confusion in our programs. This committee, which continued from year to year, now recommended a committee for further study and report. It consisted of fifteen members including six pastors, three teachers of religious education, three education directors, two women, and one layman. When the committee was appointed, there was my name as one of the six pastors. True, by the time the annual was printed, it showed my residence as Columbia, South Carolina. But, that is a story for another report. I doubt that we have fully realized as a Convention how far-reaching were the things that this Committee finally brought into being.

Of interest to my Texas ministry, a recommendation that the Convention accept the Paisano Assembly was *not approved*.

In retrospect, it seemed that as the Convention concluded, our sense of personal involvement had grown. We were to discover that this would be the fruit of every Convention.

On Saturday evening, my old Sunday School teacher at the First Baptist Church of Ada, Oklahoma, Robert S. Kerr, lawyer, governor, and later U.S. Senator, spoke on "The Book We Teach." Final registration was 8,508. After singing "The Son of God Goes Forth to War," the Convention adjourned with prayer by Dr. J. H. Rushbrooke.

Ellis Municipal Auditorium • Memphis, Tennessee

[signature: Robert Paylor]

MAY 19-23

1948

MY VERY FIRST SOUTHERN BAPTIST CONVENTION IN MEMPHIS HAD BEEN IN 1929 WHEN I WAS A STUDENT AT Southwestern Baptist Theological Seminary. Our second Memphis Southern Baptist Convention had been in 1935, and was memorable for personal reasons. Goldia and I were messengers from the First Baptist Church in Nashville, Arkansas. Now in 1948, we were messengers from the First Baptist Church of Columbia, South Carolina. How life can change between Conventions.

Three weeks after the meeting of the Southern Baptist Convention in St. Louis in 1947, I received a letter from the Pulpit Committee at the First Baptist Church of Columbia, South Carolina. This Convention report should not contain the whole story of that unexpected whirlwind, romantic sort of change of relationship that took place. Suffice to say here that the committee came to Oklahoma on the train to see a preacher whom none of them knew. We were over our heads in getting ready to go to the Baptist World Alliance in Copenhagan, Denmark. We could not have been more excited. I told this new committee that there was no possibility of changing churches and then going to the Baptist World Alliance at the expense of the former church. They replied instantly that if a relationship could be established, they would send us to the Baptist World Alliance. On a particular Sunday in July, 1947, I became their pastor, preached one sermon, and left early the next morning for seven weeks in Europe. The eight months of ministry after I returned were as full and exciting as time can be. Now we were messengers to the Southern Baptist Convention from a church east of the River.

President Louie D. Newton called the Convention to order at 10:00 A.M. on Wednesday, May 19. The theme was "Christ Is the

Answer." We were led in singing "All Hail the Power of Jesus' Name." This has been as traditional as our singing "How Firm A Foundation" at the beginning of a seminary session. The usual motions established the fact that we had 7,290 messengers registered at the opening of the Convention and that we adopted the order of business recommended by the committee. In this first session, President Newton introduced Dr. A. U. Moon of Tennessee as being in attendance at his sixty-first Convention. His commitment has more meaning for me now.

The report of the Executive Committee, then, as well as now, has a major place of importance in the Convention. The committee recommended a Convention South-wide goal of $10 million. They anticipated $2.5 million from designated gifts and $7.5 million through the Cooperative Program. The percentages of distribution included five percent to Southwestern Seminary.

Farther along in the Convention, there was a motion to reconsider the budget and committee report. In reconsideration, the percentages to Southwestern and Southern Seminaries were reduced to 4.5 percent. Would you believe that later on in the Convention, they moved to reconsider this same item? The motion was passed and these percentages were returned to their original place. People are all alike, and they really do change their minds. Of course, I thought the names of the ones making the motions were very interesting.

The Executive Committee also had a major recommendation for the capital needs of the institutions. Of the amount allocated to this, 15.99 percent was to go to Southwestern Seminary.

In moving from Oklahoma to South Carolina, I was no longer a member of the Board of Trustees of Southwestern Seminary. I came to the Convention with two assignments, namely, Committee on Church Organization and Committee to Consider the Kansas Application. The Committee on Church Organizations had been initiated a year earlier. It also had its personnel increased at the next Convention, including my name as the pastor representative on the committee. It had been a difficult assignment in that it dealt with the internal matters of the various agencies. The report called attention to the fact that our work was largely promoted through the Sunday School, Baptist Training Union, Woman's Missionary Union, and the Brotherhood. Yet, each of these agencies operated independently.

I had attended a meeting of the committee in Memphis in late January. This meeting kept me from attending the Committee on

Kansas Application which was just a week later, and also in Memphis. I was made secretary of this first committee, and the records that I kept indicated some tension in our work. Our report to the Convention was, therefore, most important. Among the recommendations was one to "set up a pattern for organizations and curriculum for the approximately 15,000 of our churches having 150-400 members; patterns for larger churches." Another recommendation that I vividly recall presented major tensions was one "unified church study course with a general diploma." It added "free interchange of comparable credit." It called for agency calendars of activities to be correlated in the churches. The thrust was to make this a working team out of diverse and independent people and units. This is a pretty good description of a Baptist church. The committee was continued, and a report was called for concerning the 1949 meeting.

The churches in Oregon presented a petition for recognition as a Convention state. The Kansas petition simply became the forefront of the tremendous expansion which was to claim all of America as a part of Southern Baptist life. The bylaws and constitution of the Convention were both amended to define membership requirements for messengers. They were largely made those from which we now operate and function.

There was a motion to consider the desirability and possibility of entering Alaska.

A report from Secretary Joe Burton indicated a record attendance of 9,525.

Foreign Mission Night was Thursday evening. In the afternoon Dr. Robert G. Lee of Memphis had been elected president of the Convention. He was introduced during this evening session.

So much of the Foreign Mission Board's report reflects multiple work in China. The shadow of Communism that was approaching was found in the report. Speakers for the report included Dr. Baker James Cauthen, secretary to the Orient. At the conclusion of this address, he gave an invitation for volunteers for mission work in foreign fields. It became a pattern for years to follow. I was greatly interested in the fact that this Convention listed in its *Annual* the names of those who responded to the invitation. I wonder how many of them finally reached our foreign fields. There were names I recognized, however, who would write a wonderful chapter of faithful missionary service.

There was Annie Hoover, of Little Rock. I had been her pastor at Arkadelphia while she was a student at Ouachita. Years later, Goldia and I were to visit in her home in Sapporo, Northern Japan. How steadfast and faithful she had been through the years; and by the force of that faithfulness, God had made her a leader of our missionary hopes for Northern Japan. There were a few others I had reason to know: Reuben Franks of Fort Worth, Texas; Kyle R. Lawrence, of Fort Worth, who dated back to the Ouachita days in Arkadelphia; and Chester L. Mason of my hometown, Ada, Oklahoma. Dr. J. Howard Williams led the closing prayer. Foreign Mission Night at the Southern Baptist Convention, as always, casts one of the longest shadows in our Baptist life.

The Committee on Theological Education brought a report. There were stirrings already for new seminaries.

Dr. Head presented the report of Southwestern Baptist Theological Seminary. You can be sure this remained my keenest interest. I was struck by the fact that there was a note of almost frantic urgency in the report of the seminary from the year before, that was totally absent from this report. Dr. Head reported record-setting enrollment, excellent morale, and the challenge that was before them. The building campaign was nearing a successful conclusion.

In the report of our Committee to Consider the Kansas Application, the Convention acknowledged messengers from that state. This meant that they were to be able to have all constitutional privileges. The committee also recommended a study of the larger problem, and a clarification of Bylaw 17 which outlined the procedure for recognizing a new state convention.

Some individual presented a resolution to the Convention expressing our appreciation for Memphis. His resolution referred to "the privilege of attending the Southern Baptist Convention with the nicest possible entertainment at a price that we pastors of smaller churches can well afford. The homes, the drink stands, the restaurants, the hotels and the business houses in general have not sought to make an extra nickel off of us."

There is also the memory of the friends, that inner circle whose fellowship you always sought at the meeting of the Convention. Our friends, the Barkers, were there from Arkansas. The Fairfield Association in South Carolina, where my own church was located, was seeking a missionary and was in correspondence with him. So, out of a lengthy discussion of South Carolina came twenty-five years plus of remarkable service in that state.

Municipal Auditorium • Oklahoma City, Oklahoma

MAY 18-22
1949

FOR THE FIRST TIME SINCE WE MOVED TO THE EASTERN SIDE OF THE CONVENTION, THE CONVENTION WAS TO meet west of the River. Just as in many previous years, we had been able to couple the meeting of the Convention with a visit with our family in Virginia, now we had the opportunity to visit with our Oklahoma family on a like occasion. When we had attended the Southern Baptist Convention in Oklahoma City in 1939, I was pastor of the First Baptist Church in Arkadelphia.

A new problem surfaced at this Convention that was to plague all of our Conventions in succeeding years. This was the number of available hotel rooms considered desirable by those of us who attended. When I wrote for reservations for the Convention, I was given accommodations in what I knew to be a second-class hotel. Fortunately, I thought I knew what to do about this. Enroute to the Convention, I called Mrs. Lucille Driggers, chief secretary in the state secretary's office. I had come to know her while I was pastor in Oklahoma. She was one of the loveliest, most accommodating, and most capable people that I knew. I told her my problem, that I wished to stay at the Skirvin, and she arranged it. So, when I arrived, I went to the new reservation and was pleased.

When my friend Barker arrived, also from Columbia, he called the hotel where I had first been given accommodations. He told the man at the desk that he wished to speak to Dr. Naylor and was told, "Dr. Naylor is not with us anymore." To which he replied, "Would you tell me where I could view the remains?" I continue to enjoy this.

The Convention opened on Wednesday, at 9:30 A.M., with President Robert G. Lee presiding. The theme was "Always Bearing . . ." (2 Cor. 4:10). Warren Angell of Oklahoma led in singing "How

Firm a Foundation." The opening registration was reported as 6,669. What an inspiration this opening moment always has been for me.

Wednesday afternoon was a busy session. A motion was adopted that read: "The Committee on Boards, Commissions and Standing Committees shall be composed of one member from each state who shall be nominated to the Convention by the Committee on Committees."

A motion was also offered: "That a committee be appointed by the President of this Southern Baptist Convention, now convened in Oklahoma City, Oklahoma, to investigate the charge that modernism now exists in the Southern Baptist Theological Seminary, Louisville, Kentucky." The motion was referred to the trustees of Southern Baptist Theological Seminary. I knew the man, Oscar Gibson, who presented the motion, and that is the other side of the story.

A report of the Executive Committee was the main focus of the afternoon. Extra appropriation was made to the Foreign Mission

Municipal Auditorium in Oklahoma City, Oklahoma, site of the 1949 Southern Baptist Convention meeting. Courtesy—Southern Baptist Historical Library and Archives.

Board to support a special effort on behalf of the "Advanced Program of Foreign Missions."

The Committee on Time, Place, and Preacher was asked at this Convention to recommend places of meeting for 1950 and 1951. When the committee reported on Friday morning, they recommended that the 1950 Convention meet in Houston, Texas, on May 10-14. A pastor moved to substitute Chicago, Illinois, instead of Houston. The substitution was approved by ballot vote. Since that time, the Convention has met in some outlying places, often with real difficulty.

Our Committee on Church Organizations made its report on Thursday afternoon. Among other things in the report, there was this sentence: "A 25% over-all reduction in the number of meetings in well organized churches is suggested as a goal with attendant emphasis on high quality and increased fruitfulness as a result of greater concentration of those held." We reported progress and finally, "we recommend: (1) a reaffirmation of the report of last year and, (2) that a committee of ten be appointed for further research and conference on the matters under consideration and other related matters, this committee to be composed of four pastors, two educational directors, two teachers of religious education, and two lay workers." I was asked by the Convention to continue service on this committee. I still consider it one of the more significant works of the years.

There were two other matters that I remember very clearly. First, there was a recommendation that two new seminaries be established, one in the West and one in the East. This was to be done as soon as suitable sites could be had and adequate plans could be made for financing without injury or impairment to our existing seminaries. I was a little horrified at the thought of more seminaries, when I was so well acquainted with the problems of one. The appropriation always seemed inadequate, and to add other institutions seemed to me an invitation to disaster. The Committee on Theological Education was continued as a committee with the special charge to seek out the place and the resources.

The second matter was a recommendation that a Southern Baptist Assembly be established at a site offered by the Chamber of Commerce in Harrison, Arkansas. Previously, there had been movement to have an assembly west of the River. My friend, Pat Murphy, was pushing for the Arkansas site. Suddenly, there was a substitute motion offered by Phillip McGahey to insert the name of Glorieta, New Mexico. The substitute was adopted and a new chapter began.

Dr. R. G. Lee was reelected president of the Convention by accla-mation. J. D. Gray of Louisiana, my seminary classmate, and Robert S. Kerr were elected first and second vice-president, respectively.

Bylaw 17 was amended to clarify the way in which state conven-tions were recognized in the future. They were to have twenty-five thousand members in their churches and following that could, in the discretion of the Convention, be represented by members on the gen-eral boards and the Executive Committee.

The Southwestern Seminary report revealed a record enrollment of 1,445. The tone was upbeat. The Convention elected me a trustee again, this time from South Carolina.

I have the warmest memories of this last of the Oklahoma Conventions. The Convention was growing rapidly and getting too large to be accommodated by the facilities there.

Chicago Coliseum • Chicago, Illinois

[signature: Robert E. Naylor]

MAY 8-12
1950

T. L. HOLCOMB, TENNESSEE, BROUGHT THE REPORT OF THE SUNDAY SCHOOL BOARD, WHICH WAS ADOPTED AFTER discussion by Harold E. Ingraham, John L. Hill, and J. L. Williams. Kearnie Keegan, the new student secretary, was introduced.

After special music by the Louisiana College Choir, Robert E. Naylor, South Carolina, spoke on "Light For Dark Places" and led in the closing prayer.

It is easy to understand that this Convention held a personal dimension for me. Early in January, I received a letter from Herschel H. Hobbs at the First Baptist Church in Oklahoma City. He was writing on behalf of the Committee on Order of Business to request that I accept a place on the program of the Chicago Convention, to speak on the subject "Light for Dark Places." It was a very warm and flattering letter indicating that I would have thirty minutes for the address. As it was my first major assignment on a Convention program, I felt the responsibility very keenly. Dr. Hobbs was kind enough to write to me afterwards to say "truly, one of the highlights of the Convention," a kindly appraisal by a good friend.

The Convention opened on Tuesday evening with President Robert G. Lee presiding. Since the theme of the Convention was "Freedom's Holy Light," the opening song was the first stanza of "America."

The registration at the beginning of the Convention was 5,027, indicating one of the first costs of going to one of the outlying states for a Convention.

After the adoption of the report of the Committee on Order of Business, the Foreign Mission Night was observed in the opening service. Dr. Baker James Cauthen of Virginia concluded the program with a stimulating address, "Souls in Shades of Night."

On Wednesday morning President Lee read a telegram from W. R. White of Texas expressing concern for the Convention, and indicating that an illness had kept him away. T. C. Gardner of Texas reported for the Committee on Common Problems with Northern Baptists, "We hereby reaffirm our conviction that Southern Baptists cannot enter into organic connection with the Federal Council of Churches of Christ in America." R. C. Campbell brought the Convention sermon.

With my involvement in theological education, I was keenly interested in the report of a Committee Concerning Future Seminaries. The recommendation was: "We recommend that the location of the western seminary be the present site of the Golden Gate Seminary." The committee also recommended that the seminary in the East be located in Wake Forest, North Carolina. Boards of trustees were elected, and the development of the recommendations was left in their care.

The Committee on Time, Place, and Preacher recommended that the 1951 session of the Convention be in San Francisco, June 20-24, 1951.

The Sunday School Board, pursuing the previous authorization by the Convention for a western assembly, was given the responsibility for a full development of Glorieta. Social Security for ministers also appeared in the Convention's discussions, urging that the right choice to participate be left with the ministry.

There was a full report given of the continuing program of Southern Baptist evangelism with a particular recommendation for simultaneous revivals east of the Mississippi River in 1951. I had participated in the west of the River evangelistic movement in 1950. The report of the Southwestern Baptist Theological Seminary was presented by President E. D. Head and was discussed by Dr. Ray Summers of the faculty.

The Committee on Church Organizations, on which I had served two years, presented their final report. It had created, by recommendation, the Inter-Agency Council, and the work of the committee turned to this group. We would hear more about this later.

The Memorial Service of the Convention included the names of B. A. Copass, my greatly beloved professor of Old Testament, and Frank Leavell, who had given leadership as well as birth to the

Baptist Student Union movement. In the times that I had seen him in public performance he had greatly impressed me with his contribution to Southern Baptist life and ministry.

Dr. Robert G. Lee of Tennessee gave the closing address for the Convention on the subject, "God's Cure for World Disease."

Chicago was a good convention city. The meeting place was not better than most. My memories of the city itself on my first visit are a bit vague. But, I remember the Loop, the stockyards, a few restaurants, and a tiny room in a great big Hilton Hotel on Michigan Boulevard. God was blessing Southern Baptists. We must be steadfast. We must pay our debts. We must address the whole world. With all of that, we offered thanks to God for new health.

Exposition Auditorium • San Francisco, California

JUNE 20-24
1951

AS WE BEGAN TO APPROACH THE 1951 MEETING OF THE SOUTHERN BAPTIST CONVENTION, THE DISTANCE WAS A major consideration. It was a long way from South Carolina to California. If I had thought that Chicago represented the outlying area, California was another matter. There was this to be said, however: California had already become a growing, maturing Southern Baptist state.

Travel in 1951 was largely by railroad. We had such excellent rail service along the eastern seaboard that I conceived the idea of making it a real train experience. Among all the traveling we have had in connection with a convention, this has to stand at the top of the list. The trip would include Washington, D. C., Chicago, the marvelous Sante Fe trains, and a return trip through Canada. This sounded wonderful. There were those in our Columbia congregation who asked if they could be a part of the trip. I explained that it was public transportation, but that I would not be responsible for any one of them. Of course, these were friends who just laughed and made their plans accordingly.

The result was that there were ten from our church who made the trip together. They included the Robert Barkers, the James Howards, Elma Towe of our church staff, Mrs. Lilly Nidifer, Dr. and Mrs. Whiteside, and the Naylors. Dr. and Mrs. Whiteside, then, must have been in their mid-seventies, but they were always the first on the train and the first off—the readiest of any for the next adventure.

We went overnight to Washington, D. C., and spent the day at the Capitol. Senator and Mrs. Olin D. Johnston were members of our Columbia church. Mrs. Johnston was one of the greatest Baptist women I have ever known, and a very personal friend. She insisted that she would have us all for lunch in the Senate dining room. There was a very personal quality to it. Senator Robert Kerr of Oklahoma had been my Sunday School teacher in my late teens, and he and Mrs. Kerr were to be present. Senator John McClellan of Arkansas had been a deacon in my church in Arkansas. I had baptized his children. He and Mrs. McClellan were also present. It was a wonderful group which gathered for lunch.

Overnight to Chicago and spending most of the day there included sightseeing and shopping. Then we boarded the Sante Fe Chief for California. When we passed through New Mexico, knowing that the train was to pass the site of our new western assembly, I took my first look out the train window at Glorieta. I must confess that it was a little forbidding then, but it was to become the scene of many wonderful experiences for us.

When we came to Arizona, our sleeping car was detached and we went overnight to the Grand Canyon. We spent a day with the first wonders of that remarkable place. That night we were taken back to the main line and on to Los Angeles. Here again, we were tourists for a little while, then on to San Francisco.

At this point, I wonder that we ever settled down to the Convention. It became, however, very much a part of the experience. San Francisco itself was an amazing city to us. To this day, we love to visit there. The beauty of the place is unsurpassed. There was a visit to the place where the United Nations came into being. Fisherman's Wharf and China Town had their own attention. The boat trips on the Bay, passing Alcatraz, and nearly freezing in the process, were memorable experiences. The Bay Bridge and the Oakland Bridge stand out in our memory.

The Convention theme was "The Whole Gospel for the Whole World." President Robert G. Lee called the Convention to order at 10:00 A.M. in the Exposition Auditorium, on Wednesday, June 20. B. B. McKinney led the singing as we sang "America" for the opening song. Secretary Joe Burton announced the opening attendance at 4,126, which I thought rather remarkable considering the distance. We adopted a report from the Committee on Order of Business that called for the Convention to conclude on Sunday evening.

In this first session, Chairman T. C. Gardner of Texas brought the report of the Committee on Relations with Other Religious Bodies.

We were at the top of the wave of ecumenical forces that had been sweeping across the world. As Southern Baptists, we had steadily maintained our individual identity. The report here is notable: "We recommend . . . that Southern Baptists cannot enter into organic connection with the National Council of Churches, the World Council of Churches, or any other unionizing organization which would compromise Baptist principles and doctrines as revealed in the inspired Word of God." That almost says it all, but there was one other line: "The idea of a Protestant Ecumenical Church has no Scriptural authority, therefore." There could come a time when Southern Baptists would need to rediscover that kind of identity.

This was one of the few times that I can remember that we had both the president's address by Dr. Lee and the annual sermon by C. Roy Angell of Miami in the same session. The existence of the two new seminaries was recognized by the amendment to our bylaws to include the names and addresses of both institutions.

A motion by John Buchanan of Alabama concluded, "No agency shall make solicitation to individuals or groups for contributions to its operating budget." Already the seeds had been sown to undermine the Cooperative Program by the determined push for special causes and special offerings. At this session, however, the Convention voted to refer the matter to the Executive Committee for study and report. At the report of our Promotion Committee there was a line: "We encourage all of our people to give increased loyalty and support to the Cooperative Program."

Thursday morning saw the report of Southwestern Seminary. As a trustee, I was present and keenly interested in the report of its record enrollment and continued blessings. Fortunately, there was no reference to the problems that we were then experiencing internally. It was a rather sad moment when the secretary was instructed to send messages of condolence to Mrs. Jeff Ray and Mrs. Ellis Fuller.

It is interesting to remember that Joe Burton of Tennessee presented a resolution on the marriage of Baptists with Catholics. F. Townley Lord, president of the Baptist World Alliance, brought the closing message Thursday morning.

The election of officers proved interesting. Those nominated for president included: W. Marshall Craig of Texas; J. D. Grey of Louisiana; R. C. Campbell of North Carolina; J. D. Storer of Oklahoma, and George B. Frazier of Washington, D. C. These were all recognized leaders and a real matter of difficult choice. There were multiple nominations also for first and second vice-president. The results were: J. D. Grey for president, my classmate and personal friend. Forrest Feezor of Texas was first vice-president and Dr. W. R. White of Baylor was elected second vice-president. There could not have been a finer group.

Thursday evening focused on the report of the Home Mission Board.

On Friday morning there was a report received from the Inter-Agency Council of Southern Baptist Agencies. This had been created by our Committee on Church Organizations on which I had served for two years, and about which I had said, "It cast a long shadow." This representation of all the agencies in a single group was without real authority over any group but worked under the mandate to bring about the teamwork and the correlation that our Committee and Convention felt desirable. I was keenly interested in what they had been able to accomplish at their initial meeting. I noted first "a correlated church study course plan had been developed." This was a major change to all the previous years. The council had also suggested and developed materials for a church council, by which a pastor could be encouraged to correlate the activities within the church. It reflected the exchange of ideas within leadership and an almost expectancy that correlation and cooperation become a fact in Baptist life.

Ralph Herring of North Carolina presented the report of the Committee on Boards, and my term on the Southwestern Board of Trustees was affirmed. The term had not expired.

Homer G. Lindsay of Florida presented the report of the Committee on Committees. Its duty was to name the Committee on Boards for the next year, and behold, there was my name as a member of the Committee on Boards at the Convention which was to meet in Miami in 1952.

Later on, the Committee on Time, Place, and Preacher presented its report. The Chairman was W. Perry Crouch of North Carolina, another seminary classmate. For the Convention preacher in 1952 the recommendation was Ramsey Pollard of Knoxville, Tennessee. Robert Naylor of Columbia, South Carolina, was chosen to be the alternate. Certainly, I had come to a time of personal involvement and privilege in the Convention structure.

Saturday morning was set aside for memorials. Dr. John Jeter Hurt, Sr., directed the Memorial Service. Among the names that were called were Hal F. Buckner of Texas, a name synonymous with Texas Baptist Life. Otto Whitington of Arkansas, whose ministry had been alongside of mine to that point, was also named. He held a meeting for my father in Heavener, Oklahoma, when I was just a child and my older sister made a profession of faith.

Ellis Fuller, the president of Southern Baptist Theological Seminary, had died suddenly. Charles W. Daniel, pastor of many great churches in our Convention, whom I had known as pastor of the First Baptist Church of El Dorado, Arkansas, had died. Just prior to the Convention, Dr. Jeff Ray, my greatly beloved seminary teacher and friend, had died. What a remarkable man he was. Suddenly, my attention focused upon that fleeting quality of time which we finally come to recognize.

The Convention closed on Sunday with an address by President Lee in the afternoon and a final sermon by W. A. Criswell.

It is a longer story than most to tell the story of this Convention. Our party promptly boarded the train again for Seattle and an overnight boat trip to Victoria, then on to Vancouver, Canada. From there, our train went through the Canadian Alps and a magnificent new country to us. We stopped in Banff Springs and Lake Louise. Then there was the long trip across Canada—its grain fields, its wonderful beauty, Niagara Falls to Washington, and finally back home. The Convention of 1951 claims its place in Convention memories.

PART TWO

Dinner Key Auditorium • Miami, Florida

[signature: Robert Naylor]

MAY 14-18
1952

GOLDIA AND I HAD BEEN BACK TO MIAMI
SEVERAL TIMES SINCE THE MEETING OF
THE SOUTHERN BAPTIST CONVENTION
in Miami in 1945. In fact, I had held revival meetings in Miami at least twice during that time. The East of the River Crusade found me at Stanton Memorial Baptist Church. Then, there were vacations that I had always enjoyed, and we were returning to Miami with anticipation. It was such a different world from the one of my native Oklahoma.

The Convention was to meet in the Dinner Key Auditorium. I remember it well because it became my responsibility to preach in it. It was a huge airplane hangar that had been converted into an auditorium, about five miles south of the business district. It was big and barny, a difficult place in which to speak.

Though I had no knowledge of it, I should have known that this was to be a year of change. It seemed that in those years, in my experience, they always became times of increased, intense denominational activity. It was to be so here. I was a member of the Board of Trustees of Southwestern Seminary. At the San Francisco Convention, I had also been named to the Committee on Boards to report to this Convention. The Convention had honored me with the assignment of being the alternate preacher of the Southern Baptist Convention sermon. I had also been asked to preach at the closing session of the Convention on Sunday evening at the Training Union hour. So, I went with a sense of being at work.

Two of these ought to be discussed here. First, there was the seminary. It had been a year of difficulty and internal struggle there. It is alright to say at this point that a great many of the faculty had

81

sought to assume administrative control of the seminary. Dr. Head was such a gentle spirit and shunned the confrontation this involved. As trustees, we had been very supportive of the president and were in fact adamant that the administrative structure not be changed. The trustees were to meet at the Convention, and in fact met at least three times. One of these sessions lasted far into the night, and to this moment, I remember that it was a stormy session. I saw men greatly agitated with the gravity of our problems who were normally quiet and reserved. Dr. Summers was elected dean of theology again, which evidently indicated that in his support of the president, he, too, had come under fire.

Then, this was to be my second experience with the Committee on Boards. Our structure is very simple. The Committee on Committees is named at the opening session of the Convention. It is composed of representatives from each of the states. Any committees called for by the actions of the Convention are named by this committee. In addition, they name a Committee on Boards to report at the next session. This committee nominates people to the Convention to fill all the vacancies of the boards of institutions and agencies.

It was such a period of freedom and Baptist liberty that it was very vulnerable to manipulation and corruption. As a member of the committee from South Carolina, it would be expected that where state representation was required in a committee, I would have the principal weight in nominating that particular person. I remember a prominent pastor from a neighboring state that undertook to fill not only the positions of his responsibility, but for all of the rest of us. We just quietly took care of him and went along and respected the responsibility of each other.

It would be expected, I think, that a man would nominate people that he knew, and that it could even be a close friend, or as in many cases, a neighboring pastor in the same city. There was nothing wrong with this, and the system works in our Baptist way. Our present difficulty is that there are those who come to this responsibility and allow their decisions to be made from without. They bring lists of approved people when they come. This is not only not Baptistic, it is the corruption of a very real privilege. I enjoyed my service on the committee, and I look back now and read the names that I had suggested with a sense of pleasure, and with history indicating that they did a good job in carrying out their assignments.

The Convention opened on Wednesday morning at 9:30 and was called to order by President J. D. Grey. The theme was "Magnifying the Church" (Eph. 5:25). We began with singing "All Hail the Power of Jesus' Name" and "Faith of Our Fathers." The formal motion that constitutes the Convention came with the announcement that 3,820 had already enrolled as messengers. The Committee on Order of Business presented its report, previously published in our denominational papers. It was quickly adopted.

It was in this morning session that the concluding item was the hour of worship in which Ramsey Pollard of Tennessee preached the Convention sermon. The item in the minutes read, "Robert E. Naylor, South Carolina, read the Scripture passage and Ramsey Pollard, Tennessee, preached." The theory is that the alternate preacher will be ready to preach at the last moment, even if the appointed preacher is not able to continue. I am sure that I had a sermon in mind. I have no idea at this point what it was. I do remember that it was a point of high privilege and spiritual involvement.

In the afternoon, the report of the Executive Committee, with its many recommendations, was presented. The Cooperative Program goal recommended was $10 million. Recommendation 11 said: "An agency or institution shall not create any liability or indebtedness except such as can be repaid out of its anticipated receipts within a period of three years." We were all still very sensitive to the great burden of debt from which we had been freed in 1943. It is a pity that the memory cannot always stay that sharp. However, this recommendation was one I had to live with as president of an agency in the years that followed.

In kindred vein, a recommendation was adopted that "neither shall any agency approach any agency or group for special solicitations without approval of the Convention or its Executive Committee." We were trying to protect the Cooperative Program.

There was an affirmation of the Cooperative Program as "the fundamental, effective and indispensable channel of providing for the needs of all our work." Also, there was a reference made "to the gravity of the non-resident member problem among Southern Baptists." If it was grave then, I wonder what it is now.

Wednesday evening was Foreign Mission Night. In making a report to my church after the Convention, I said that the sound of airplanes overhead and the outlines of the hangar that were still evident made me sensitive in a very special way to the fact that the whole world was our task. This made Foreign Mission Night tremendously significant and moving. One of the sermons was "Churches Around the World." Missionaries home on furlough were presented at the meetings. There are names among them that you would recognize.

Thursday morning C. Roy Angell of Florida announced that the registration had reached 9,845, exceeding previous attendances.

In the election of officers, J. D. Grey was reelected without opposition. C. C. Warren of North Carolina and Edgar Patton of Virginia were elected first and second vice-presidents. Wayne Dehoney presented a motion which asked the Convention "to guarantee seating for all messengers at all sessions of all future conventions."

Thursday evening was the Home Mission Board program. It closed with a missionary message by W. A. Criswell.

The Friday morning session was certainly eventful. Dr. W. R. White of Texas brought a motion on Boy Scout work. Many of our Baptist churches, then and now, had Boy Scout troops. I became a member of such a group when I was twelve years old, in the earliest days of scouting. At this time, however, there were some who felt the promotion of Boy Scout work by a church would damage the promotion of Royal Ambassador work. So, when Dr. White offered a motion that encouraged Boy Scout work, E. E. Eller of South Carolina brought a substitute motion, calling for a committee of five to confer with the Woman's Missionary Union about the promotion of Royal Ambassador work. They were also to confer with the Brotherhood Commission about the Man and Boy movement and bring a report of that work at the next meeting of the Convention. An amendment offered included Boy Scout work, and suddenly a very significant committee came into being.

Later, when the committee was named by the Committee on Committees, to my surprise, I had been chosen chairman of the committee. It was to be a pleasant and meaningful assignment. Out of it came the transfer of Royal Ambassador work to Baptist Brotherhood. I mention those who served with me on the committee. They include Dr. White; Carlyle Marney of the First Baptist Church, Austin; Robert Hughes, whose pastor I had been when he was at Ouachita College; and J. Perry Carter, a pastor from Coral Gables.

Also in that morning session, "Robert E. Naylor, South Carolina, presented the report of the Southwestern Baptist Theological

Seminary which was received." Dr. Head was ill and could not come to the Convention. Strangely enough, he had asked me to represent him and the seminary and to present the report. With this, I was also to be the speaker at our Southwestern Seminary alumni luncheon. What a glorious hour that was. I talked to them about Abraham, who set out to rescue Lot with 250 men "trained in his household." I insisted that it was not time for hirelings but for those who loved the seminary. My friend Roger Smith, of the Foreign Mission Board, and now deceased, later told me that following that meeting, he told his father-in-law, chairman of the Pastor Search Committee of Travis Avenue Baptist Church, Fort Worth, that Naylor was the man he ought to consider. There is no room for a discussion of that here.

On Saturday morning, T. C. Gardner of Texas brought the report of the Committee on Relations with Other Religious Bodies. There was this item in it: "That we warn our children of the dangers to harmonious married life of a Baptist and a Roman Catholic if promises are made that are not in a civil marriage ceremony."

Finally, on Sunday evening, I was to preach on "Christ Speaks on Training." I tried to pay a bit of my debt to the Training Union as an undergirding foundation to a vital New Testament church.

What a busy, responsible Convention it had been for us. In my report to the church on the following Sunday, I chose as a text Ephesians 5:25, "Christ loved the church and gave himself for it."

Sam Houston Coliseum • Houston, Texas

Roberts Taylor

MAY 6-10
1953

WITHIN TWO MONTHS AFTER THE SOUTHERN BAPTIST CONVENTION IN MIAMI, I WAS HAVING URGENT conversations with the Travis Avenue Baptist Church in Fort Worth, Texas. My own memories of the church were a little vague, and I certainly had no intention of going back to Texas. In fact, the chairman of the committee, A. O. Melton, came to Columbia, South Carolina, to see me and to talk about the church. I hope that I was courteous, but when we were together and he started to open a briefcase containing the papers about the church, I asked him not to do it. Thanking him for the interest of the committee, I explained that I had no reason to leave South Carolina or to go back to Texas. He departed, having earnestly requested that I make it a matter of prayer.

So here I was, barely nine months later, a messenger from a church in Texas to the annual meeting of the Southern Baptist Convention in Houston, Texas, This story is too long for detailed account here. From my moving date in October until my leaving for Houston, all had been busy, busy months. Twenty years after leaving the seminary and becoming pastor of the First Baptist Church in Nashville, Arkansas, I was back in Texas.

Lest anyone reading this find it too negative, I do need to record that I was always mindful of my Texas roots. My paternal grandparents came to the state in 1850 from Tennessee. My preacher father was saved in his twenties, called to preach, and ordained, all in Texas.

At this Convention, Houston was to be established as one of our main places to gather. Like a great city, it had made preparations for conventions. Dr. J. D. Grey, president of our Convention, called attention in his presidential address to the fact that we were meeting in a city named for a man who was a Baptist. Sam Houston was baptized in 1854 into the Baptist Church at Independence. My Tennessee forbears undoubtedly knew Sam Houston.

My time between the Conventions had been taken up with two Convention responsibilities. There was always the seminary. I was still a trustee simply by virtue of the bylaws that allowed a trustee, even in transition, to serve out the year. The time of stress at Southwestern had culminated in Dr. Head's poor health and his resignation as president to become effective August 1. This meant that the annual meeting of the trustees, well remembered, was one of tremendous importance, and there was a sense of heartache at the change.

There was always the Committee on Royal Ambassadors, Man and Boy Movement and Scouting, of which I was chairman. Much correspondence and a formal meeting of the committee to prepare its report to the Convention constituted the year.

The Convention began its ninety-sixth session in the Sam Houston Coliseum with President Grey presiding. The theme was "That the World May Believe" (John 17:21). Edwin McNeely, of the seminary, led us in singing "How Firm a Foundation." Secretary Burton made the opening motion that constituted the Convention and indicated a registration already of 8,205. Ultimately that was to be 12,976, by far a record to that date. The Committee on Order of Business presented its report, previously published, which was adopted. There were new innovations. There would be no afternoon sessions. The reports of the Home Mission Board and the Foreign Mission Board, traditionally each given an evening, were both on the same Thursday night.

Thursday morning brought the report of the Executive Committee. The constant increase in the importance and responsibilities of this committee were apparent. Agencies submitted their budgets to the Executive Committee for review before being presented to the Southern Baptist Convention. The fiscal year of the Convention and its agencies were established as January 1 to December 31, except in the case of the seminaries.

A special committee of the Executive Committee appointed to study the relationship of the WUM Training School, recently renamed the Carver School of Missions and Social Work, to the Southern Baptist Convention, made a report. On the basis of this report, the Executive Committee recommended that a special committee be appointed by the Convention to make a study of our total program of theological, religious, and missionary education as it involved financial support from the Southern Baptist Convention. They added that this special committee should be composed of members from the Executive Committee and seven members to be appointed by the president. It speaks to my involvement in Southwestern, and of my commitment, that I was named to this committee.

In the report of the Promotion Committee, I noted that Recommendation 7 read: "That the Bible doctrine of the Atonement be given emphasis by all means possible in 1955." I cannot imagine what produced a resolution that certainly was an axiom.

The report of the Committee on Study of Royal Ambassador, Man and Boy Movement and Scouting was on Thursday morning and was presented by me. The report itself commended the growth of male leadership, even under the direction of the Woman's Missionary Union. It also commended the progress made by Royal Ambassadors. Our recommendations to the Convention were twofold. First, the continuance of the committee to meet with representatives of the Executive Committee, Woman's Missionary Union, and representatives of the Baptist Brotherhood of the South, together with the executive secretaries of these agencies, to study the advisability of the transfer of Royal Ambassador work to Brotherhood sponsorship. Concerning the first recommendation, John Buchanan of Alabama, the pastor of many of the south-wide WMU leadership, offered an amendment that would have just referred it to the Woman's Missionary Union. The amendment was defeated and the recommendation of the committee was adopted.

Concerning Scouting, the committee did not feel the need to promote another program for Southern Baptist boys. They did recommend that the committee be instructed to prepare guidelines for awarding the "God and Country Award" by Scouting, as such guidelines might be needed in our churches. This called forth a great deal of discussion which was finally tabled.

The Memorial Services of the Convention, always meaningful, contained the names of M. E. Dodd; W. T. Conner; B. B. McKinney—these were the ones closest to my own life.

Officers elected included J. W. Storer of Oklahoma, president; Hermond Westmoreland of Houston, first vice-president; and Dr. R. C. Campbell, second vice-president. The missionary evening, though unusually long, was very moving. In all of these years, there had been no change in the fact that at the heart, we are a missionary people.

The proceedings indicated that E. D. Head presented the report of Southwestern Seminary and introduced William W. Barnes, professor of church history for forty years, who would retire June 1, 1953. President Head announced that his own resignation had been accepted by the Board of Trustees, effective August 1, 1953. The Convention stood in recognition of Dr. Head's service to the denomination at the suggestion of Duke K. McCall of Kentucky. The last line in this final report by Dr. Head reads, "All in all, the spirit at Southwestern was never better; the prospects never brighter. To God all the praise and glory."

So with our Committee on Royal Ambassador work continued, the responsibility of the new Special Committee on Theological Education, and continuing concern and involvement with the seminary, the Houston Convention concluded. Houston, we will be back!

Kiel Municipal Auditorium • St. Louis, Missouri

Robert Taylor

JUNE 2-5

1954

THIS WAS ALREADY OUR THIRD SOUTHERN BAPTIST CONVENTION IN ST. LOUIS, MISSOURI. THIS INDICATED that it had been a good Convention city. The auditorium was adequate. Most of the hotels were within walking distance of the Convention. There did not seem to be exciting tourist attractions. Yet, when I think of the arch alongside the Mississippi River that marked the western movement of our American people, I can get excited.

It had been a busy year in personal ministry. It had also been a year of continuing Southern Baptist involvement. There was the Committee to Study Theological Education, to which I had been appointed at the last Convention. One of our chief concerns had to do with the Carver School of Missions, formerly the Woman's Training School at Southern Seminary. We were to report to the Executive Committee. That recommendation will be mentioned later. As far as the seminary was concerned, it had been the first year of Dr. Williams' presidency, and that proved to be an exciting involvement. I had been elected chairman of the Board of Trustees, which put me in a very intimate relationship with the administration of the institution. The final report of our Committee on Royal Ambassador work was to be made. The previous Convention had made me a member of the Southern Baptist Foundation Board of Directors, as a representative of Southwestern Seminary. All of this meant that the Convention was to be business for us.

It is also time to mention again the growing anticipation for fellowship in the Convention. Moving from state to state, the intertwining of lives and ministries with a constantly increasing group, meant that I would see them only at the Convention. There was always that inner circle that dated back to the beginning. We wrote to each other to set up a time and place for getting together, and each one of these periods made the Convention more important and very worthwhile.

The Convention was called to order by President J. W. Storer of Oklahoma in the Kiel Municipal Auditorium in St. Louis at 9:00 A.M. on Wednesday, June 2. The theme was "Forward . . . in Christ Jesus." An innovation in procedure marked the order of business. For the first time, there was to be no Sunday session. The Convention was to adjourn Saturday at noon. Of course, a great many of the messengers had always adjourned the meeting sometime Saturday anyway. But, It was a formal recognition of the desire of the Convention messengers that the schedule be changed. Secretary Burton reported 5,023 messengers registered, and before it was done, the number would be in excess of 10,900.

President Storer delivered the opening address on the subject, "The Making, Meaning, and Mission of the Southern Baptist Convention." It is a document worthy of reference. The report of the Executive Committee dealt with the matter of interim appointments by Convention agencies. These appointments could be made in the case of a vacancy, but only until the next session of the Convention.

The Executive Committee recommended that the Southern Baptist Convention accept the invitation to Miami, Florida, for the meeting of our 1955 Convention. In a previous year the Convention had voted to meet in Washington, D. C., but they were unable to provide adequate auditorium facilities. I had looked forward to going to Washington, but you can understand how I already felt about Miami.

There was a recommendation that our Committee on Theological Education, that was appointed at the Houston Convention in 1953, be continued. This underlined to me the importance of theological education in Southern Baptist life.

Dr. T. L. Holcomb presented the report of the Southern Baptist Foundation. He had been made director of the foundation after his retirement. The report reflects its growth. I had discovered, in being a member of the foundation, that there was a real future involved. Some of the finest leaders I met were in that early board.

There were no afternoon sessions of the Convention. The first evening session was Foreign Mission Night. Dr. George Sadler spoke on "We Have Advanced in Africa." Among the new missionary

Kiel Municipal Auditorium in St. Louis, Missouri, site of the 1954 Southern Baptist Convention meeting. Courtesy—Southern Baptist Historical Library and Archives.

appointees presented to the Convention were Mr. and Mrs. Keith Parks of Texas who were appointed to Indonesia. One of the veteran missionaries presented was Bertha Smith, China. Almost thirty years later, she would still be veteran missionary Bertha Smith.

Thursday morning, it was my responsibility to present the report of the Committee to Study Sponsorship of Royal Ambassadors. We recommended that Royal Ambassador sponsorship be transferred from Woman's Missionary Union to the Brotherhood Commission. In doing so, WMU requested that the Brotherhood Commission employ a Royal Ambassador secretary. For a period of three years, WMU would continue to contribute to that person's salary and expense. During this time, a joint committee of the two agencies would supervise the work. There was a word of alert that insisted the Royal Ambassador program continue to be a missionary organization. We also recommended that the Convention adequately finance the work. The report was approved and there began a new period of growth, both in Royal Ambassador and Brotherhood work.

Both of our boys had been members of the Royal Ambassadors. It was in connection with the Scripture memorization that Dick was saved. I felt a personal debt to the organization, and felt that God was indeed leading in the recommendation.

This Convention was marked by live debate. A dozen times a motion was made to extend the time for discussion. There were three separate occasions in which an action of the Convention was called back under reconsideration. In an unusual way, it did emphasize the democracy that is basic in Southern Baptist gatherings.

This Convention changed the name of the Radio Commission to include the word "television." There was also a recommendation that the commission pursue its study of a change of location. Living in Fort Worth, I was already aware that this was "in the works," so to speak. The Convention simply said that the place of the location was to be left open for further study.

On Thursday morning, Dr. James L. Sullivan concluded that session with an address on the subject, "A Million More in '54." In the years since, I have heard people make snide remarks about Southern Baptist slogans. They particularly love to cast some kind of aspersion on "A Million More in '54." I took it seriously and so did a multitude of other Southern Baptists. It was one of the greatest years in winning people to Christ in the history of the Convention.

The report of the seminaries was given on Friday morning. Apparently, all of the presidents of the seminaries spoke to the report. All of the years that Dr. Head was president, I was a member of the trustees. This meant increasing involvement, as I steadfastly supported his leadership. In his final years, and at his request, I met him in Nashville, Tennessee, at the meeting of the Executive Committee, to assist in the request for funds from the Cooperative Program. This was always a meeting of stress, and it introduced me to a new part of the Nashville life. I had been involved in the Sunday School Board and its various programs, crusades, and such for fifteen years. I had also been a writer for Sunday School Board periodicals. Therefore, this kind of meeting was the very heart of the work of the Executive Committee.

When Dr. J. H. Williams was elected president of the seminary, I was elected president of the Board of Trustees. The report of the seminary became a very personal affair.

It might just be alright to place a personal note at this point. Dr. A. J. Holt had been president of the trustees until the time that Dr. Head resigned. He appointed the committee that was to be the

Search Committee for a new president. Later, he told me with a bit of an apology that he did not appoint me on the Search Committee because he thought I would be a prime consideration for president. I had no thought of such, but appreciated his friendship and evaluation of my services.

The report of Southwestern reflected a banner enrollment for the year. There were the names of new faculty members who had been added. There was a general spirit of optimism and progress that was so characteristic of Dr. Williams.

One of the key matters discussed at this Convention was that of our westward expansion as a convention, and in particular, the development of Southern Baptist churches in Canada. Dr. R. E. Milam brought a recommendation to the Convention that employees of our mission boards be granted the privilege of giving assistance to the churches in Canada that asked for such help. There was a point of order by someone suggesting that this was out of order by our Constitution. We were limited to our own country, except as a foreign mission enterprise. The Convention overruled the ruling of the president and gave hearty approval to the motion from Dr. Milam.

Those early pioneers in our Southern Baptist work in the West had already written a noble chapter. I had been out there for their programs, meetings, and encampments. I often said that the people paying the price for that expansion were those wives of these pastors and missionaries. I was personally committed to the fact that western Canada was a mission territory for us that should not be neglected.

Saturday morning was to be the closing session, but it turned out to be one of the busiest sessions. That could have been the reason we finally reached the place where no new business was on the agenda for closing sessions.

The report of the Committee on Time, Place, and Preacher was reported by Chairman Harold W. Seaver of Alabama. It called for the Executive Committee to study the advisability of the Convention meeting from Friday through Tuesday. It also suggested that the place of the Convention meeting be determined as far as three years in advance. This committee brought recommendations about meeting at Kansas City in 1956 and Chicago in 1957.

This Convention met in a time of change. Not only were we looking to new territory and accepting new challenges, but we were finding the size of our structure increasingly difficult as an area of unity.

$\mathscr{S}$outhern $\mathscr{B}$aptist $\mathscr{C}$onvention

Dinner Key Auditorium • Miami, Florida

Robert Taylor

MAY 18-21
1955

IT WAS CERTAINLY DIFFICULT TO BE TOO DISAPPOINTED THAT THE CONVENTION WAS NOT MEETING IN WASHINGTON, D. C., as originally planned. The year before, the place had been changed due to inadequate facilities in the Capitol. Feeling as I did about Miami, it seemed a good decision. This was to be the third Miami Convention.

There was another factor involved. We had already made plans to go to the meeting of the Baptist World Alliance in London in July. This trip was to include our first trip to the Holy Land. We were very excited about it; and even in the midst of building a tremendous auditorium and going to the Southern Baptist Convention, the Alliance meeting could not be put away from our minds. This would be a special meeting of Baptists from around the world.

The ninety-eighth session of the Southern Baptist Convention, meeting in its 110th year, was called to order at 9:00 A.M., Wednesday, May 18, by President J. W. Storer. We were meeting in the Dinner Key Auditorium, which I have not forgotten. It was not the best. Secretary Joe Burton reported 2,083 messengers as having registered by the opening of the Convention. By the time we were through the number would rise to over 10,800.

This was one of the Conventions in which I kept the notes for reporting to my church in Fort Worth. The notes call attention to the theme, "Giving God the Glory." They also indicate that the Scripture basis was "Let the Lord be glorified" (Isa. 66:5b). It was clear that I had been impressed in this opening session by the Convention sermon which was preached by Monroe Swilley using the text, "For Christ did not send me to baptize, but to preach the Gospel, not with eloquent wisdom, lest the cross of Christ be emptied of its power" (RSV).

95

A fine note sounded in the Convention was that of Dr. Herbert Gezork, the vice-president of the American Baptist Convention, as he brought a fraternal message on the theme, "Things Baptists Have in Common." He spoke of convictions held in common as to the authority of the Scriptures, regenerated church membership, the universal priesthood of believers, our freedom of conscience, and the separation of church and state. Does that sound familiar?

Then there was the report of the Committee on Theological Education, brought by Dr. Louie D. Newton of Georgia. It provoked one of the major discussions of the Convention concerning accepting the Baptist Bible Institute at Graceville, Florida, or the Baptist Institution at Clear Creek, Kentucky, as Southern Baptist agencies for which the Convention would become responsible. Before the discussion was through, the Carver School of Missions in Louisville had been brought into the discussion. It was virtually decided that we had enough institutions to care for. Later on, there was a recommendation that a new Baptist hospital be established in Los Angeles, California. This, too, was delayed on the same grounds.

The report of the Foreign Mission Board was on Wednesday night. Dr. Baker Cauthen used his area secretaries to present a report from their areas, and to introduce missionaries present from those areas. (There is never a more impressive moment for me than that in which they finally present the new appointees.) Husband and wife, they came by, each to give their name and the place from which they came. There were single missionaries, to be sure, always among the families. There would be some children in arms. Tommy Halsel was one missionary I knew. I had been his college pastor when he was in Ouachita College. In fact, God had allowed me to be a part of his understanding that God was speaking to him for ministry.

The highlights of the Convention that I noted included the first time in history that the Convention had one thousand missionaries under appointment. Now the number was 1,002. At the same time, there were more than 1,300 home missionaries.

There were Four Major Milestones in the report. For the first time, our membership exceeded eight million. Six million members were enrolled in Sunday School, and two million in Training Union.

This was the year that we would hear a report from the 1954 evangelistic emphasis, "A Million More in '54." It was reported to the Convention that in 1945, there had been 256,699 baptisms. In 1954, the Convention had baptized 396,857 people. This was a fifty-five percent gain in nine years. It does pay to get serious about the goal that you adopt. Thirty-three years later, with almost twice as many members, Southern Baptists failed to baptize this number.

I was personally involved in the report of the Southern Baptist Foundation. Dr. T. L. Holcomb continued to report growth in this work. On my part, I had been able to see that some of our Southwestern Seminary endowment funds had been placed with the Southern Baptist Foundation. It proved to be a fruitful investment.

In the report of the seminary itself, Dr. Williams reported 2,375 students enrolled; this was a record for the seminary. There was a spirit of optimism in the report concerning the development of the building program and other things to be done. God had used Dr. Williams in a wonderful way to inject a forward-looking spirit in the institution.

As usual with Miami Conventions, we returned saying, "This was a good Convention." We would go to Kansas City in 1956.

Municipal Auditorium • Kansas City, Missouri

Robert Naylor (signature)

MAY 30 - JUNE 2

1956

THIS WAS TO BE OUR FIRST CONVENTION IN KANSAS CITY, AND WE LOOKED FORWARD TO A NEW PLACE. WE WERE to meet our friends, the Barkers, in Enid, Oklahoma, and drive to the Convention. The hotel reservation was at the Hotel Muhlbach, a storied hotel in the Midwest.

The Convention's theme was "Righteousness Exaltheth a Nation— A Crusade for Christian Morality" (Prov. 14:34). The opening moment was one of particular inspiration.

In this first morning session, President C. C. Warren brought the president's address. As I recall, almost as an afterthought to his message, he said, "We ought to double the number of preaching stations in the Southern Baptist Convention in the next five years." First reaction would be that he was carried away by his own message. It became, however, a five-year program, and a constantly repeated slogan in the Convention. The emphasis was upon preaching stations, which allowed chapels and missions to be counted, and it undoubtedly added momentum to the next five years.

Porter Routh reported record Cooperative Program gifts, and in a high moment, the Convention adopted a budget both operating and capital in the total amount of $11 million for 1957. Southwestern Seminary was to receive $499,000 for operations and $242,000 for capital. The Convention operating budget for that next year was set at $160,000. How far we had come! The years 1959 to 1964 were essentially designated as "The Baptist Jubilee Advance."

A recommendation was adopted which "emphasized unity for all of our Denomination work, both South-Wide and State." It reaffirmed the principles of cooperation set forth in 1934. Many sessions later in the Convention, a resolution was adopted endorsing again the action of the Southern Baptist Convention entitled "Relation of the Southern Baptist Convention to Other Baptist Bodies." It was an action taken by the Convention of 1928. The need to reestablish the building blocks of our Convention became evident. The next time we would meet in Kansas City, we would be examining even our basic doctrinal identity.

The Foreign Mission Board was allowed to increase its number of directors from fifty to one hundred. Golden Gate Seminary was noted as approving the Articles of Faith adopted by the Convention in 1925. My old professor, Dr. Leslie Carlson, was named fraternal messenger to the Swedish Baptist Convention.

The Sunday School Board wanted to change its name to "The Board of Education and Publication." Long discussion followed, and the request was referred. It seems that ever so often, somebody wants to change their name within the Convention.

To my consternation, there was a motion to approve the establishment of a new seminary. Of course, the clause was attached, "as soon as one is allowed." The five seminaries then were struggling to exist. When the committee named finally reported in 1957, sure enough, the new seminary was to be in Kansas City.

In like fashion, the WMU Training School, now the Carver School of Missions, became a Convention agency with trustees elected by the Convention.

The election of officers bespoke the unity of the Convention. C. C. Warren was elected president for another term by acclamation. The nominations for first and second vice-presidents were several. They were all divided by standing vote. It seemed it was no big matter. We were all brothers and sisters.

The Convention expressed unity, commitment to world evangelism, and momentum in grace. Perhaps the final recorded action says it best: "Following prayer . . . the 99th annual session of the Southern Baptist Convention was, by vote of the majority, finally adjourned."

International Amphitheatre • Chicago, Illinois

MAY 28-31
1957

WHILE WE DID NOT QUESTION OUR ATTENDING THE SOUTHERN BAPTIST CONVENTION, I WAS NOT TOO enthusiastic about going back to Chicago. There would be room to be sure. The city was so large that it would remain unimpressed by our presence.

There was a personal side to this. At Travis Avenue we were engaged in an epic endeavor, building what was to be at that time the largest auditorium in the Convention. I often thought we were making bricks without straw. God had so abundantly blessed, but I was going at a time when the building stage was most pressing.

Still, it was the Convention. President Casper C. Warren called the Convention to order on Tuesday night, May 28. The theme was "That the World May Know" (John 17:23). The Convention was to run from Tuesday through Thursday night. The opening registration announced by Secretary Burton was 6,749 messengers. At the close of the Convention, this enrollment had reached more than 9,100. We were getting ever larger.

The opening session was to be a joint presentation by the Foreign Mission Board and Woman's Missionary Union. Dr. Baker Cauthen presented the reports from the different fields, and then a great host of forty-five new appointees. Dr. J. Howard Williams brought an excellent closing message for the missionary evening on the subject, "Christ Calls Now."

On Wednesday morning in the report of the Southern Baptist Foundation, of which I was still a member, there was a resolution authorizing the foundation to accept the trust funds of the Carver School of Missions and Social Work. The Convention had already voted to accept and to fund this institution as one of its agencies.

100

At this same session, Dr. W. Douglas Hudgins presented a report recommending the establishment of a new theological seminary. The usual condition was attached that "as soon as a place could be determined, and at a time when such an undertaking could be financed without impairing our present seminaries and our Cooperative Program allocations." At this distance, it seems almost humorous. We already had two new seminaries, and the Convention "committed" to Southern Baptist theological education embarked on a program that was to be a financial struggle all the way.

In the amendments that were offered and their substitutes, it was determined that this new seminary would be located at Kansas City, Missouri. It would limit its scope of work to a School of Theology. The capital investments for the institution would be limited to $2 million. There was a real effort to choose other sites before Kansas City, but the matter was passed. Suddenly a Convention meeting in a marginal area of the Convention became one of long-range and long-term significance.

The recommendation by the Executive Committee for the approval of the new Cooperative Program budget always seemed most routine. We seemed to little realize that the life blood of our witness was involved. Capital needs and operating funds in excess of $13 million were adopted by this Convention. All of the above required much time. It was necessary to establish, by resolution, that the order of business should bring the Convention sermon on time.

We rarely had a more interesting election of officers. There were six different people nominated to be president. These included Forrest Feezor of Texas, Roy Angell of Florida, W. R. White of Texas, Ramsey Pollard of Tennessee, C. Vaughn Rock of Arizona, and Brooks Hays, Congressman/layman from Arkansas. For one of the few times in my memory, the rules were suspended and the election was by standing vote among these six men. Without any evidence of stress, people stood up and voted for the man they preferred. Hays was elected, and a motion that it be unanimous was adopted. Somehow, I feel that this is the way that a Baptist convention ought to function. Noel Taylor, chairman of the Host Arrangements Committee, was elected second vice-president of the Convention.

There was a recommendation concerning the change of name for the Sunday School Board. At this point we seemed to embark on a long-running discussion as to the name of the Convention, and sometimes we would focus on one of its agencies.

My friend, James E. Coggins of Texas, presented the Memorial Service. Among the names that were called were C. E. Matthews of Texas, B. H. Duncan of Arkansas, and J. Gilliam Hughes of Tennessee. All of these were warm, personal friends, and in my heart I thank the Lord for each of them. I thought, "How heaven multiplies."

Dr. J. H. Williams, reporting for Southwestern Seminary, spoke of the completion of the new library and our Memorial Building. The financial campaign for student housing had been successful. A total enrollment of 1,849 was reported. How little we realized that this would be his last report to the Convention.

On a more personal note, G. W. Bullard presented the report of the Committee on Time, Place and Preacher. The Convention chose Robert E. Naylor as preacher of the Convention sermon in 1958 in Houston. The alternate was to be my close friend Harold W. Seever of Alabama. I first had known him as a warm friend in South Carolina, and later in his church, Dauphin Way, at Mobile, Alabama.

There was one other emphasis in this Convention that should be remembered. The proposal that we establish thirty thousand new churches and missions received its impetus and definition here. It would include twenty thousand new preaching places.

Sam Houston Coliseum • Houston, Texas

[signature: Robert Naylor]

MAY 20-23
1958

IF THERE WAS TO BE ONE CONVENTION THAT WOULD BE MORE PERSONAL THAN ANY OTHER, MORE MOMENTOUS in its sweep than any other, it would have to be the 1958 Convention. There was a movement in the Convention both as to the Convention itself and in my personal life that gathered force. Preceding events reached a climax at the Convention.

On April 20, 1958, I was conducting a revival meeting at the First Baptist Church of Spartanburg, South Carolina. It was really a bit of respite from pressure. The building of the new sanctuary at Travis Avenue had reached a climax. All that remained was interior completion; pews had been ordered, and the financing of the building was at its most critical stage.

Suddenly that morning a telephone call informed me, as president of trustees at Southwestern, that President J. H. Williams was dying. I immediately called Mrs. Williams at the hospital, and she confirmed the sad news. Along with the church, suddenly the weight of the seminary responsibility fell upon me.

That same morning, there was a call from another trustee, a friend of the years, who said, "God is moving to make you the president of the seminary." To say that I was upset would be to understate the matter. In the days that followed, the trustees asked me to be the interim administrator, acting as president. A Search Committee was appointed. The committee almost immediately indicated to me that there was a prevailing conviction that God had chosen me. When we came to the Convention, just thirty days later, the committee was ready with its report.

As if this was not enough, I had been chosen by the previous Convention to preach the Convention sermon at this very session.

Only a preacher and pastor will understand that this is a great moment in the ministry of a Baptist preacher. For twenty-five years I had been attending the Convention; now I had been chosen to give the central message.

On arriving in Houston, I found that the number one item of discussion was the seminary and its search for a new president. There were those who did not feel that I should be president. At no point did I suggest to anybody that I wanted to be president of the seminary. On the other hand, there were others who insisted that this should come to pass. I could not leave my room in the hotel without being surrounded by people who wanted to discuss it with me.

You say that is enough. We should add to this bill of particulars that it was the Golden Anniversary of Southwestern Seminary. Dr. Williams had made great plans for the Convention and for the presenting of our fifty years. Suddenly the responsibility for all of that was added to these other things.

The Convention opened on Tuesday night with Congressman and President Brooks Hays of Arkansas presiding. The Convention theme was "Go . . . Make Disciples" (Matt. 28:19).

William J. Reynolds was the music director for the Convention. Secretary Joe Burton announced that 6,439 messengers had been accredited at the opening moment of the Convention. The first session was concluded with an address by W. A. Criswell of Texas on "Jubilee Advance," and a pageant depicting the spirit and objectives of the Jubilee Advance.

On Wednesday morning the Executive Committee of the Convention made its report with recommendations. I will refer to some of these matters later. The morning was to climax for me with the hour for the Convention sermon. Almost sixty people had come from our church at Travis Avenue to be present for this hour. Virginia Seelig sang "Blessed Redeemer" with that marvelous introduction "Up Calvary's mountain one dreadful day." It was simply magnificent. My friend, Harold W. Seever of Alabama, read a Scripture, John 1:43-51, and I preached from John 2:23-25: "Jesus knew what was in man, but died for him and saved him anyway."

When the service was done, I was exhausted. I said to my friend Bob Barker, "The afternoon session is routine. True, it is time for election of officers, but Brooks Hays is due by all tradition, as well as by a good performance, to receive his second term as president. I just must get away. Let's be tourists this afternoon." So we left immediately with our wives and spent the afternoon at the San Jacinto Monument. My historical blood flows faster in the presence of that particular monument. Only later was I to learn what went on in our absence.

The time came for the election of officers and Brooks Hays was nominated, as would be expected. He was nominated by one of my closest friends, J. D. Grey of Louisiana. A woman came to the platform who was unhappy with some of the rulings of the chair, and with some of the things being done in the Convention. President Brooks Hays tried to explain to her gently that she was out of order, and that the order of business was upon the election of officers. She persisted in her discussion. At last Hays said to her, "Madam, this is the time for the nomination of a president. You will have to make a nomination, or I will have to declare you out of order." Upon which she said, "Very well, I will nominate that man who preached this morning." She did not even know my name. What should they do? I was not there to defend myself or withdraw my name, as we customarily did in the Convention. My friends would not do it because I was not there to assent. So Robert E. Naylor was nominated for president of the Convention. Later in the minutes, I learned that "Mrs. Mary Odom of Texas nominated Robert E. Naylor of Texas." So the vote was cast, and of course Brooks Hays was elected. I was told by my friends, as they laughed about the matter, that two or three thousand people voted for me under those circumstances.

Now to the things that transpired in that first session. The charter of Midwestern Seminary was approved and final action was taken concerning its government. Of particular significance was the adoption of a Cooperative Program budget, and for a very particular reason not routine this time. Dr. Williams had asked me to go with him to the meeting of the Executive Committee in February. As chairman of the trustees, he wanted me to assist him in the plea that had to be made. Space here does not allow description of the meetings, but I was present when the presidents of the seminaries could not agree upon the distribution, and so reported to the committee. The committee in turn refused to make an appropriation and sent them back into session saying they must agree. Agreement only came when Dr. Williams made concessions to the other seminaries that was to cost Southwestern important funds. When asked about my feelings on the matter, I simply said to the presidents, "I always support my president." I think the distribution is unfair, and if invited to another meeting, I can in that context, say that I will not agree. In this case, surely Dr. Williams' vote is my vote. The result had been that the appropriation made by the committee cost Southwestern at least $25,000. I was most concerned about the fact that Dr. Williams seemed very distressed about it. By the time this moment came in this Houston Convention, Dr. Williams was dead, and Dr. Roland Q. Leavell of New Orleans was broken in health and had retired for health reasons. It was a meeting that cast a long shadow.

The time for the report of the presidents of the seminaries came on Thursday morning. As a first matter, Ellis L. Carnett of Texas, trustee of the institution, presented a resolution adopted by the trustees of Southwestern on the passing of former President J. Howard Williams. The Convention stood while the resolutions were read following a period of silent prayer.

A few moments later, as chairman of the trustees, and acting for the president, I presented the report of the seminary. It consisted of presenting the three deans, each of whom addressed the Golden Jubilee Anniversary of the seminary.

It can be indicated parenthetically that it had also been my responsibility to speak to the gathering of our alumni, as Dr. Williams would have done had he been present.

As a final responsibility, a time had been set apart in the program of the Convention for the formal recognition of the Southwestern Seminary Jubilee Program. Southwestern Seminary Oratorio Chorus, Robert L. Burton, conductor, assisted by the Cowboy Band, sang "Hallelujah." The fifty-year history of the seminary was presented in picture and story. Finally, it was mine to bring the closing message that would have been brought by Dr. Williams. John Haldeman of Florida made a brief statement for the trustees.

What had happened to the matter of electing a president? The special committee came to me to say that they were unanimous in their choice. They would not take a formal action at the Convention, since it had been only one month. They would meet in Fort Worth one month later and confirm their decision. How could I leave Travis Avenue? Was this certainly the will of God for my own life, as well as for the institution? Subsequent events would say yes.

Thus far, the report has been altogether personal. The Convention was far more significant than just that. There was the Foreign Mission

Board report by Dr. Baker Cauthen on Wednesday evening. There were thirty-eight newly appointed missionaries presented, and they were made the object of a prayer of dedication and blessing.

A report that had been headlined preliminary to the Convention was given by a special committee to study the total Southern Baptist Convention program. It was indeed far-reaching. A new agency called the Stewardship Commission was created. A structure for the organization of the Executive Committee was adopted. A recommendation stated that the Executive Committee should be provided with facilities which will serve its needs fully. It was resolved that Woman's Missionary Union should be continued as an auxiliary to the Southern Baptist Convention. Cooperation would be provided through the Inter-Agency Council, a fellowship of agency executives that had been created only a few years before by a committee on coordination. Membership in the Inter-Agency Council was spelled out. For the first time, it was determined that committees, boards, and commissions should include both ordained and laypersons as members, and that not more than two-thirds of the members of any group should be drawn from either category.

The first steps were taken toward making hospitals and their ministries a function of the state conventions. Of particular interest was a recommendation, "Allocation of Cooperative Program funds should be related more directly to the number of students the seminaries are expected to train." Another said, "The seminary presidents should adopt a revised formula for distribution of Cooperative Program funds." There were further safeguards established against the formation of new seminaries. The details are a little full, but you can see that it had breathtaking scope, and even yet is referred to as a "milestone in the life of the Convention."

The Convention finally closed on Friday evening, with an address by President Hays on the special program concerning the present world crisis and a sermon by Dr. Theodore F. Adams, president of the Baptist World Alliance. The actions taken by the Convention are here only in barest outline. We turned away with a sense of God intervening in our own lives in such a personal fashion, in the life of the seminary to which we had always been devoted, and in the life of the Convention, which was the ultimate channel of fellowship.

Kentucky State Fair and Exposition Center • Louisville, Kentucky

[signature: Robert Naylor]

MAY 19-22

1959

FOR US, THIS CONVENTION MEETING IN LOUISVILLE, KENTUCKY, HAD TO BE A NEW CONVENTION, SET IN A NEW context. For almost a year I had been president of Southwestern Baptist Theological Seminary. For all of the years to follow, going to the Convention was to be tied up with an agency of the Convention in a very personal way. During the years, the six seminary presidents had held many meetings, some of them quite serious and quite important. The very life of the institution, which was our responsibility, seemed to be at stake. Out of those meetings had come a new understanding that was reflected in the action of the Convention concerning appropriations for the institutions.

It could be said here that I had a special sort of conviction about the new relationship. I assigned all of the honors and many of the personal privileges of service in my mind and heart to a pastor. There were certain things that a man who directed the affairs of one of the agencies of the Convention ought not expect. With those statements being made, let us begin the new chapter.

For a very special reason, this time the Convention was meeting in Louisville. This was the centennial year of the founding of Southern Baptist Theological Seminary, our oldest institution. The school had arranged its calendar so that its graduation exercises could be made a formal part of the Convention procedure. All of us graduates of the Southern Baptist seminaries felt a keen and personal interest in the proceedings.

In addition, this was the sixth meeting of the Southern Baptist Convention in Louisville, Kentucky, since its founding in 1845. In 1857, the attendance was officially listed as 184. In 1870, after the seminary had moved to Louisville, the registration was 399. In 1887, the attendance was 689; in 1899, it was 869. In 1927, when George W. Truett was president, the attendance had been 4,424. So, this was the first of my ministry in Louisville. It was also the largest registration in Louisville, finally becoming 12,326. It was the second largest attendance in the history of the Southern Baptist Convention. This would mark the last Convention here because of the lack of facilities.

We had an enjoyment-plus this Convention, because of the fact that Dr. and Mrs. Joe Steger accompanied us to the Convention in our car. Dr. Steger was our personal physician and also a trustee for the seminary. He was a tower of strength in my pastorate at Travis Avenue Baptist Church, and they were both very personal friends. Traveling to the Convention and returning home was a delight. After our first day in Louisville, I remember Dr. Steger saying to me, "You know these preachers want to get me aside and marvel about the fact that Naylor can bring his personal physician to the Convention." I laughed and explained to him that that was the privilege of being a seminary president.

The Convention theme was "Teaching Them to Observe" (Matt. 28:20). The Convention opened on Tuesday evening and was called to order by President Brooks Hays. We sang "All Hail the Power of Jesus' Name." It seems a far cry to yesterday that we concluded the Convention singing "Amazing Grace, How Sweet the Sound." We have lost something in the changing of the music in our Convention.

This Convention was in truth the seminaries' Convention. At the opening session, five of us presented reports from our institutions with no discussion. The Convention had agreed that opportunities for questions would come later in the course of the Convention. Then Southern Seminary presented its graduation exercises in which we all participated. It was a memorable evening for me. We all entered as a seminary processional. The graduates were presented the degrees they had received, and all of the regular formalities of commencement were observed. Paul Caudill of Tennessee preached the Convention sermon, which was also the commencement address.

On Wednesday morning, the report of the Executive Committee was the main order of business. As is true even now, the committee first presented the new Cooperative Program budget for adoption by the Convention. The total budget, including its Advance Challenge provision, totalled $18 million. In the seminary appropriations, it was observable that Southwestern, almost for the first time and in recognition of its size, was given the largest appropriation of the six seminaries.

Dr. Naylor speaks to Southwestern Baptist Theological Seminary alumni during 1959 Southern Baptist Convention meeting in Louisville, Kentucky. Courtesy—Texas Baptist Historical Collection.

This same Convention is the one that first recommended that at least one-third of the members of the boards and commissions of the Convention be laypersons. That is to say that no more than two-thirds of the members of the boards and commissions should be ordained persons, nor more than two-thirds laypersons for that matter. This recommendation was to bring far-reaching changes. In fact, the changes adopted in the structure of this Convention, even though some of them were very constructive and progressive, sowed the seeds for division, and the struggles for power and leadership which plague our Convention to this day.

Among the recommendations was one which indicated that "when the membership of cooperating Baptist churches in a given state shall have reached 250,000, there should be elected an additional member of the Executive Committee." This was rapidly extended to other boards and the increasing size of the Convention recognized thereby.

The Inter-Agency Council, which had grown in its usefulness for the Convention, was a product of a committee on which I had served for many years. It was officially made the organization through which the various agencies of the Convention would correlate their work.

The outreach of the Convention was underlined by a recommendation that Baptist churches, in a state or territory having twenty-five thousand members, may apply for representation on the Executive Committee and the boards of the Convention.

Ramsey Pollard, seminary classmate and a recognized leader in the Convention, was elected president of the Convention. W. R. Pettigrew of Kentucky was named first vice-president, and Bruce Price of Virginia was named second vice-president.

Wednesday night was Foreign Missions Night. The dynamic leadership of Dr. Baker Cauthen was already evident.

The Convention debated the status of the Carver School of Missions and Social Work. There was an attempt to make it a part of Southern Baptist Theological Seminary. Strongly resistant, the Convention finally voted to leave it as an institution apart, and to proceed to support it.

On Thursday morning the seminaries' reports were again presented and, on this occasion, discussed. There were remarks and questions raised even then; among them a man named James W. Bulman of North Carolina made an unsuccessful effort to extend the time in order to offer a substitute motion. The reports of the seminaries were approved. A footnote says that a little later in the Convention, this same man tried to get recognition to speak, and by vote of the Convention was refused.

A dominant discussion of the Convention for two or three years was the report of the Committee to Study the Total Southern Baptist Program. It had already reported in Houston in 1958, and now was to bring its final report in 1959. Many of the changes were technical and relatively unimportant. There were others, however, that had far-reaching significance. The first eight recommendations concerned the Home Mission Board; they simply affirmed, identified, and strengthened the work of the board.

There was much discussion about the establishment of a new Stewardship Commission. An effort was made to amend the recommendation in order to make the Stewardship Commission a part of the Sunday School Board. This effort was defeated, and the new commission came into being.

A long discussion took place concerning recommendations that the seminaries do more about financing their own institutions. Three recommendations called for us to practically seek out individual sustenance. All of these recommendations were defeated, and the Convention reaffirmed its total commitment to theological education.

The Convention adjourned on Friday evening, having made some far-reaching decisions. A characteristic of previous Conventions was present here. In the midst of serious discussions, there was a spirit of harmony, fellowship, and willingness. Even though there were differing opinions, there was still a common fellowship. When we closed on Friday evening singing "Amazing Grace," the Convention had come to its most mature expression of oneness.

On the way home we stopped some place in West Tennessee to eat supper. For many miles we had seen an advertisement suggesting a wonderful fish place on the River. We pulled up to the place after dark, went in, and ordered catfish. Mrs. Steger said that as we were sitting there, a woman came in from the kitchen, looked at us, and said, "Reverend Naylor!" We laughed about it, and I have often thought, this is "going to the Convention."

Miami Beach Exposition Hall • Miami Beach, Florida

MAY 17-20
1960

MIAMI BEACH WAS A GREAT CENTER FOR CONVENTIONS. AS PREVIOUSLY INDICATED, IT WAS A PLACE THAT I had always enjoyed; and every Convention had been like a few days in a different world. Miami Beach had built a great new Exhibition Hall, and the Convention had accepted an invitation to hold its sessions there. Even though our plans were to go to the Baptist World Alliance in Brazil in just two months, Miami still held its own in our expectations.

John Seelig, whom I had brought to Travis Avenue Baptist Church as minister of education, had become director of public relations at the seminary. The plus of this trip to the Convention was that he and Virginia were to accompany us to the Convention in our car. On the way, we were to stop Sunday in Tallahassee. Virginia was to sing, and I was to preach at the First Baptist Church. It was always a special joy when Virginia sang. They are not only great friends, but delightful spirits. At every point, the journey was a real joy.

The Convention theme was "Required of Stewards . . . Found Faithful" (1 Cor. 4:2). The Convention opened on Tuesday evening, May 17, with President Ramsey Pollard, my longtime friend and seminary classmate, presiding. C. Roy Angell, pastor of the Central Baptist Church in Miami, welcomed the Convention. The secretary reported that there were already in excess of nine thousand messengers present. The president announced the committees and I noted that my lifetime friend, E. C. Brown, had been made chairman of the Committee on Committees. On this opening night, Ralph Herring of North Carolina preached the Convention sermon on "Lifting Life's Limitations." A memorial service had preceded the message, and the evening concluded with "God Be With You 'Til We Meet Again."

113

One of the major activities of the Convention concerned the newly authorized and organized Stewardship Commission as a new agency of the Convention. In 1959, there had been much discussion about making this work a part of the Sunday School Board. The Convention had voted to make it a separate agency, so many of the actions taken, beginning with Wednesday morning, concerned the structural alignment of the agency. The programs of the commission were approved. The first secretary, Dr. Merrill D. Moore, was introduced. He began his work auspiciously by paying tribute to the beginnings of the Cooperative Program.

The Executive Committee made its report and offered its recommendations on Wednesday morning. The Public Affairs Committee was created with fifteen members. What a long shadow it would cast.

The Convention adopted a recommendation that provided "the President, in conference with the Vice Presidents, shall name the Committee on Committees and the Committee on Resolutions." This was more significant than intended.

One of the major debates occurred over a recommendation that said, "No executive or member of the staff of any Agency or the Executive Committee shall initiate recommendations to the Committee on Boards regarding places to be filled." In the meeting of the Executive Committee the previous February, this recommendation had been hotly debated. I was amazed and a little insulted that they thought it unethical for the head of an agency to make a suggestion of any kind to the Committee on Boards about the trustees that were needed. I entered into the fray there and lost. It seemed to me that of all the people in the world that ought to be vitally interested in the kind of trustee chosen, it would be the head of a particular agency. I certainly did not believe in dictating the personnel of the trustees, but to express interest seemed to me absolutely necessary. After the debate, the Convention in Miami refused to adopt the recommendation.

For the first time that I can remember, this Convention also adopted a recommendation establishing a goal for contingent reserves. How far we had come from those dark days when it seemed that the Convention would come to bankruptcy. I noted that Southwestern Seminary was asked to establish a goal of $350,000 for contingency reserves.

In the recommendation concerning the operating budget of the agencies, a new formula that we had hammered out for distribution of funds to the seminaries bore its first fruit. Southwestern Seminary increased in a single year from $562,000 to $698,000 recognizing the size of the institution.

The seminaries reported on Thursday morning. Millard Berquist, president of Midwestern Baptist Theological Seminary and chairman of the Inter-Seminary Council, brought the report. This Inter-Seminary Council was the result of that first action that I initiated, suggesting that we all meet together and frankly discuss our different problems and differences. Dr. Berquist presented all of us who were presidents of seminaries; the reports from our institutions were adopted; and Dr. Berquist brought the address on theological education on behalf of all of us.

Another recommendation adopted by our Convention said that the Committee on Boards, because of the increasing size of the task, would have at least two called meetings prior to the Convention.

Foreign Mission Night was Thursday night. Fifty-nine new missionaries were presented, and their names were printed in the *Annual*. Many of these names have become almost household names for those of us who regularly pray for our missionaries.

This Convention extended an invitation to the Baptist World Congress to hold its 1965 session in Miami Beach, Florida. We were there.

Foy Valentine was introduced as the new secretary of the Christian Life Commission. The death of R. S. Jones, formerly with the Relief and Annuity Board, was announced, and a letter of sympathy was sent to Dr. Kathleen Jones in Indonesia.

Billy Graham and George Beverly Shea closed the Convention on Friday night.

This summary of the Convention suggests growth; inevitably, such growth meant bureaucracy. As a president of a seminary, even though I shall always be a pastor, there was a new intimate focus upon a Convention that chooses to work together.

Kiel Auditorium • St. Louis, Missouri

MAY 23-26
1961

HERE WE WERE IN ST. LOUIS AGAIN. I HAD BEEN THERE FOR THREE PREVIOUS CONVENTIONS. IN 1936, THE CONVENTION had met in St. Louis; and that was the only one that Goldia had missed in these years. I sorely missed her, and my memories of the Convention are not that significant.

In 1947, when the Convention was there again, it was just prior to my experience with the First Baptist Church of Columbia, South Carolina. I was still a pastor in Enid, Oklahoma, and St. Louis seemed a part of our world.

On the other hand, when the Convention came to St. Louis again in 1954, we were in Fort Worth. We were involved in a great church building program, and intimately tied to the affairs and needs of the seminary. Much of this is reflected in my response concerning the Convention.

St. Louis was a great convention city. The auditorium was fully adequate and our hotel accommodations were not far away. As the doorway to the West in the development of our country, St. Louis was always an attractive tourist city. Now president of Southwestern, already experienced in the Convention in that role, we came to St. Louis with delight and anticipation of the fellowship that the Convention had always provided.

President Ramsey Pollard called the Convention into session on Tuesday evening, May 23. The Convention theme was "My Church . . . Reaching Out." We began with singing "All Hail the Power of Jesus' Name" and "Blessed Assurance Jesus is Mine." The initial enrollment was reported as 8,557 messengers. There was great emphasis in the 1960 Convention upon the creation of the

Stewardship Commission. In the first session, the Stewardship Committee report was presented by Merrill D. Moore of Tennessee. Their first recommendation, I am sure with the sense of a new charter, was "urge all Baptists to join in giving the Cooperative Program their loyal and undivided support."

Following this report, my friend A. V. Van Arsdale of Alabama preached the Convention sermon on "The Everlasting Gospel."

It would be expected that my own priority would have shifted to a concern for the programs through the seminaries. On Wednesday morning, the 1962 budget was presented and adopted by the Convention. Again it reflected the new formula for the distribution of funds which had been arrived at by the presidents, with the approval of the Convention. The predominant size of Southwestern is reflected in those figures. It also indicated a major support of the Southern Baptist Convention, unusual in the world of theological education.

The seeds of the Inter-Agency Council had been sown in the last Convention. As indicated, this gathering of the agency executives, without formal structure, was an outgrowth of the new "presidents of the seminaries sessions" which had proved fruitful in fellowship. The Inter-Agency Council received new structure, new limitations upon recommending capacity, and a new emphasis upon the fellowship feature of the agency.

We were already reaching out for structural identities. We had begun a long program of program statements. This was to define the purpose and parameters of the work of each agency. This Convention would emphasize the Historical Commission, the Education Commission, and the Christian Life Commission. We were to discover that these were not in concrete, and would be subject to continuing definition. This was also found in the program statements of the Sunday School Board and the Radio and Television Commission.

One of the recommendations that was to cast a long shadow said, "we recommend the following to be the interpretation of the Convention of the service to be performed by the Public Affairs Committee in cooperation with the Joint Committee on Public Affairs." We are still working on those relationships.

There were constitution and bylaw changes, part of a continuing process. A first reading of the constitutional provision allowed exceptions to be made in terms of office for local members of the boards presented whose technical services were in demand.

An amendment was adopted defining ordination and ministerial services, made necessary by government regulations concerning Social Security.

The election of officers has always been of great interest in a body that is altogether autonomous and free. The world assigns an authority to a body that does not actually exist. We Southern Baptists take pride in, and pray for, the people chosen to be our leadership for a particular year. In 1961, there was no one running for office. There was no requirement by the Convention that prior willingness to be nominated be secured. People were nominated as the messengers felt moved to nominate. An individual who did not choose to be a part of the election process could withdraw his name at that point.

With that bit of history and background, you will understand that it had always been a very pleasant procedure. The nominees for president this year included Roy O. McClain of Georgia, Herschel Hobbs of Oklahoma, and W. O. Vaught of Arkansas. McClain asked that his name be withdrawn. Later the announcement was made that Hobbs had been elected. This same procedure of fellowship for first vice-president and second vice-president was followed. Out of it came people respected in the Convention, trusted by the messengers, and honored in recognition of prior service.

It was interesting to me that as late as 1961 we were presented with a motion that the Convention "ask or instruct our Southern Baptist seminaries to welcome publicly, and openly, qualified students of any race." As a matter of fact, that was already the policy for the seminaries. The motion was referred to the Committee on Resolutions, but something, already an adopted norm in our Southern Baptist life, was becoming a matter of demand.

The report of the six seminaries had been given under the direction of H. Leo Eddleman, president of New Orleans Baptist Theological Seminary and chairman of the Inter-Seminary Council. All of the presidents were recognized, and brief reports were given from each institution. The apparent unity was remarkable.

Sermons during the Convention were delivered by R. G. Lee of Memphis, W. A. Criswell of Dallas, Carl Bates of North Carolina, and others.

In leaving the Convention, I reflected upon the strain of size, the increasing demands of secular structure, and the basic unworldly fellowship of the people of God called Southern Baptists. The final enrollment was 11,140. We would go to San Francisco in 1962.

Civic Auditorium • San Francisco, California

JUNE 5-8
1962

THE TRIP TO THE 1951 SOUTHERN BAPTIST CONVENTION IN SAN FRANCISCO, CALIFORNIA, HAD BEEN such a special event in our lives. The trip itself was one that we will always cherish. Ten of us from the First Baptist Church in Columbia, South Carolina, had adopted an itinerary that included Washington D. C., Chicago, the Grand Canyon, Los Angeles, Portland, Vancouver, and a wonderful train trip across Canada to Niagara Falls. Placed in the middle of that, the 1951 Convention itself had been far-reaching. In the first place, it affirmed publicly the national dimensions of our Convention fellowship.

Now we were going to San Francisco again in 1962. We decided that a train trip might again be possible. Not only did we have a train connection directly from Fort Worth to Denver, but there was also a special train through the Rockies which was still in operation. This trip was a magnificent experience. The beauty of the mountains was never more apparent. We came to this second "far off" Convention with great anticipation, and were not disappointed.

The Convention opened on Tuesday evening, June 5, with President Herschel H. Hobbs presiding. The theme was "Sharing Christ." It is always an inspirational moment when the announcement is made that the Convention is in session. After the inspirational singing, there was the customary announcement of messengers. The enrollment was at 3,100 when the Convention began. The number would reach 9,396 qualified messengers who were elected by the churches.

In this opening session careful notice was taken of 130 persons killed in an airplane crash in Paris, France, some of whom were from Atlanta, Georgia. A dramatic presentation, "Sharing Christ through

119

the Cooperative Program," was presented. This presentation had been written by Albert McClellan of Tennessee. The climax of the evening was the Convention sermon by Franklin Paschall on the subject, "The Gospel of Our Time," using Romans 1:16 as the text.

Wednesday morning we heard the president's address. Later, a motion was made that the address be printed in the minutes of our meeting, and in full in the *Baptist Program*. I will conclude this Convention account with some things which were said by President Hobbs.

The report of the Executive Committee brought us to the heart of the business of the Convention. The amendments to the constitution proposed in the previous Convention were continued for second reading, and new ones were introduced. This structural struggle to reshape and redefine the body was evident. The composition of institutional and agency boards was restated, not to conflict with basic charters. The executive head of an agency was made responsible to its directors. It seemed necessary to specify in the constitution that "all officers and members of all boards, trustees, institutions,

Dr. and Mrs. Naylor honored in 1962 by the unveiling of his official portrait as president of Southwestern Baptist Theological Seminary. Courtesy—Texas Baptist Historical Collection.

commissions, and missionaries of the Convention appointed by its boards shall be members of regular Baptist churches cooperating with this Convention."

There was approval for removing previous exceptions concerning board memberships so that they might be continued for technical reasons. For the first time, printed ballots were authorized for each messenger. Indiana was recognized as having met the requirements for state identity in the Convention.

We presidents of the seminaries, like any of the other agencies, were vitally concerned with the budget. There was no way for the minutes to reflect the struggle that always preceded the presentation of the budget. For most of the year, we had been struggling to anticipate the stewardship of the people and the needs of the agency. It always amazed me that in the midst of the discussion of lesser things, suddenly a Convention like ours could adopt a $19 million budget without a dissenting voice. The formula for the distribution of theological education funds continued to favor Southwestern as the largest of the seminaries. This was true in spite of the fact that more than one thousand of the students received no financial recognition in the budget allocation.

In the previous Convention, the adoption of program statements for each agency was begun. This was continued in San Francisco with a recommendation for each agency involved. These agencies had program structures approved for them. The Southern Baptist Foundation and all of our Southern Baptist hospital programs were adopted.

In the light of subsequent history, there needs to be a word about the election of officers. President Hobbs was elected to another term by unanimous vote. In selecting a first vice-president, four nominations were presented. There had been no previous announcements in the press and no one was running for the office. In the best of fellowship, four names were presented. No majority being received, two of these engaged in a run-off, and Grady Cothen was finally elected as the first vice-president. The election of officers was more an expression of fellowship than a division of intent and purpose.

There were two far-reaching actions of the Convention which subsequent history would underline. Recommendation 14 of the Executive Committee called attention to the Statement of Baptist Faith and Message as adopted in 1925 by the Convention: "We recommend, therefore, that the President of the Convention be requested to call a meeting of those now serving in the various state conventions . . . by Bylaw 18 to present to the Convention in Kansas City some similar statement which shall serve as information to the churches and which may serve as guidelines to the various agencies of the Southern Baptist Convention." There was the usual disclaimer that there was any intent to establish a creed. History should have taught us sooner that the peculiar genius of Baptists is that fellowship can only be fractured by creeds.

An interesting commentary is that following the adoption of this recommendation, K. O. White of Texas "moved that the messengers to this Convention, by standing vote, reaffirm their faith in the entire Bible as the authoritative, authentic, infallible Word of God; that we express our abiding and unchanging objection to the dissemination of theological views in any of our seminaries which would undermine such faith in the historical accuracy and doctrinal integrity of the Bible; and that we kindly, but firmly, instruct the trustees and administrative officers," etc. What a prolific harvest this seed was to bring!

In all of the discussion and motions to amend that followed, the final adoption was substantively as offered. Amended by Dr. White, it read, "We express our abiding and unchanging objection to the dissemination of theological views in any of our seminaries which would undermine such faith in the historical accuracy and doctrinal integrity of the Bible, and that we *courteously request* the trustees and administrative officers of our institutions and other agencies to take such steps that shall be necessary to remedy at once those situations where such views now threaten our historical position." There would not be a time again when our seminaries would be removed from this subtle aura of suspicion. The fact that a basic tenet of authority was raised is almost secondary to that.

Foreign Mission Night was an inspiration. New missionaries were presented to the Convention, and a ringing challenge was presented by Baker J. Cauthen, secretary of our Foreign Mission Board.

A request which had special meaning to the seminaries was that the Southern Baptist Theological Seminary was requested to accept the assets of Carver School. Along with that request it was asked to operate its programs in such a manner as would, in good faith, seek to achieve the purposes set forth in the Carver School charter. God had wrought a wonderful work in that which we call the Woman's Missionary Union Training School. In the closing session, there was a line that said, "Joann Shelton sang "Saved by Grace." How often God spoke to me through her unusual gift. The minutes were concluded with this phrase "The 105th annual session of the Convention was adjourned finally." I only wish it could have been *finally*.

The president's address was worth publishing, and it is worth reading now in light of all of our divisions. I will quote just a few lines. "Neo-Orthodoxy in its extreme form makes its claim to Orthodoxy, but is it a valid claim? It avows to be a Bible centered theology, but it still tends to make the Bible subservient to the autonomy of physical science. It speaks of the transcendence of God. It insists that the supernatural shall be subject to a natural interpretation." There is an excellent reference to Bultmanism.

"Southern Baptists must recognize and practice the principle of unity in diversity. The unity within the faith of Southern Baptists is a modern theological miracle. With no creed to bind them, yet they have remained remarkably one in their basic body of beliefs. This has been due largely to two things: their restricted geographical location and their insistence on the New Testament as their final rule of faith and practice.

"When one speaks of 'Baptist Doctrine,' he is usually understood. There are Baptist confessions of faith. Southern Baptist seminaries have abstracts of principles. The Convention itself adopted a statement of 'The Baptist Faith and Message.' But, none of these is a creedal statement binding upon all Southern Baptists. They still hold to the priesthood of believers which extends to every Baptist both the privilege and the responsibility of interpreting the Scriptures for himself." These remain sound statements.

Municipal Auditorium • Kansas City, Missouri

[signature: Robert Taylor]

MAY 7-10
1963

THE LAST WORD OF THE MINUTES OF THE SAN FRANCISCO CONVENTION WAS "FINALLY." WE SHOULD HAVE known better. It was true that the Convention had ended. In our Baptist way, the Convention could exist only for its time in session. A motion at the beginning had constituted the Convention, and a motion at the close made it history. This is our Baptist way.

In reality, however, at least two of the actions of the Convention became absorbing discussions in the year that followed. The Committee on Baptist Faith and Message, composed of the president of the Southern Baptist Convention and the presidents of the state conventions, were often in the news during the year. Many thought that we needed to bring our statement of faith up-to-date. The action that asked the seminaries to see to it that all of their faculty and staff were committed to an infallible Book served only to cast some doubts in the fellowship.

Now we were going to Kansas City for the next annual session of the Southern Baptist Convention. Kansas City had already proved itself to be a fine convention center. It was not too far removed from the population center of the Convention. The meeting place was close to adequate hotels that made the attendance a pleasure.

On Tuesday evening, May 7, President Herschel Hobbs of Oklahoma called the Convention into order as the 106th session of the 118th year under the theme, "To Make Men Free." Throughout the years, we had gone to great effort to be sure that we were present for the opening. It had always been, and is now, a most inspiring moment. The congregation sang "There is a Fountain," "Jesus Paid It All," and "Amazing Grace." Claude Ray of Louisiana sang "Speak to My Heart." The report of opening enrollment was 9,010 messengers.

By the end of the Convention the attendance would rise to 12,971. With the opening organization details finished, the Convention had anticipated a special feature, the 75th Anniversary of Woman's Missionary Union. A historical pageant commemorating this event was presented, under the direction of Mrs. Ned P. King of Texas. Following this event, the Convention sermon was preached by Carl E. Bates of North Carolina on the subject of "Trouble Makers in a Troubled World," and his text was Acts 17:6. We began the Convention with high inspiration.

The next morning President Hobbs presented his President's Address to the Convention on "God and History." His Text was Acts 17:22-23. I do not recall the Convention sermon and the President's Address ever before being taken from this chapter of the Scripture. Sam Scantland of Oklahoma moved that the President's Address be carried in full in the *Annual*. It was done so and was well worthy.

The Executive Committee presented its report under the leadership of Porter Routh, the executive secretary. The large part of the proceedings of the Convention is to be found in these actions. It was determined that an amendment to the constitution should be approved by two successive Conventions. There was a limitation placed upon any person resigning from an agency and becoming at the same time a trustee/director of another agency. Colorado, Oregon, and Washington were recognized as conventions having arrived at the required strength. The adoption of the budget for 1964 was, as usual, without objection. The total budget adopted was $19,248,500. The seminaries received $3,250,000 to be divided by the formula agreed upon by the presidents and the Convention.

The practice of the year before of adopting program statements for Southern Baptist agencies was continued. This year the Annuity Board program was adopted.

A major surprise in this Convention, never quite repeated later, was in the election of officers. The election of the officers of our Conventions had always had full attendance. It was not a year-long contest, but often was an expression of the appreciation of certain individuals by constituencies in the Convention. Any regularly elected messenger to the Convention could be nominated for any office of the Convention.

This particular year there were fourteen nominees for the office of president of the Southern Baptist Convention. This was most unusual and everyone enjoyed it. Finally, nominations ceased and these fourteen nominees went before the Convention. Immediately

Dr. Herschel H. Hobbs (left), outgoing Southern Baptist Convention president, presents the gavel to the new president, Dr. K. Owen White, in 1963. Courtesy—Southern Baptist Historical Library and Archives.

before voting, five of the fourteen withdrew from consideration. However, nine remained on the list. Before the vote was taken, there was a motion that the run-off balloting be between the top four men instead of the top two. The motion failed and the vote was cast.

That evening when the Convention met it was announced that Carl Bates asked that his name be withdrawn. Our president ruled that his name could not be withdrawn at this point. To this ruling Dr. Bates replied respectfully that if elected he would not serve. This was high drama indeed. S. L. Staley offered a motion that Dr. Bates be allowed to withdraw his name, and that the third highest man be considered in the run-off ballot. This motion failed. Dick Hall of Georgia moved that as a substitute the first ballot be considered null and void, and that a new ballot must be taken. This motion carried.

President Hobbs ruled that since he was not a registered messenger at the Convention, Billy Graham could not be considered part of the ballot. With that the ballot for president was taken, with the seven men whose names had not been withdrawn. After the vote, it was announced that K. O. White and W. O. Vaught had received the highest number of votes and that the run-off election would be between these two men. Later, it was also announced that K. O. White would be the new president of our Convention.

You would have thought that the election drama was over. Yet, on Thursday afternoon, when the time came for the election of a first vice-president, there were seven names presented for the office. So again it was a choice between the seven. The result of the ballot was a run-off election between Paul S. James and W. O. Vaught for vice-president. In the final ballot, Vaught was chosen. In the election for a second vice-president on Thursday evening, four names were presented. Mrs. R. L. Matthis and John Huss were the names voted on in the run-off. Mrs. Matthis was chosen second vice-president, an important achievement for Baptist women.

Out of all of this drama came two significant actions. First, a motion made and approved by vote of the Convention that henceforth any nominee should have expressed a willingness in advance to be nominated. This sounds reasonable, except that it is entirely contrary to our Baptist way and history. Once a willingness is expressed prior to the fact, that individual becomes a candidate for the office. In our Baptist doctrine of equality in discipleship, candidacy is a mistake. We prefer our brother. No action concerning our Baptist polity casts a longer shadow than this one which made us "of the world."

There was also an action taken to require that the ballot be announced and that the actual vote be recorded. This made necessary the recording of the presidential vote of 4,210 votes for K. O. White, and 4,053 votes for W. O. Vaught. What is wrong with that, you may ask? The answer is that it heightens the significance of the election beyond that which was intended.

We had now come to a consideration of the report of the Committee on Baptist Faith and Message. In all previous notes about the anticipated Convention, this report had been highlighted.

After all of the considerations, the report was changed little from the 1925 Statement of Baptist Faith and Message. The exception to that statement is a lengthy preface which became a part of the body in the discussion. This preface disclaims any creed for Southern Baptists. It gives full attention to the diversity among us, and inevitably becomes a weather vane of all doctrinal irregularities.

The first motion following the reading of the report was that the report be amended "by striking out all of the report except the Scripture references." The motion failed. Another wanted to make a motion expressing gratitude to the committee. This motion was ruled out of order. There was a motion to strike the last paragraph, which also failed. Then there was a motion that prevailed. It ruled that the introductory material be included in the vote on adoption. Not only was the report to be printed in whole in these proceedings of the Convention, but the report was to be shown in parallel columns between 1925 and 1963.

My first reflection, not for the first time I am sure, was that it seemed very reasonable that we should take recognized leadership and ask for a doctrinal statement of what we believe. Surely a person cannot expect a body as large as the Southern Baptist Convention, that is made up of individual believers, to stand on common ground with his own statement of faith, and all be committed to the Scriptures. The truth is, that is exactly what we expect. It does not appear reasonable, but it sure does appear miraculous and recognizes the work of God in grace that draws us together.

The major attention given to these items would be enough for this kind of Convention report. We would not fail, however, to call attention to the Stewardship Commission, with its major insistence that the Cooperative Program was our lifeline. We again recognized the 75th Anniversary of the Woman's Missionary Union. The tribute to Mrs. Marie Matthis in her leadership in Woman's Missionary Union was worthily given. A full page detailing acknowledgement of President Hobbs was also worthwhile.

Lest we forget, there had been a motion expressed in 1962 requesting a progress report from the Executive Committee with reference to actions of the seminaries and agencies in carrying out the wishes of the Convention. As was suggested then, doubts linger and fingers were pointed. The seminaries seek to give every possible assurance of our doctrinal commitment, Southern Baptist loyalty, and the blessings of God upon the enterprise.

Not until Friday morning were the seminaries given time for their report. Sydnor Stealy of North Carolina, president of Southeastern Seminary, presented the report from the six seminaries and the Seminary Extension Department. Reports were discussed by all of the presidents. There being no recommendations, these reports were accepted by the Convention.

There is a personal note concerning Southwestern that I would like in these memoirs. William Fleming, who was chairman of our trustees, a great personal friend, and through all the years a steadfast supporter of Southwestern, died just at the time of the Convention. Since the committee was still in session, it was suggested that his successor on the Board of Trustees be named by the Convention. I was consulted and asked to suggest a successor. Before suggesting the name of F. Howard Walsh, son-in-law of William Fleming, I called him. We wanted Howard Walsh in his own right to be a trustee. He very soberly assured me that he would serve. Let it be recorded that for ten years he gave faithful fulfillment to every promise.

This is noteworthy in the Convention minutes, because a sentiment was growing that executives of Southern Baptist agencies should have no suggestion to offer in the election of their trustees. I opposed the idea when it was first presented, and I think it is utter foolishness now. Should an executive officer of a Southern Baptist agency name the trustees? Not at all, but to fail to consider suggestions of an executive officer would be foolishness in my view.

The Convention in Kansas City remains a fertile seedbed in Southern Baptist life. Before adjournment, President Hobbs presented the gavel to K. O. White, who, expressing appreciation to the Convention, concluded the meeting by quoting 1 Corinthians 15:58.

Convention Hall • Atlantic City, New Jersey

MAY 19-22

1964

THE BAPTIST JUBILEE ADVANCE WAS A FIVE-YEAR (1959-1964) PROGRAM THROUGH WHICH SEVEN BAPTIST bodies in the United States and Canada undertook to work coopera- tively, to witness effectively, and to celebrate worthily the 150th Anniversary (1814-1964) of the organization of Baptist work on the continental level. These seven independent Baptist groups were: the American Baptist Convention, the Baptist Federation of Canada, the National Baptist Convention of America, the National Baptist Convention, U.S.A., Inc., the North American Baptist General Conference, the Seventh Day Baptist General Conference, and the Southern Baptist Convention. It was truly a gigantic concept of cooperation for groups of Baptists to share. The Joint Cooperative Fellowship meeting of these seven Baptist bodies was to be held immediately following the adjournment of the Southern Baptist Convention on May 22-24. The movement itself was worthy of this emphasis, but to introduce Atlantic City, we need to understand the special dimensions of the gathering. This was indeed reaching out to the perimeter of our Southern Baptist Convention.

Atlantic City may not be familiar in terms of denominational conventions, but it was certainly a convention city. Known world- wide for its casinos, hotels, and dramatically for its boardwalk, Atlantic City was quite a place for Southern Baptists to gather. The Convention Hall was located alongside the scenic boardwalk.

The inspiration of the opening moment remains constant. President K. Owen White called the session to order on Tuesday night, May 19. Leroy Till of Texas led the Convention in singing "To God Be the Glory," "Glory to His Name," and "Blessed Assurance."

Following the welcome and response, the organizational motion was made by Joe Burton with the announcement that at the opening of the Convention, there were 11,726 messengers. By the close of the Convention this number rose to 13,136. Underlining the size and the intent of the Convention, the president's address and the Convention sermon were both preached on this Tuesday evening. K. O. White presented the president's address on the Convention theme "For Liberty and Light." At the close of this session, my long-time friend, Enoch Brown, preached the Convention sermon "The Church Fulfilling Her Mission in World Crisis," using as his text Matthew 28:18-20.

The Executive Committee of the Southern Baptist Convention is described as being the Convention "ad interim," that is, between the meetings of the Convention. The Committee carries out instructions, conceives plans, takes actions, all of which are finally ratified or dis-ratified by the next Convention.

Wednesday morning, we moved immediately into business, and, as usual, the Executive Committee recommendations occupied a great deal of the attention of the Convention. There was a motion almost immediately to limit the term of office for the president to one year. This would require a constitutional amendment. A later time was assigned for this discussion which was long and varied, but the Convention refused to limit the office to one year.

Joe Burton made a motion that a special committee be appointed to study the bases of representation in the annual sessions. This motion was significant mostly in that it represented again the stirring within the Convention to adopt itself a new structure and authority.

The Convention voted to use *Robert's Rules of Order* rather than *Kerfoot Parliamentary Law.*

Much time was consumed in the discussion of a motion to amend the bylaws so that they would read "six ordained clergymen" rather than the present phrase "six pastors." It seemed innocuous to me. The Convention was so divided that after a long debate, it voted and declared that the motion had prevailed. Then a request was made from the body questioning the count, so a ballot vote showed that the motion had indeed failed. In like vein, there was a recommendation that we try a new time sequence for the sessions of the Convention. This motion was lost.

Of far larger and perhaps more personal concern, was a recommendation concerning the Capital Needs Budget for 1965-1968. In the report I noted that $300,000 was allotted to renovate Fort Worth Hall, $50,000 to complete the Memorial Building, and $300,000 for the renovation of Barnard Hall. The Capital Needs Budget was approved, and, later, the time of distribution from 1965-1968 was indicated. The total Capital Needs program was $8,955,000. Southwestern's distribution was a "breath of hope."

The Cooperative Program operating budget for 1965 was adopted at a total of $20,335,600. An attempt to amend the recommendation failed. The seminaries' reports were received as a final matter in the Wednesday morning session. It was my year to be chairman of the presidents. As such, I presented the report of the seminaries and spoke briefly. Then I presented Duke McCall from Southern Baptist Theological Seminary. One after another the seminary presidents were presented and given time for a brief word, until all six presidents had been recognized.

Joann Shelton sang "Someday the Silver Cord Will Break." Robert Naylor brought the closing message of the session on "The Cutting Edge of Theological Education." The commitment of Southern Baptists to theological education remains a wonder of the theological world. This was but one moment, but I would not forget to say that God has blessed theological education among Southern Baptists. We are eternally grateful for the support of the people, and we will carry always a sense of responsibility for those things we most deeply cherish.

The election of officers continued to be a very exciting time in the Convention. Again it was not a case of people running for office, but it was a moment in the Convention when we thought about those who proved their leadership and considered the nominations that were presented. First was the period for the nomination of the president. Thirteen names were offered for nomination. Forest Hicks requested that his name be withdrawn, leaving the ballot for president based upon twelve names. By the adjournment on Wednesday afternoon, it was announced that Theodore F. Adams of Virginia and Wayne Dehoney of Tennessee had received the highest number of votes, though not a majority, and would be voted on in the next ballot.

The ballot was taken at the close of the Wednesday evening session. It was followed by the announcement that the run-off results could be released to the press ahead of the Convention meeting on Thursday morning. The announcement was made at the Thursday morning session that Dehoney had been elected president of the Convention. And he would become a fine moderator at the 1965 Convention.

Five nominations for the office of first vice-president of the Convention followed. It was announced that Roy Gresham of Maryland and Nane Starnes of North Carolina were the two receiving the highest number of votes. Gresham was elected.

Nominations for second vice-president were called for in the afternoon session. Seven nominations were presented. The two receiving the highest number of votes, calling for a run-off, were Owen Cooper of Mississippi and Gregory Walcott of California. You would know that most of the people nominated for any office were not only people whom I knew, but whom I counted as friends. There is an interesting side-note about Gregory Walcott. In 1963, we had gone to Japan for a great crusade. There I met Gregory Walcott, a nationally recognized actor and consistent Christian. Interviewed by the press, he indicated that he had two birthdates, the day he was born physically, and the day he was born spiritually. Walcott was elected.

Convention Hall in Atlantic City, New Jersey, site of the 1964 Southern Baptist Convention meeting. Courtesy—Southern Baptist Historical Library and Archives.

Dr. Naylor speaks at Naylor Student Center ground-breaking at Southwestern Baptist Theological Seminary in 1964. Courtesy—Texas Baptist Historical Collection.

On Wednesday evening, Mrs. R. L. Mathis of Alabama, the Convention's second vice-president, was called on to preside. This was the first time a woman had presided over a session of the Southern Baptist Convention. She did an excellent job.

Other actions of the Convention included permission for the Radio and Television Commission to borrow against the current appraised value of its property. There was a motion that would plan toward "more grassroots involvement in planning." Houston, Texas, was then approved for the Convention site, May 20-23, 1969.

A special paragraph ought to be devoted to the resolutions presented. It is understood that resolutions represent the sentiment of that particular Convention only. They cannot speak for an individual church, nor for another Convention, only for this Baptist body.

Bearing that in mind, there was a recommendation concerning race relations. In 1964, it provoked much discussion. Finally, a substitute resolution was adopted representing the more moderate reservations of our Southern Baptist people. Notable was its claim "that the final solution to these problems must come on the local level, with Christians and churches acting under the direction of the Holy Spirit and in the Spirit of Jesus Christ. This must be in full recognition of the autonomy of each Baptist church."

The Cooperative Program received major affirmation by the Convention. The American Bible Society also was a subject of a resolution of affirmation and approval. C. C. Warren of North Carolina presented and discussed the report of the Jubilee Advance Committee to which reference has been made.

The seminary presidents had worked with the Executive Committee throughout the year in preparation for a program statement and structure for the seminaries. There was an unsuccessful effort to amend the recommendation concerning the program, but the adoption was wholehearted. Note here in this discussion the objective of Southern Baptist seminaries: "The objective of Southern Baptist seminaries is to provide theological education, with the Bible as the center of the curriculum, for God-called men and women to meet the need for trained leadership in the work of the churches. The seminaries have utilized scholarships with reverent concern and dependence upon the guidance of the Holy Spirit. They shall be distinctive Baptist institutions, witnessing to the truth revealed in the Holy Scriptures. They shall help the Convention by study of its life and by involvement in its programs."

Programs of leadership training in theology, in religious education, and in church music were approved. Individual seminaries were recognized in that part of the program that was assigned to them, and the degrees to be granted as approved by the Convention. Atlantic City came to be the place of the largest outreach of the enterprise that claimed our lives, Southern Baptist theological education.

The last note of the proceedings said, "The 107th session of the Convention was adjourned, finally." That kind of conclusion seemed strange to me, but we moved into the celebration of the Baptist Jubilee Advance. One hundred and fifty years after the 1814 rise of the Triennial Convention, a group of Baptists called Southern Baptists met to affirm their faith and to make a commitment to world witness.

Dallas Memorial Auditorium • Dallas, Texas

JUNE 1-4
1965

FOR THE FIRST TIME, THE SOUTHERN BAPTIST CONVENTION MEETING WAS A "HOME" EXPERIENCE FOR US. WE HAD come back to Fort Worth in 1934 with a real sense of nostalgia. Then I served as president of the institution that was the basis of the nostalgia, and it was sure to be a new experience.

The first session began on Tuesday night, June 1, when President Wayne Dehoney called the Southern Baptist Convention to order for its 108th session. We began with "All Hail the Power of Jesus' Name" and "The Solid Rock." The secretary reported eleven thousand messengers in attendance. By the end of the session, 16,053 messengers were recorded. The Convention theme was "Proclamation and Witnessing."

We had decided to stay in Dallas because of the complexity of time. I had been named as a member of the Resolutions Committee, a committee that appears frequently in the minutes. We were completing the beautiful new Student Center at Southwestern Seminary. For months, we had been in the midst of plans for the meeting of the Baptist World Alliance in Miami Beach in July. Every moment seemed to be unusually precious. At the first evening session, after the naming of the committees, John H. Haldeman preached the Convention sermon on "The Essentials for Our Proclamation and Witness." President Dehoney concluded the evening session with his presidential address on "Issues and Imperatives."

We began with a strong resolution concerning the imprisonment of our Southern Baptist missionaries, Herbert Caudle and David Fite, in Cuba, along with some pastors and other Christians. The opening prayer had been a petition on their behalf. Now we reached out to them as a major concern of the Convention. (David Fite would

136

become a member of the faculty at Southwestern, and his family remains a choice part of our missionary history.)

The Convention was also asked to make a choice early in the meeting concerning the place for our 1970 session. The choice was between Denver and St. Louis, with the merits of each set forth. In almost a three-to-one vote, the messengers chose Denver.

Several motions and recommendations concerned changes of Convention procedure. They were not major matters, and were most important as an indication of a need to sharpen our Convention process.

Two of the agencies of the Convention had programs presented and approved, the Brotherhood Commission and the Sunday School Board. Both agencies are important, of course, but the Sunday School Board is major with us. There was a lengthy resolution recommending that the churches support the materials of the Sunday School Board. Profits from the sales of these materials had become a financial asset in the Convention for the promotion of our Southern Baptist programs. Later in the Convention, there would be a motion commending the Sunday School Board for acknowledging errors in the publication procedures. This error was an apparent reference to the publication of Professor Ralph Elliott's *The Message of Genesis*. There was general approval given to the way in which the Sunday School Board had responded to the Convention in all of these matters.

Messages of concern were sent to families that had lost loved ones who were leaders in the Convention. A message was sent to the family of J. N. Barnett, a giant in the work of the Sunday School Board who was entirely worthy of this memorial.

Michigan was recognized as having achieved the size that made it eligible for representation on various agencies of the Convention.

The Cooperative Program budget goal for $21,800,000 was adopted. There was an attempt, however, to amend it that would reduce the appropriation for the Christian Life Commission. Further along in the Convention, an unhappiness was noted concerning the Christian Life Commission. There was even one motion made that the Commission be terminated. Much of this reflected the difficulty of making adjustments in our understanding of race relationships. Otherwise, there was no discussion of items within the budget.

It is to be expected that the seminary allocation would be a matter of very personal concern. The seminary allocation continued to grow, and Southwestern continued to be favored by the formula.

I was warmly receptive to a motion that would recognize the 150th Anniversary of the founding of the American Bible Society. This recognition would be held on May 13, 1966. A committee was established to give special emphasis in that Convention.

When the time came for election of officers, there was a sudden subsiding of the fervor of the previous Conventions to nominate a host of individuals. Wayne Dehoney was nominated as president and was chosen by acclamation. Likewise, M. B. Carroll of Texas was chosen by acclamation as first vice-president. There were four nominations for second vice-president, and one of these nominees withdrew before the ballot. Major General Robert Taylor and Leobardo Estrada were in the run-off for the office, with Estrada being elected.

We were told that Jacksonville, Florida, would not be able to complete its buildings in time for the Southern Baptist Convention to meet there in 1968, so the Convention voted to go to Miami Beach instead on May 21-24, 1968. It was traditional that Wednesday night was the night that the Home Mission Board made its report, and the Foreign Mission Board reported on Thursday night. Both sessions were tremendously inspirational. More than one motion and Convention item centered upon a new evangelistic thrust in the life of Southern Baptists. Of more mundane consideration, a motion failed again and again to extend time when we were discussing a certain item. There seemed to be a determination to get on with business. There were three or four moments that time was extended when a present concern of this particular Convention was revealed.

The seminaries made their reports on Thursday morning. Duke McCall was now our chairman. We other presidents were briefly introduced, but Dr. McCall brought the major morning address on "Theological Education."

The songs we sang deserve comment. The selections chosen simply say that the difference between 1965 and the 1990s is a chasm indeed. We sang "My Jesus I Love Thee," "I Love Thy Kingdom Lord," "Saved, Saved," "Jesus Saves," and "I Will Sing of My Redeemer." Surely my feeling about these songs is not just a matter of age.

The Friday afternoon session closed with Ramsey Pollard preaching on "The Priesthood of Christ." Friday night W. A. Criswell preached on "Our Mandate from Heaven." God had graciously endowed these brethren, and the sermons were a true blessing.

Two personal matters close my recollections concerning this Convention. One was the centrality of interest in Southwestern

Seminary. Strangely enough, there were Southern Baptists who had never seen the seminary. Many of these cared enough about the institution to make plans to see it during the Convention. Although we were involved in the sessions, our people at the seminary spoke of a great host of people who came. There was also the returning seminary "family." I spoke at the outset about my nostalgia of 1934. There were hundreds of messengers, graduates of Southwestern, who had not been back since the days of their participation in "the family." The depth of their feeling was reflected in the gathering of the alumni.

The other matter concerned one of the closing items of the Convention. "The premier was presented of 'Proclaim the Word.'" This was a cantata which was commissioned by the Church Music Department of the Sunday School Board, composed and conducted by T. W. Dean of Texas. The fact that I had written the libretto for this composition was not a part of the Convention minutes. Dr. Dean requested that I do so, and much to my own surprise, I had complied.

Instead of "going" to the Convention, we stayed home for this one; and it proved to be a rich and rewarding experience.

Cobo Hall • Detroit, Michigan

MAY 24-27
1966

THERE HAD BEEN SENTIMENT IN THE CONVENTION FOR SOME TIME THAT A SESSION OF THE CONVENTION SHOULD be out on the perimeter, in what we termed our new territorial expansion. Atlantic City did not quite meet that criteria, because it was a meeting which celebrated a fellowship between national Baptist bodies. Detroit, however, seemed to be the ultimate. As we prepared to go to the Convention, I thought, "What are we doing, going to a place that has so few Southern Baptists?"

The city itself proved to be interesting. We may not have been to Detroit, but all of us knew about the Model T. We knew about Auto City, and about the economic power of the area. Our hotel reservation was in the Headquarters Hotel. It was customary to see to it that the executive officers of the agencies stay in this hotel in order that they be available for committee meetings and such. Although our hotel was a part of a national chain, I think it was the smallest room we have ever stayed in. We almost needed a map to get around the bed to the bathroom, or to the door.

About the time I was not too happy about our room, we began to hear comments from others. For some, there were no hotel rooms available at all. They had been compelled to go across the river to Canada to get rooms. On top of all of that, the resultant transportation problem was indeed a headache. On the other hand, our longtime friend, Bob Barker, had simply filled out the forms for a hotel request. He had been assigned a hotel whose name we had not heard of. He was suddenly in the midst of luxury and plenty—but on with the Convention.

President Wayne Dehoney called the Convention into session on Tuesday evening, May 24, under the theme "God's Word for a New

140

Age." After the usual beginnings, the secretary reported the registration of 9,590 messengers, and moved that these messengers constitute the Convention. This number would become 10,414 at the close
of the Convention. This was one of the only times in my memory
that there was a motion protesting the seating of a church, the First
Baptist Church of Russellville, Arkansas, because of the departure
from traditional Baptist practices. Our president ruled the motion out
of order and cited the constitution, which does not clearly assign this
area of determination to the Convention. The report was accepted,
the Convention was constituted, the report of the Program
Committee was accepted, and we were in business. As in other years,
the first session concluded with the Convention sermon by Ray
Roberts of Ohio on "The Unpaid Debt of Southern Baptists," and the
president's address, "The Living God at Work in His World."

Wednesday morning, we seemed to be trying to do everything
that we came to do. There was a continuing reference to changing the
name of the Southern Baptist Convention. The 1971 date and place of
meeting were determined to be St. Louis, Missouri, June 1-4.
Landrum Leavell was asked to preach the sermon in the 1967 session.

The budget adoption was always amazing. Our largest goal to
date was $24,200,000 for the Southern Baptist Cooperative Program.
This included $3,833,000 for the seminaries. The adoption of the bud-
get was done without objection, and in relatively short time.

In the previous two Conventions, we adopted a Statement of
Programs for our institutions. On Wednesday morning, in one single
session, we adopted program statements for the Historical
Commission, Stewardship Commission, Radio and Television
Commission, Annuity Board, Baptist Joint Committee on Public
Affairs, Southern Baptist Hospital, Southern Baptist Foundation,
Christian Life Commission, Education Commission, American
Baptist Theological Seminary Commission, Foreign Mission Board,
Home Mission Board, and the Woman's Missionary Union. This con-
stituted a tremendous body of material which was not read in the
adoption, but which was printed and available to the messengers.

These programs, both then and now, are worth reading carefully.
The purpose of a program statement is definitive, directive, and, all
too often, defensive. The underlying aim, of course, is to have cooperation between all of the agencies. I read with interest the objective
under the Foreign Mission Board for hospitals and Medicare, "To provide medical assistance to people in foreign countries as an expression

Seminary presidents during
1966 Detroit Convention
include, from left, Dr. Duke
K. McCall of Southern, Dr.
Harold K. Graves of Golden
Gate, Dr. Robert E. Naylor
of Southwestern, Dr. Millard
K. Berquist of Midwestern,
Dr. H. Leo Eddleman of New
Orleans, and Dr. Olin T.
Binkley of Southeastern.
Courtesy— Southern
Baptist Historical Library
and Archives.

of Christian love, and as a means of witness, in order that they may
be brought to God through Jesus Christ." Rebekah, our only daughter, was finishing her pre-med program at Baylor, and her life
remained subject to this direction. For Woman's Missionary Union,
the objective was said to be, "To promote Christian missions
through the organizations of Woman's Missionary Union in the
churches of the Southern Baptist Convention."

An action of the Convention was to change the place of meeting
in 1967 from New Orleans to Miami Beach. This was made necessary
by their failure to complete an auditorium in New Orleans.

A committee had been appointed in 1965 to plan a celebration of the
150th anniversary of the founding of the American Bible Society, founded
in 1816. The committee had done its work and the organization which
was faithfully supported by our Convention was recognized.

In the election of officers, it appeared to me that the recognition
of leadership was significant. There were twelve people nominated
for the office of the president of the Convention. None of these
twelve asked that their names be withdrawn. Later, the president
announced that three people had received the majority of the votes:
Owen Cooper, Jess Moody, and H. Franklin Paschall. When the time
for run-off had arrived, it was announced that Cooper and Paschall
would be on the ballot. Paschall of Tennessee was chosen.

In the nominations for first vice-president, Owen Cooper asked
that his name be withdrawn. Fred Hubbs of Michigan was elected.

In the nominations for second vice-president, four were nominated. Among those was Jess Moody of Florida. Later, the president announced that Moody had indicated that he could not serve if elected. The president then ruled the first ballot invalid. The messengers cast another ballot for the three nominees; and finally, Howard H. Altman was chosen as second vice-president. All of this is interesting only as it indicated the unlimited freedom of our Southern Baptist fellowship. For us to misuse that liberty is an ultimate transgression.

The seminaries were the Thursday afternoon session of the program. All of us presidents were given an opportunity to speak. Millard J. Berquist, president of Midwestern Seminary, addressed the Convention on the field of theological education. I found that the body of my remarks to the Convention on that occasion were published in some newspapers. Perhaps it is worth a quotation in these memoirs: "Last Friday morning at Southwestern Seminary, we came to a moment that is always new to me. The Commencement Sermon had been preached. The diplomas had been awarded. The degrees had been conferred. The President had presented the graduating group to God in dedication and commended them to His care and direction. Then, as we waited, these graduates turned away down the aisles to a world that so desperately needed them, and to the appointments which God had for them with the multitudes. A drop of water in a sea of need, you say? No, these are the leaven making life palatable, the light which the darkness cannot resist."

Foreign Mission Night on Thursday evening was a high hour of inspiration as Dr. Baker Cauthen addressed the Convention on "How Shall They Hear?" There is a personal note at the end of the proceedings of the Convention. Item 169 reads, "Mrs. Virginia Seelig of Texas sang 'Oh, What A Day!'" How many, many times in these years Virginia has blessed and inspired me personally when it was my responsibility to speak before a Convention.

Southern Baptist Convention

Convention Hall • Miami Beach, Florida

MAY 30 - JUNE 2
1967

MIAMI HAD BEEN ONE OF SOUTHERN BAPTISTS' FAVORITE CONVENTION CITIES. MY FIRST VISIT TO MIAMI HAD occurred when the Convention first met there in 1946. In pre-air conditioning days, we stayed in fine hotels with cross-window ventilation, if you were lucky enough to have a corner room. The sessions of that Convention were held in Biscayne Park, and they were exciting.

When we went back to Miami in 1952 and then in 1955, we met in a large air hangar, south of the city, which, as a building, left something to be desired. We also went to Miami Beach in 1960. During this Convention of 1967, Mrs. Naylor and I stayed in the Fontianbleau Hotel. My fascination for the ocean was simply a plus for the Convention. There were so many hotels that all of the messengers could walk to the Convention session.

President H. Franklin Paschall called the 110th session of the Southern Baptist Convention to order at 7:00 P.M., May 30, 1967, in the Convention Hall at Miami Beach. We began with "All Hail the Power of Jesus' Name," "Oh For a Thousand Tongues to Sing," and "My Jesus I Love Thee." By motion, the Convention was constituted with 12,770 messengers already enrolled. This spoke to the favor of the Convention city. The final number enrolled was 14,794.

There are some observations in advance. I remember there being more motions to extend the time. Some were passed and some were refused. There was also a "busyness" about the Convention that was reflected by the changes in the order of the program. This was beyond the usual.

The theme of the Convention was "Mandate to Minister." The chief feature of that opening evening was the Convention sermon by Landrum Leavell on the theme, "The Church with a Future."

144

The first business session was on Wednesday morning with a series of motions. These motions were usually referred to the Committee on Order of Business for a featured discussion, or to some other committee to consider the resolution. Vietnam was very much on the mind of all of us. There was a motion by Rufus Spraberry of Texas relating to our nation's involvement there. There was also a motion that the Christian Life Commission be discontinued. The address of the commission to the social order has, along with its blessings, produced some sharply critical moments in the fellowship.

The report of the Executive Committee constituted the heart of business. Douglas Hudgins recognized the Fiftieth Anniversary of the Executive Committee, and the Fortieth Anniversary of the Committee as then constituted for a totally democratic organization. The Executive Committee represented our authoritative compromise with the way the world does business. Early on we decided to meet in Philadelphia in 1972. The recommendation of $26,800,000 for Cooperative Program allocations was without dispute or discussion. The seminaries were to receive $3,833,000 of that amount. I will write more about this later. Apropos to the observation about time, Duke McCall moved that the president's address be made a fixed order at the time originally stated. This motion being passed, we proceeded at once to hear a very fine message.

In the afternoon session, there was the first election of officers. H. Franklin Paschall was elected to a second term as president with no opposition. Four nominations for first vice-president resulted in the election of Landrum P. Leavell. Most of the recommendations of the Executive Committee were non-controversial. That does not mean without discussion. The report from the seminaries was the closing feature of the Wednesday afternoon program. Each one of us made some brief report to the Convention. Southwestern's report emphasized an enrollment that had grown beyond 1,800. It called attention to the death during the year of Dr. Leslie Elliott, who had been the librarian of the seminary for thirty-eight years. Dr. Elliott was a supportive friend. I was delighted to find that I had made full reference to a faculty salary increase. H. Leo Eddleman was to have made the final address on theological education. The minutes simply say, "H. Leo Eddleman made brief remarks, due to lack of time, in lieu of a scheduled address related to theological education."

Wednesday night was featured by the report of the Home Mission Board by Secretary Arthur B. Rutledge. In this Convention, the report included an appointment service for missionaries. The missionaries' testimonies made the hour inspirational.

In the Thursday morning session there were five nominations for the office of second vice-president. It was of personal interest to me that John Abernathy of Arkansas was chosen. Why was this unusual? Abernathy was a retired foreign missionary whose service had been a remarkable chapter in our Baptist life. He was in China when the Communists took over, and for a while, he was interned. He was also there when our work opened in Indonesia. I had known him through the years and counted him one of God's finest.

There was no Thursday afternoon session so that the time could be given to our seminary luncheons and other special institutional meetings. I will not try to make that a part of these Convention reports.

Thursday night was simply Foreign Mission Night. The announcement of new missionary appointees and the testimonies of missionaries presently on furlough was highly inspirational. The evening was climaxed with a great message by Baker James Cauthen.

Friday morning was traditionally the time for our Resolutions Committee. There was always an expression of gratitude to the whole city. We spoke on church and state, peace, and support of the American Bible Society. I noticed a request from the Committee on Order of Business that they seek to provide more time for matters of miscellaneous business. J. D. Grey concluded the morning's session with a sermon on "The Fellowship of Kindred Minds."

This was one of our better Conventions. The setting in a city soon to change, the sense of openness to a world that was at our very door, the high order of sermon and commitment—all marked a Convention to be remembered by all who attended.

The Coliseum • Houston, Texas

[signature: Robert Naylor]

JUNE 4-7
1968

IT HAD BEEN TEN YEARS SINCE THE SOUTHERN BAPTIST CONVENTION HAD MET IN HOUSTON. THE CONVENTION had met there in 1915 and again in 1926. Then, when the Convention met there in 1953, we had already moved to Fort Worth. The concerns for the seminary were overwhelming. A president had been chosen to succeed Dr. E. D. Head. J. Howard Williams brought fresh, new leadership to the seminary. The year 1958 became the epochal, determinative Convention in my own life. All of this is reflected in the minutes of Convention meetings.

Ten years later, God had wondrously blessed the seminary. Enrollments were at a record high. An element of understanding and fairness had come into the distribution of the Cooperative Program. In this decade, Mrs. Naylor and I had looked at a world of which we had not dreamed. The mission fields were so present. Houston formed a perfect background for reaching out to the frontiers.

President H. Franklin Paschall called this 111th session to order at 7:00 P.M. on Tuesday, June 4, 1968. Every Southern Baptist needs to remember that this was a Convention unto itself. It could speak only for itself. That was our Baptist way. For that reason, I enjoy recording the registrations. The secretary said that when the Convention opened the number of messengers was 12,449. At the time of adjournment, the number had reached 15,071.

The thrill of the opening singing was like a first Convention as we sang "All Hail the Power of Jesus' Name," "The Solid Rock," and "How Firm a Foundation."

After those inspirational moments, the first session was occupied with the routine announcements of committees and other business.

The focus of the evening was the Convention sermon by W. Douglas Hudgins from the First Baptist Church, Jackson, Mississippi. My friend and professor, John P. Newport, was the alternate. The sermon by Hudgins was preached on "Christ Our Hope."

On Wednesday morning, with Vice-President Landrum P. Leavell II of Texas presiding, the Executive Committee presented their report and recommendations. This was always the main thrust of the business. A new procedure was introduced. As the agencies brought reports, before the report, the Committee on Boards brought the names of the people who were nominated for election to that board by this Convention. They were then elected and became a part of the report.

In the beginning, the Executive Committee's recommendations represented the same structural changes and struggle that had been present in the previous conventions. For example, "No person shall be nominated to serve as trustee or director who receives any part of his salary from the agency he would serve," or "The members shall be divided into four groups as nearly equal as possible." Messengers approved meeting in Portland, Oregon, in 1973.

All of this was interesting, but it became vital when we came to the adoption of Cooperative Program goals and distributions. Without dissent, the Convention adopted a Cooperative Program goal of $27,670,480. I can assure you that this amount represented vision in 1968. A five-year Capital Needs Program of $5,000,000 for the agencies was presented and adopted. This was of vital concern to all seminaries because each one was engaged in some building enterprise.

In any Convention, there is always a moment of consuming interest to the messengers which becomes its focus, and often is a surprise. Remembering the national climate, I suppose we should not have been surprised that the Executive Committee brought a report on "A Statement Concerning the Crisis of Our Nation." The time set for its consideration was Wednesday afternoon. When the time came for this report, there was immediately a rather detailed amendment offered which changed some of the wording. This amendment was passed, but not without great discussion. There was another amendment offered that began, "We recognize and deplore the infiltration of Communism into the racial movement that increases daily division between the races." There was more, but this amendment lost. There was another amendment which was amended, and the amendment and its amendment both lost. This is to indicate that the discussion occupied the afternoon. There were motions to extend the time that was lost. There was one for five minutes which passed. It had been previously voted by the Convention that when we voted on this one, we would vote by ballot. It was finally done and adopted.

One comment should be made here. The Convention adopted a motion that said that the results should be given in terms of actual voting strength. A vote that had been called decisive was 5,687 approving, and 2,119 against. Decisive? We sometimes ask whether such issues are ever decided? Vice-President John Abernathy of Arkansas presided over the Wednesday evening meeting. As had been our practice, it was home missions evening. Testimonies were given, wonderful music was sung, and an address was given by C. E. Autry of Georgia.

In the midst of everything that was happening, Wednesday afternoon we also began the election of officers. W. A. Criswell of Texas, Gerald Martin of Tennessee, and C. Owen Cooper of Mississippi were nominated for president of the Convention. Cooper asked that

The Coliseum in Houston, Texas, site of the 1968 Southern Baptist Convention meeting. Courtesy—Southern Baptist Historical Library and Archives.

The faculty of Southwestern Baptist Theological Seminary in 1968. Courtesy—Southern Baptist Historical Library and Archives.

his name be withdrawn. A ballot was taken in which Criswell was chosen as president. The nominations in the afternoon for first vice-president included four names. Owen Cooper was elected, and on Wednesday evening, Lee Porter was elected second vice-president of the Convention.

The report of the theological seminaries was presented on Thursday morning under the direction of Harold K. Graves. Then, each one of us was given an opportunity to speak for our institution. Personnel from the six seminaries were recognized. President Graves then addressed the Convention on "The Work of Theological Education."

Foreign Mission Night on Thursday evening was a great hour of inspiration. The theme of the Convention was "Good News for Today's World." It was around this theme that we looked at our world and at that which God was allowing us to do in the midst of it.

The Convention expressed itself in the report of the Committee on Resolutions. Included in the expressions of appreciation were resolutions on highway safety, beverage alcohol, the Lord's Day, and the church. One on church-state relations was amended but passed. In 1968, there was reference to "the insane trafficking of guns."

The seminary reports always get second reading and emphasis. Our report began with a statement that during the sixty years of Southwestern, twenty-five thousand students had matriculated and 11,500 had received degrees and diplomas. In the current year there were 388 graduating, and 397 degrees and diplomas were received. New members of the faculty were named and recognized. A recurrent theme was that salary structure was again revised upwards "bringing it into line with median compensation for theological education in America." Gratitude to God was the overwhelming emotion.

Billy Graham brought the closing message of the Convention on Friday evening. The 111th Convention was finished.

Rivergate Exhibition Center • New Orleans, Louisiana

JUNE 10-13
1969

THIRTY-TWO YEARS HAD PASSED SINCE THE SOUTHERN BAPTIST CONVENTION HAD MET IN NEW ORLEANS IN 1937. In my previous account of that meeting, I talked about the eagerness with which a young pastor attended the Convention. Accompanied by our WMU president, it was a memorable journey in every respect. Now thirty-two years later, I was no longer a pastor, but a denominational servant.

This sounds significant, but in reality, I was simply an executive officer of one of our Southern Baptist institutions. This Convention represented a far more personal journey. It provided me an opportunity to compare my attitudes concerning the Convention, as a young pastor and as a denominational executive. At this point, I am glad to report that my attitudes had not basically changed.

I still saw the Southern Baptist Convention as a miracle of God, much the same as the New Testament church. It was not an authoritative body which ruled over the churches. The participation of the messengers from the churches was entirely individual. All of the actions taken by this Convention represented this meeting only. The Convention was a worldwide enterprise through which people voluntarily reached out to a lost world. Every messenger was equally significant, and every cause was deserving of the fullest consideration.

I will write a personal word about New Orleans. It was at the first, and it is now, a great tourist city. The exploration of the city was always a temptation. Riding in the historic streetcar had to be an event in the midst of it all.

The 112th session of the Convention in the 124th year of its history was called to order by President W. A. Criswell on Tuesday

152

evening, June 10. The number of registered messengers when it began was 12,475, and by the time the meeting was concluded the number was 16,678. This was a record attendance with great music. The congregational singing of "We're Marching to Zion" made it an exciting evening. That first evening had the announcement of the committees. President Criswell presented the past Convention presidents to the Convention.

Scott Tatum of Louisiana preached the Convention sermon on "The Autonomy of Baptists and the Authority of Christ." J. D. Grey, pastor of the First Baptist Church in New Orleans, was my seminary classmate and the chairman of the Committee on Arrangements. He warned all of us about the parking regulations on the streets. The evening concluded with the address of our Convention president on "Christ in Faith and Work," which was also the Convention theme.

If being a denominational employee made a difference, the beginning of business on Wednesday morning demanded total attention. This first session could largely be the report of the Executive Committee. There were reports on items committed to their consideration during the year by the previous Convention, and suggested directions for the Convention. The authority was entirely with the Convention.

Our attention was called to the fact that the year of 1970 would be a celebration of the 125th Anniversary of the Southern Baptist Convention.

A recommendation from the Executive Committee reported no particular interest expressed in changing the name of the Southern Baptist Convention, which put this matter largely to rest. The action of the Convention naming Dallas, Texas, as the host of the 1974 Convention, of course, had personal overtones for the seminary.

The presentation and adoption of the Cooperative Program allocation budget for 1970 was of vital interest to each of the institutions of the Convention. A total goal of $26,756,800 reflected the favor of the churches. The division made among the seminaries indicated that working of the formula recognized the basic factors of need in the individual institutions. I remember that we presidents used to refer to "an equal distribution of an inadequate appropriation"; and to our credit, we always added a smile. As usual, the adoption of the Cooperative Program goal was without objection.

The restlessness about the doctrinal integrity, which actually means the lingering suspicions we sometimes have about others,

continued to thrust itself forward. Those of us who date the present
Convention problems to 1979 should read the minutes again. For
example, there was a motion that "we urge the Sunday School Board
to have all writers to sign a statement with each manuscript of belief
in the infallibility of the entire Bible; that the seminaries secure from
the professors a like statement annually; and that the Sunday School
Board and the seminaries be urged to report to the President of the
Convention as to the implementation of this motion."

When the time for consideration of this motion arrived, a substitute was offered by James L. Sullivan, president of the Sunday
School Board, "that this Convention called to the attention of its
agencies the doctrinal statement framed after careful study and
much discussion at its annual session in Kansas City in 1963 and
vigorously urged the elected trustees responsible for these agencies
to be diligent in seeing that the programs assigned to them are carried out and so forth." All of this brought much discussion. Many
proposed amendments were offered and lost. Finally, a vote was
taken that was considered uncertain as to its results. In the ballot
taken upon a motion that the actual numbers be included in the
minutes, we learned that the substitute motion offered by President
Sullivan prevailed with 5,470 to 3,416 votes.

For the first time, we had a motion that only registered messengers be admitted into the auditorium until it had been ascer-
tained that all messengers who desired to be seated were seated.
We will hear this many times in the conventions that will follow.
Finally, the church of which we were members had more messengers than they had seats allowed; and Mrs. Naylor was not a messenger after all of these years. The Convention was suddenly
opened to me as a messenger and not to her, in its early moments
at least. We have not reconciled to that condition. The report of
the Home Mission Board was also received in this session.
Secretary Arthur B. Rutledge had the opportunity of presenting
Mr. and Mrs. Herbert Caudill and Mr. and Mrs. David Fite, missionaries to Cuba who had recently been released from prison.
They were wonderful people.

Wednesday afternoon was the time for the election of officers.
W. A. Criswell of Texas was nominated, as was W. C. Smith, Jr., of
Virginia. There was an interesting aftermath to the election. First,
it was announced that Criswell had been chosen as president.

There was then a motion that the actual ballot be placed in the minutes. When this was done, the results were that Criswell had 7,482 votes, and Smith had 450. Where were the other votes? Alastair Walker was listed as saying to the Convention that his name had been presented for president without his knowledge, and that he wished to be withdrawn. No consideration was shown in the minutes. The man who had nominated Smith explained that he was not aware of the policy that requires a consent of the person nominated. I have already offered my opinion that this policy was a mistake. To be nominated as an officer is an honor. To be elected is a call to service, not to be denied. Consent obtained in advance places the person in the realm of a candidate. This does not fit Southern Baptist polity or life.

Much of Wednesday evening was devoted to the report of the Sunday School Board. An interesting by-line in my memory is the new name that had been given to the Baptist Training Union— "Quest." If ever we did anything as a Convention that was comparable to the Ford Motor Company's failure with the Edsel, this was it. Nobody liked the name "Quest." It was an object of ridicule and discussion by the messengers, and finally, it was quietly withdrawn by the Sunday School Board.

Thursday morning began the report of the Committee on Resolutions. The list was longer this time, indicating the preoccupation of the messengers with the world in its secularity. The usual resolutions were offered, namely, appreciation for the host city, the American Bible Society, and others. To this list were such items as family life, sex education, use of young people in organized Baptist life, conscientious objectors, the church's educational curriculum, and the United States Ambassador to the Vatican. More important than the items was the fervor with which they were discussed, passed, rejected, or amended. There was constant demand for an extension of time.

Concerning the election of officers, four were nominated for first vice-president. Of these, Lee Porter and Harper Shannon were in the run-off ballot, and Porter was elected.

The report of the seminaries was given on Thursday evening. A total of thirty minutes had been allowed for all six of the seminaries. Olin Binkley was our chairman, but we obviously all had time to simply make a quick statement to the Convention. Concerning

Southwestern, it needs to be noted that for the first time, we had more than two thousand students enrolled in 1968-1969. Some remarkable blessings are reflected in the minutes.

Foreign Mission Night on Thursday evening was, as usual, a high point. The willingness of a host of individual people to be one witness to a lost world is a testimony to the powerful grace of God. Since our first Convention in New Orleans, Mrs. Naylor and I had been over much of the world two times. We had personally seen hundreds of missionaries in the places where they worked. This evening could do nothing else but reach deep into our hearts.

The Convention closed on Friday night with a great night of evangelism. John Bisagno of Oklahoma preached the sermon and gave the invitation. The warm hospitality of the city that so recently had been largely Catholic, and in which God had made a Baptist witness fruitful, was a blessing. We went away anticipating the next Southern Baptist Convention meeting in New Orleans.

$\mathcal{S}$outhern $\mathcal{B}$aptist $\mathcal{C}$onvention

Exhibition Hall of the Convention Center • Denver, Colorado

JUNE 1-4
1970

WITH MY SENSE OF HISTORY, THE CELEBRATION OF 125 YEARS OF SOUTHERN BAPTIST LIFE, MARKED BY the favor of God and the growth of a great denomination, was an exciting prospect. I had known this same excitement as we approached the 1945 session of the Convention when we were to celebrate our centennial, only to have it dashed by the cancellation of the Convention due to the war. Now in a beautiful "mile high" city, Southern Baptists were gathering in the West on one of our frontiers to celebrate 125 years. The Resolutions Committee expressed it well when they said, "It has been our good fortune to celebrate our 125th Anniversary in beautiful Denver, Colorado, the 'mile high' city, where the great central plains and the towering Rocky Mountains meet." From that point, they expressed the Convention's appreciation for that kind of welcome that is a part of the nature of the West, open-hearted, generous, and hospitable. True, the hotels were crowded, but the heart was there.

The Convention theme was "Living the Christ Life." The Convention began on Monday night, June 1, as President W. A. Criswell called to order the 113th session of the Convention, and the Program Committee outlined the anticipation of celebration. On that opening evening, following President Criswell's message, there was an audiovisual presentation of the last 125 years.

There were two other audiovisual programs in the Convention that I thought were directly a matter of celebration. On Tuesday evening, there was a forty-five-minute film on "The Denomination Serving the Local Churches." The seminaries' audio presentation on Wednesday morning focused on "The Seminaries Serving the Churches." That was a thrilling report.

157

For me, the Tuesday morning presentation, "Projecting the Program of the Seventies," might also have been a part of the celebration. It was a new decade into which we had entered. Any celebration by the people of God should have a high anticipation for the future.

Now to the Convention as it unfolded. We began with that note of inspiration that I knew so well. As we were called to order by President Criswell, there were already 9,907 messengers registered. This number would become 13,692. We sang together "All Hail the Power of Jesus' Name." The Convention being formally constituted, the Program Committee presented its recommendation and outline, and the former presidents of the Convention were presented. After we sang "How Firm a Foundation," President Criswell's daughter sang "Set My Soul Afire, Lord." Dr. Criswell spoke on "The Rock From Which We Were Hewn."

On Tuesday morning, we discovered the kind of Convention that we were to have. The first recommendation of the Executive Committee seemed innocuous enough. It had to do with the use of student workers by the Home Mission Board. Immediately, a substitute motion was offered describing in greater detail the ones to direct the work of these students. The substitute was lost, and the first recommendation was adopted.

The second recommendation presented a Cooperative Program budget for 1971, a challenging $29,146,883. There was an immediate motion to amend the budget by striking out the allocation to the Christian Life Commission and making other distributions of the monies. This controversy will be dealt with in later detail. A new amendment received immediate discussion. R. Archie Ellis of South Carolina moved the previous question. The motion was adopted, the amendment was defeated, and the Cooperative Program budget for 1971 was approved. The unhappiness of some of the messengers was significant, and the cutting off of the debate grew more difficult.

There was also the election of the president. Five nominations were offered. A ballot was taken, and it was announced later that Carl E. Bates of North Carolina had been elected. When a recommendation was presented selecting Miami Beach, Florida, for our 1975 Convention, a substitute motion deleted any reference to the 1976 Convention; and the Miami Beach Convention was approved.

Typical of the Convention was the next recommendation which related to when the Convention would begin in 1971. There was a motion to amend by substituting. There was a point of order raised, but not sustained by the chair. The motion to amend was lost, and the recommendation was finally adopted.

In completing the election of officers, Fred Rhodes of the District of Columbia was elected first vice-president. After a run-off ballot, Russell Dilday of Georgia, a member of the present Resolutions Committee, was elected second vice-president of the Convention.

There were three major controversies that surfaced during the Convention. The seed for them had been sown in earlier conventions. Attention has already been called to it in passing. These controversies, which are still not settled, remain basic divisions among us. First, let us deal with the matter of the Christian Life Commission. The attempt to remove the appropriation for this agency is an old device for doing away with an agency. When this idea was rejected, there were other motions offered. Dick Roe of California moved that the Christian Life Commission be abolished in accordance with the constitutional provision. Later, Bertha Smith of South Carolina moved that the Convention call for the resignation of the elected staff of the Christian Life Commission. Still later, Harold Coble of California moved that "the Convention take note of the fact that a great number of our people and our churches have been sincerely offended by the Christian Life Commission's Atlanta Conference, and that as a matter of Christian conscience, this offense be considered by our Christian Life Commission."

Perhaps the best summary indicative of the storm was the statement presented to the Convention and signed by four previous presidents of the Convention, Ramsey Pollard, H. H. Hobbs; J. D. Grey, and H. F. Paschall. It read, "It is our sincere judgement that the issues concerning the Christian Life seminar in Atlanta have been fully exposed, and that nothing of real value can be contributed by additional discussion. Your convictions have been heard, and they have registered. It is good to know that no effort has been made to limit debate on this vitally important matter. There are good, intelligent, and loyal Baptists who question the motive of those responsible for such a program. However, we are well aware of the fact that many Southern Baptists strongly resent the presence of these men on the program. We would urge that it be the sense of this body that the Southern Baptist Convention does not commend or condemn the program of the Atlanta seminar. We would urge our boards, agencies, and commissions, to be exceedingly careful in arranging future programs so that the harmony and cooperative spirit of the Convention not be destroyed." There was more to the statement, but this brought us to the final action of this Convention on the matter. The minutes read, "The motion by Bertha Smith was tabled, the motion by Dick Roe was tabled, the ruling of the chair was appealed, the chair was sustained in the ruling." Most significant, I think, was that we still had leadership commanding enough respect in the Convention that their appeal was heard and the discussion was finally closed.

The second controversy, using almost the identical language of previous conventions, was a motion by J. R. Jones of Ohio, "The Messengers of this Convention instruct the Executive Committee of the Southern Baptist Convention to obtain annually, as a condition of continued employment, a written statement from all employees of each board, commission, or other agency receiving funds from the Cooperative Program; said statement to be a reaffirmation of the individual employee's personal acceptance and belief in the Bible as the authoritative, authentic, inspired, infallible Word of God; said Executive Committee shall report the results annually." When it finally came the time to discuss this motion, it was ruled out of order by the chair because of structural demands that were unconstitutional. The ruling was challenged but the Convention sustained it.

Glennon Culwell of California made a motion that all seminaries require all of their teachers to affirm annually their belief in the entire Bible as being the only infallible, inerrant, inspired Word of God through a signed statement to this effect. The motion continues in the later half, "the Sunday School Board requires all writers and or contributors to their publications to affirm commitment to the entire Bible as the only infallible, inerrant, inspired Word of God." Suddenly a basic fact of life among Southern Baptists had acquired a new vocabulary.

The Sunday School Board, caught up in the controversy as were all the agencies involved, made its response through its Chairman, Landrum Leavell II of Texas: "With regard to the action of the Southern Baptist Convention in New Orleans in 1969 concerning the Baptist Faith and Message the Sunday School Board is taking the following actions. (1) The elected Board, in its July meeting, instructed employees to carry out programs or tasks in a manner consistent with and not contrary to the Statement of Faith." There was a fuller explanation of the actions taken implementing this basic commitment.

The 1963 statement of the Baptist Faith and Message had become, and remains, that which it was not intended to be in Baptist polity. It is a law, a defensive bastion, subject to suspicion. Southern Baptists, by all that they are and do, begin and end with the Scriptures.

The third question that remains is a motion concerning *The Broadman Bible Commentary* which requested the withdrawal of Volume 1, the Genesis volume. Later, in a motion to publish a new volume, a statement was made by the Sunday School Board, and was approved, that attention had already been given to the matter.

Regarding the spirit and activities of the Convention, the resort to multiple devices was constant. This could be expected in a free-wheeling structure such as ours, but it is not worthy of our Baptist faith and fellowship. These phrases convey my meaning: "motion to amend," "motion to substitute," or "motion to table." These terms were constantly used to shut off debate. They prevented others less skilled in parliamentary procedure from having an opportunity to speak. It became commonplace that every declaration of a result of a vote be challenged and become a ballot. There was even a matter of personal privilege in the Convention when a man chose to rebuke the president for making remarks about items being considered that were out of keeping with the chair's responsibility. None of it reads very well.

There is a very unusual tribute to President Criswell in the minutes for the manner and spirit in which he presided. In their expression of appreciation, the Resolutions Committee had recommended a paragraph "thanking Criswell, Porter, and Shannon for their statesmanship in presiding . . . it has made this a memorable Convention one not to be forgotten." Let us not forget there were some high moments in the Convention. Foreign Missions Night always stirred us. In the midst of our inadequacies, it remains the heartbeat of Southern Baptists who reach out to a lost world.

Let us conclude this Convention report with Resolution 5 "On Anniversary Reaffirmation," an important resolution, indeed:

Whereas, In this 125th Anniversary year of the Southern Baptist Convention we stand at a significant milestone in our pilgrimage of following the leadership of our Lord, and

Whereas, There is an unprecedented need for a distinctively Christian witness and ministry in our troubled nation and world, and

Whereas, God has given Southern Baptists a unique opportunity to function as Christ's servants in every state of our nation and in an ever expanding number of foreign nations and,

Whereas, We are aware of certain tensions and misunderstandings among us, due in part to honest differences of opinion with regard to the interpretation of certain points of belief enunciated in 'The Baptist Faith and Message,' and due in part to sincere differences of opinion concerning certain aspects of the programs of some of our Convention's agencies and institutions, and

Whereas, Throughout our history we have been united in sharing a broad body of basic Christian convictions, and in a common commitment to carrying out the missionary imperative of the Great Commission,

Be it therefore Resolved, that we the messengers to the 125th Anniversary Sessions of the Southern Baptist Convention, meeting in Denver, Colorado, June 1-4, 1970, hereby rededicate ourselves to the high calling of taking the good news of new life in Jesus Christ to every person, and that we call upon churches to join us in that rededication, and

Be it further Resolved, that in this historic meeting we reaffirm 'The Baptist Faith and Message,' as adopted in Kansas City in 1963, as the common statement of the faith that unites us, recognizing that it accords each Baptist appropriate latitude to develop his own understanding of it in the light of God's Word and the leadership of the Holy Spirit, and that we urge our institutions and agencies to carry out their assigned ministries in a manner fully consistent with our historic beliefs, and that we urge our churches to be diligent in teaching our Baptist people the biblical basis for our statement of faith.

Be it further Resolved, that we both express our confidence in our Convention's agencies, institutions, and leaders and at the same time call upon them to devote their best energies and full resources to helping our churches fulfill their mission of reaching our sin-ridden, tormented world with the saving power of the gospel.

PART THREE

Kiel Auditorium • St. Louis, Missouri

JUNE 1-3
1971

IN 1871, THE SOUTHERN BAPTIST CONVENTION, IN THE TWENTY-SIXTH YEAR OF ITS HISTORY, MET IN ST. LOUIS, Missouri, with 360 messengers in attendance. One hundred years later, the Convention, in its 126th year, was meeting again in St. Louis. St. Louis proved to be a popular convention city with Southern Baptists. They met here in 1913 with 1,400 messengers. Then in 1936, I attended my first Convention here. This was the only Convention that Goldia had missed. The 1971 meeting of the Convention in St. Louis was to be my fifth. We had also met there in 1947, 1954, and 1961.

St. Louis was a delightful city for most of us. I personally was always impressed by the towering arch which was a memorial to the westward expansion of the American people. The Mississippi River, the "father of waters," was meaningful. The auditorium was adequate, and most of the hotels were within walking distance. I think that these physical circumstances made a contribution to the meeting of the Convention.

President Carl E. Bates called the Convention to order, in its 114th session, on Tuesday morning. The Convention theme was "In the Spirit of Christ." The minutes record that we sang "God of Grace and God of Glory," "Amazing Grace," and "Nothing but the Blood." The motion constituting the Convention was made and passed, and the number of registered messengers at its opening was 9,626. The final tally would be 13,716.

New in procedure was the fact that the first morning session was devoted largely to business. There was no president's address nor Convention sermon for this Tuesday morning. The report of the

165

Committee on Order of Business officially established the order of procedure for the Convention. Interestingly enough, at least in my memory, was that the president called to the attention of the ushers that only messengers be seated in the auditorium prior to the time a given session was called to order. Hitherto, it was "everybody come," messenger or not. Committees were announced, former presidents of the Convention were recognized, and our present officers were greeted. There was a citation for Porter Routh and Mrs. Routh for recognition of twenty-five years of service in the Convention.

The Executive Committee report became the primary matter of business. Different from the Denver Convention the year before, it seemed to proceed quietly with little disposition to amend. The fourth recommendation was a change in our bylaws to strike out "the hospital agency of the Southern Baptist Convention." Southern Baptists were getting out of the hospital business. There were proper expressions of appreciation for the hospital ministry.

Norfolk, Virginia, was chosen for the 1976 Convention meeting.

Under the theme "Share the Word Now," a specific plan for the 1973-1974 promotion in the Southern Baptist Convention was approved. With that, a recommendation was adopted which provided a statement of Cooperative Program principles. These principles emphasized the "essential unity of all denominational work." The independence of state convention boards was affirmed, along with the convenience of contributions being made through those agencies. The Southern Baptist Convention has no authority to allocate funds or divert funds from any state project or program. Continued conferences were called for between state conventions and the Southern Baptist Convention boards and committees looking for fuller cooperation.

The 1972 Cooperative Program budget was adopted. This time the budget was to be only a nine-month budget in the amount of $24,630,589, because of the change in the fiscal year. No discussion is recorded, and a unanimous vote was accepted.

Carl Bates was elected president of the Convention, with no other nominations. There were six nominations for the office of first vice-president, which resulted in a run-off ballot between James Landis of Texas and W. Ross Edwards of Missouri. Landis was chosen. There were likewise many nominations for second vice-president, with Warren C. Hultgren being chosen in a run-off ballot. The election of officers sessions were in succeeding periods.

Numerous resolutions were presented in this first morning session. Either they were referred to the Executive Committee, or the appropriate agency, or to the Committee on Order of Business for further discussion. Some of these resolutions cast longer shadows than others. For the first time, there was a resolution on abortion. Later, there was a motion to amend, which lost. There was a second motion to amend, which also lost. Finally, the previous question was moved and passed, and the resolution was adopted. The resolution called for legislation that allowed for the possibility of abortion under carefully stipulated conditions.

There was a motion that said, "Since *The Baptist Program* has carried two articles which present acceptance of fallibility and errancy in the Scriptures and no articles of an opposite viewpoint, and since the Baptist Faith and Message of 1963 declare that Baptists believe the Bible to be 'truth without any mixture of error,' the Convention respectfully requests the Executive Committee and the editor of *The Baptist Program* to provide equal space. . . . " It is notable that the issue did not die. The suspicion that is created by these carefully worded phrases on the Scriptures continued. As suggested previously, the 1963 Baptist Faith and Message continues to be "authoritative."

The second session Tuesday afternoon was notable in that the seminaries were allowed to make their reports that afternoon. We were all presented and given a few minutes in which to present our work. I noted that in Southwestern's report enrollment had continued to climb. There were 2,171 students. In fact, our report began, "continuing growth in enrollment, expanding emphasis upon continuing theological education, and an intensified restudy of curriculum, together with innovative teaching methods mark the entrance into the Seventies of the Southwestern Baptist Theological Seminary." There were 428 graduates reported during the year. When our alumni gathered on Wednesday noon for their annual luncheon, it was evident that "the family" was spreading over the earth.

The day was concluded with an hour of worship, and a bringing of the Convention sermon by John R. Claypool of Kentucky. The theme of the sermon was "The Challenge of This Hour."

Wednesday morning we returned to the resolutions presented by the committee. There was a resolution on the American Bible Society. There was another on beverage alcohol which caused discussion, amendments, and the final adoption of the resolution as presented. In this session, there was a presentation of theological education by Southern Baptist theological seminaries on behalf of the six theological seminaries to set forth their ministry through varied and diverse means.

There was a motion that would have dropped the name "Broadman" from *The Broadman Bible Commentary* because of controversy. In this connection, recognizing a continuing controversy, there was a motion "that the Sunday School Board be advised that the vote of the 1970 Convention regarding the rewriting of Volume 1 of *The Broadman Bible Commentary* has not been followed and that the Sunday School Board obtain another writer and proceed with the Commentary according to the vote of the 1970 Convention in Denver." This motion was followed by a later motion asking that this be a matter of order of business for the Convention. This the Convention agreed to do. The previous question was moved and called for. The vote was taken and a division was called for. Only after the ballot was it announced that the motion had passed. Upon further motion and passing, the actual tallies included in our minutes were 2,672 for the motion, and 2,298 against.

The foreign mission hour on Wednesday night was a great hour of inspiration. New missionaries were presented under the general theme of "Our Mission." There was a joint commissioning service for missionaries of the Home Mission Board and Foreign Mission Board, conducted under the leadership of our secretaries.

Resolutions on world peace, public funds and non-public education, prejudice, and voluntary prayer reflected a world at unrest. St. Louis Convention number five was just as exciting as the first.

Convention Hall, Civic Center • Philadelphia, Pennsylvania

JUNE 6-8

1972

PHILADELPHIA, "CITY OF BROTHERLY LOVE" AND THE "CRADLE OF AMERICAN LIBERTY," IS ALWAYS worthy of a visit. We had always enjoyed the city as a family and as tourists. Now the Southern Baptist Convention would meet there in its 127th year, and the large attendance reflected the anticipation of our people. As Baptists proclaiming ourselves a free people, the city would have special attraction. We had personal reasons to anticipate the Convention because our oldest son and his family lived in Wilmington, Delaware, just a few miles away.

On Tuesday, June 6, President Carl E Bates, pastor of the First Baptist Church in Charlotte, North Carolina, called the Convention to order at 9:30 A.M. As we sang "Amazing Grace" and "All Hail the Power of Jesus' Name," the inspirational tone was set. "Proclaim Liberty to All" served as the Convention theme.

The registration secretary reported that 8,100 messengers had registered as the Convention began, made the motion that these messengers constitute the Convention, "and that duly accredited messengers from churches in cooperation with the Convention who arrive later be recognized as messengers." The final total would be 13,153.

The Committee on Order of Business presented their report that had been published in our denominational papers, and it was quickly adopted. The Presidential Address was among the first in this order of business. With Vice-President Landes presiding, President Bates brought the address on the subject, "Hitherto-Henceforth." He is a peerless preacher. He used as his text the erection of the stone by the Prophet Samuel who named the stone "Ebenezer," meaning "Hitherto hath the Lord helped us."

169

Later in the Convention there was a motion that this address be published as part of the minutes, and we are indebted to that motion for some very choice quotations. Much of the first part of the address concerning "hitherto" was a reflection of the preacher's pilgrimage. The Convention had met in Nashville in 1914, when Bates was born, and in 1934 in Fort Worth. That was the year he was converted and became a Southern Baptist. Against that background, he reminded us of some great chapters. He spoke of the $75 Million Campaign. There was thanksgiving for the Cooperative Program as something that God had given us.

Dramatic was Bates' statement, "If I have learned anything about us during the past two years, it is this: Our churches are in trouble! I hasten to say that this has been true for us for 127 years." Does that sound like present tense? He said, "Twice in the past ten years we have fought the battle of Genesis." Most timeless was this, "Let me remind every messenger in this Convention that any individual or group that is determined to have theological and ecclesiastical sameness, he has one of two choices: he may join another denomination, or he may deny the basic democratic principles for which our people have been known across the years." It was indeed a stirring address.

The Convention now began with its matter of business. Multiple resolutions were offered and referred to the Committee on Order of Business for a time of discussion. The Executive Committee began to offer its recommendations. Then, as now, we were seeking to amend the bylaws, and to refine our procedure to make it more businesslike. After the recommendation which presented our 1972-1973 Cooperative Program budget, there was not a dissenting voice as we adopted the goal of $33,042,506.

There was a motion "that because a large segment of the material of *The Broadman Bible Commentary* is out of harmony with the spirit and letter of 'The Baptist Faith and Message' adopted by this Convention, we request the Sunday School Board to withdraw from further sale the entire set. . . . " The motion failed for adoption.

The time for the election of officers was on Tuesday afternoon. Jerry Clower, a layman from Mississippi, nominated for president Owen Cooper, who was from the same state. It was my first contact with Jerry Clower and his attractive humor. Few of us there will forget the nomination. It was so well received by the Convention that the election that followed was determined. Others nominated were

James Pleitz of Florida, James Coggin of Texas, Mrs. R. L. Mathis of
Texas, Fred Rhodes of the District of Columbia, James Westberry of
Georgia, and Dotson Nelson of Alabama. After a run-off between
James Coggin and Owen Cooper, Cooper was elected.

Program statements for the Baptist Sunday School Board and the
Education Commission were a part of that afternoon's business.

The time arrived for the presentation of resolutions, and the
multiple interests across the world were represented. There was
even one on taxation and freedom of conscience, which will be
mentioned later.

A pageant, entitled "Philadelphia Heritage," had been prepared
by the Historical Commission and was presented on Tuesday
evening, with accompanying music by the Centurymen directed by
Buryl Red and members of the Philadelphia Symphony. The
Convention sermon by my friend E. Hermond Westmoreland concluded the evening session.

Wednesday morning we began with the election of the first vice-
president. There were four nominations, and my own pastor and
friend, James Coggin, was elected.

Documents! You would expect that there would be one on religious liberty. An interesting note was the introduction of a motion
proposing to change our Constitution by changing the name of the
Southern Baptist Convention to Cooperative Missionary Baptist
Convention. When the motion came up for discussion, it was ruled
out of order as being too late for constitutional consideration.

Our seminary luncheons followed this morning session. We were
personally blessed at our Southwestern luncheon by the presence of
our son and his wife and their eight-year-old son. Mrs. Naylor
remembers that Rob III was a little put out that he did not fit at the
head table with his grandfather, grandmother, and parents. This was
really taken care of by the fact that Jack Coldiron looked after him at
a special table. This luncheon is always a most significant gathering
of the Southwestern family.

The actual hour for the seminaries was on Wednesday evening.
Grady Cothen of Louisiana was acting as our chairman as the reports
of the six seminaries were presented. Each of us, assisted by visual
features, music numbers, questions, and testimonies, presented the
ministry of theological education, emphasizing the call to Christian
ministry.

Following this report, Cliff Barrows led us in singing "Amazing Grace" and "All Hail the Power of Jesus' Name"; and Billy Graham preached the evening's concluding sermon.

Thursday, the last day of the Convention, was given largely to all of the business that remained, together with the concluding ceremonies. In the discussion of many resolutions, the freedom of the messengers to discuss is notable. We do not appear to our best advantage in those discussions, but they remain a vital part of our freedom. The discussions on individual conscience and war have an interesting history. There was a motion to adopt, a motion to amend, a motion to extend the time, and a motion to table. All reflected our activity. The motion to table lost. The motion to amend lost, also. Finally, the resolution itself lost.

Thursday afternoon, James Irwin, the astronaut, brought the final address of the session.

After all that had transpired, one would have thought that the closing session would have been anti-climactic, yet this was our great mission night. Baker James Cauthen presented a report of the Foreign Mission Board. A processional of missionaries to the platform dramatized our involvement in the work around the world; and new missionaries were presented. The Convention in this historic city closed with a note of victory, fellowship, and anticipation.

Memorial Coliseum • Portland, Oregon

[signature: Robert Taylor]

JUNE 12-14
1973

PORTLAND, OREGON, REPRESENTED IN 1973 THE OUTLYING PERIMETER OF THE SOUTHERN BAPTIST CONVENTION. JUST as Jesus had made the perimeter Caesarea Philippi the platform for a new miracle—a New Testament Church—Southern Baptists had also staked out the United States as its home mission territory. Five years earlier, when Portland was chosen as the 1973 Convention City, this recognized the fact that in the birth of the Northwest Convention, a new dynamic had come to our missionary impulse. There had been remarkable growth and sacrifice.

President Owen Cooper of Mississippi, the first layman to preside as president of the Convention since Brooks Hays had presided in 1959, called the Convention to order at 9:15 A.M., June 12, 1973, in the Memorial Coliseum in Portland. It was more than traditional. It was entirely fitting that we began by singing "All Hail the Power of Jesus' Name."

The theme of the Convention was "Share the Word Now." The Program Committee had invited James L. Sullivan to lead a period of meditation on the Convention theme in most of the sessions. It was an inspiration to hear him speak on subjects entitled "The Different Book," "America's Way Up," "The Bible for Christian Growth," and "A Book Without Bounds."

The registration secretary announced that 6,638 messengers had been registered, and moved that they constitute the Convention along with those of like credentials who would yet register. The final total was 8,871, the lowest in twenty-five years. Surely we expected this, yet I noted that North Carolina had more messengers present than Texas.

The Program Committee structure was approved. Dan Stringer welcomed the Convention to the Northwest Baptist Convention and spoke of God's wonderful blessings there. After the announcement of committees, we moved to the main business of our Convention, the report of the Executive Committee and their recommendations.

One of the earliest recommendations had to do with the 1973-1974 proposed Cooperative Program budget. The final amount was $33,042,506. It was a challenging budget, and it was adopted without dissent. Southwestern was to receive .0576 percent of this amount, the largest participation we had ever had.

Commenting on previous Convention notes, I underlined the importance of the program statements, the adoption of which had always seemed routine. Of course, these statements had been hammered out in other sessions of the Executive Committee. Yet over a ten-year period, the statements were casting a long shadow. They were not only defining the areas in which the various agencies would work but also were opening doors to them, the likes of which we could not imagine. In this Convention there were program statements for the Brotherhood Commission and the Home Mission Board, the latter of which was intricate and involved. The Sunday School Board program statement was amended and enlarged. There was also a program statement for the Christian Life Commission and the Radio and Television Commission, using terminology concerning the work of Southern Baptists.

Even at this early date, my notes speak of the adoption of the promotional emphasis for 1975-1976 entitled "Let Christ's Freedom Ring." This first morning session concluded with the president's address making an appeal for faithful and zealous personal witnessing as we "Share the Word Now."

In the afternoon session, Owen Cooper was reelected president of the Convention by acclamation. Four nominations for first vice-president required a run-off between James Harris and Clifton Branham, with Harris being elected. The liveliest discussion concerned the Stewardship Commission. Duke K. McCall of Kentucky had made a motion that the Commission be dissolved, and the work of the commission be carried on as part of the work of the Executive Committee. I remember the division well, and it was only after a lengthy session that the motion was defeated.

Foreign Mission Night had historically been a great high hour of inspiration for us. That remained true during this Convention under the leadership of Secretary Baker Cauthen, as Nelson Fanini, president of the Brazilian Baptist Convention, spoke to us. New missionary appointees were presented. Dr. Cauthen brought an excellent, stirring appeal to close the session.

Wednesday morning began with eight nominations for second vice-president. The final result was the election of Clifton Brannon of Texas. The report of the Baptist Sunday School Board received major attention. The twentieth anniversary of James L. Sullivan as president of that board was appropriately recognized.

We began consideration of the resolutions presented by our committee. These always reflect the current crises in the Convention. There was one concerning those returning from the Vietnam War. There was a communication from President Nixon. There was a call for integrity and morality in the American political system. For the first time we had a resolution on the study of the aging. The opening statement said, "From 1900 to 1970 the population of citizens over 65 has risen from approximately 4% to 10%." There was also a resolution concerning the place of women in Christian service.

The fellowship of our luncheon on Wednesday afternoon was memorable. All of the seminaries were upbeat in their reports. On Thursday afternoon, Southwestern's blessings were notable in the school's account, which noted that "all-time records for the Institution" had been broken. Concerning enrollment, "no accredited theological seminary has ever sought to minister to as many bonafide, full-time students as this Institution is presently. There were more students on the Southwestern campus in the fall, than in any time in the history of the Institution." The Doctor of Ministry program was inaugurated, and Dr. Joe Davis Heacock was recognized in his retirement.

Mrs. William Fleming of Fort Worth, a personal friend and benefactor of the seminary in large measure, was present at the Convention. She had been a helper to so many of our Southern Baptist causes which were taking root in Canada. We had agreed to go with her following the Convention to visit these places of ministry. We flew to Calgary, Canada, and rented a car. For the next four days we went from place to place. It is not surprising these years later that Southern Baptists have a seminary in Calgary, and an increasing number of churches. The Flemings' faithful involvement in the Canada expansion should be remembered.

Portland, Oregon, always reminds me that "they went everywhere preaching the Word." This was a good Convention.

Convention Center • Dallas, Texas

JUNE 11-13

1974

DALLAS, TEXAS, HAD CERTAINLY PROVED ITSELF AS A SOUTHERN BAPTIST CONVENTION CITY. FORTY years before, the Convention had met in Fort Worth, Texas; and we had returned for our first "at home" Convention with keen anticipation. It was thought at that time that we were meeting on the perimeter. In 1965, the Convention came to Dallas as though we were meeting at the very heart of the Convention. It was not surprising that a new attendance record was set at that time.

Along with the meeting in 1974, we had made every plan at Southwestern to make the most of the open door that the Convention provided to involve multitudes in the life of the institution which was theirs. No place or institution would be allowed to overshadow the meeting of the Convention itself; however, it certainly added an intensity for Southwestern to have the Convention meeting in our own front door.

President Owen Cooper of Mississippi called the Convention to order in the 117th session in the 129th year of the Convention, on Tuesday, June 11, 1974, at 9:30 A.M. The sounding of the gavel to this hour has an electrifying quality. After the special music, the Convention sang "All Hail the Power of Jesus' Name." Immediately following, Carl E. Bates of North Carolina presented a period of meditation on the Convention theme, "Share His Love Now." He spoke on the topic "Share His Love Now by Teaching the Bible." This succession of interpretative devotions made for high inspirational moments.

The secretary reported that 12,927 messengers had registered at the time of opening, and made the motion that constituted the

Convention. The final number would be 18,190, which was a new record. The Committee on Order of Business presented a program which had long since been published in our denominational papers. President Cooper requested that resolutions be limited to one hundred words by unanimous consent.

The presidential address on "The Declaration of Cooperation" sounded a keynote for the Convention.

Proceeding immediately to business, the Executive Committee presented its recommendations. Recommendation 1 called for a Cooperative Program budget for the 1974-1975 fiscal year in the amount of $40,000,000. How far we had come! We will save the Southwestern appropriation for a discussion of the seminary itself.

There were recommendations concerning the structure and the program statements of various agencies. The struggle of the Convention to adapt itself to the fast pace of growth, and to the organizational pattern of the world about us, was quite evident. A recommendation that was to cast a long shadow was one to "authorize the Convention officers in 1974 to appoint a committee of seven persons, widely experienced in denominational life, to study and evaluate the Executive Committee in light of bylaw 9." Later, W. A. Criswell was to move that a "committee of seven members be appointed to study the possibility of changing the name of the Convention with instruction that the Committee report to the Convention next year." When these recommendations were discussed, there was a substitute that made the matters of their consideration to be cared for by the first committee. The Convention had appointed other committees. It may be a simple matter of hindsight. It seemed to me that it marked a new commitment to the idea that a committee could take care of our denomination's concerns. The trouble with this procedure is that Baptists simply do not settle their problems in committee. Finally, all must speak. The matters themselves were important, of course. The proposal to change the name of the Convention was not new, but this motion was close to the end of the line for that consideration.

The chief thrust of this Convention could be better identified by the themes introduced, than by specific recommendation detail. For example, there was a motion made under the title of "Missionary Qualifications" that said, "All appointments, endorsements, and so forth (including the military and industrial chaplaincy) whose function will be that of a pastor, which is restricted to males by Scripture, must meet the requirements as outlined in the New Testament." The underlying problem was the affirmation of male dominance in ministry. Southern Baptists would be debating the place of women in ministry for all of the years to come. This particular motion was defeated, after it was given full discussion and many amendments were offered. It required a ballot because the vote was so close. There was a resolution presented on "unisex and the Scriptures" which was never given full discussion. The place of women in ministry would continue to be a growing discussion in Southern Baptist life.

A resolution was presented calling for "black representation" on Convention boards. In the discussion that followed, it became larger than black representation, and addressed itself to the representation of minorities. It did not call for quotas, but in the form finally amended and adopted, it declared that minority representation should be encouraged on all boards. We even began the long discussion about "the physical universe" with a resolution on "the stewardship of God's creation."

In addition to these, there were many resolutions presented on abortion and the sanctity of human life. The number of resolutions presented simply made a promise and an agenda for the future. When dates begin to be assigned as to the origin of discussion, this should be remembered.

Tuesday afternoon began with Dr. W. A. Criswell interpreting the theme, "Share His Love Now by Remaining Faithful to the Church."

The election of officers was a Tuesday afternoon concern. There were seven nominations for president presented. Those nominated were W. O. Vaught, Landrum P. Leavell, Clifton W. Brannon, Kenneth L. Chafin, Dotson M. Nelson, Jr., Daniel Sotelo, and Jaroy Weber of Texas. After a run-off between Weber and Chafin, Weber was elected. The Fiftieth Anniversary of the Cooperative Program was to be officially recognized at the Convention in 1975 by the Committee on Order of Business.

An amendment to Bylaw 7 was adopted which would require that not more than two-thirds of the members of any group shall be drawn from either category that is ordained or a layperson.

Like previous conventions, Tuesday evening featured the work of the Home Mission Board. The evening concluded with an emphasis on the challenge of home missions, by Russell Dilday.

The sessions on Wednesday would be held only in the morning and evening. The afternoon was reserved for the seminary luncheons, an emphasis which will receive major attention in this discussion. H. Franklin Paschall of Tennessee spoke on the topic "Share His Love by Serving People" in theme meditation. The election of a first vice-president became the first order of business. There were seven people nominated, and Stewart B. Simms of South Carolina was elected. The subjects previously discussed received major attention in this session with resolutions and recommendations. The Convention sermon was preached by R. J. Robinson of Georgia on the subject of "Hope from That Dawn."

We had made preparation at Southwestern for our finest homecoming. In that superb fashion which was peculiarly his, John Seelig rolled out the welcome mat for our ever-growing Southwestern family. A large tent had been erected on the seminary mall in front of the memorial building. Here buffet lines were opened and multitudes of people were fed. Buses from Dallas had been arranged for, and the event turned into a major fellowship.

The seminary report itself, made later to the Convention, was indicative of the high tide that God had given to us. "All previous records of this, the largest seminary, were broken this year. The total enrollment for 1973-1974 is 2,622." Details followed as to the degree programs in which these engaged, "the successful conclusion of the two-year self-study required and the accreditation by the Southern Association of Colleges and Schools is announced."

"The Goldia and Robert Naylor Children's Center, made possible by a personal gift together with an appropriation from the capital needs program of the Convention, was completed and dedicated on March 14. It is a facility having the capacity for three hundred children in daycare and kindergarten programs. . . . " Mrs. William Fleming had made it all possible by making the gift. She also required that the building include my wife's name, Goldia, in its name. You know that I thought such naming entirely appropriate.

I noted in the report also the line which read that "50 single young women who could not find accommodations in Barnard Hall were enrolled duirng the last session." All of this is to say that Southwestern could not have had a finer hour, both on Wednesday afternoon and in the entire development of the Convention program and plan.

Wednesday evening was Foreign Mission Night. How appropriate it was that we should be featuring foreign missions at the same time as a seminary gathering that had been given the privilege of a foreign mission mandate. Dr. James Cauthen concluded a magnificent evening on the subject of "Share His Love Now."

Thursday morning began with the resolutions. The new subjects in the list included "abortion and the sanctity of human life," "population explosion," and, strangely enough, "appreciation to the News Media."

The seminaries were also given an hour on Thursday morning under the leadership of Milton Ferguson of Midwestern Baptist Theological Seminary, who was the year's chairman of the President's Fellowship. The six seminaries made their reports to the Convention. Ferguson recognized Olin T. Binkley, retiring as president of Southeastern Baptist Theological Seminary, and W. Randall Lolley as the president-elect.

In the Thursday afternoon session, C. Kenneth Mann of Texas was recognized as the eighteen-thousandth messenger to the Convention.

Thursday evening, Mrs. Marie Mathis of Texas presented a resolution on the Cooperative Program which had been previously adopted by Woman's Missionary Union. It recognized June 8-9, 1975, as a special time for the Cooperative Program. It gave every encouragement to a total participation in the Cooperative Program as a channel for Southern Baptists to world witness. It is called "Life Line of Southern Baptist Missions Work." In this session, President Owen Cooper presented Paul Cates of Texas with a Declaration of Cooperation. In it appears this quote: "In 1925 our forbears committed themselves to a new level of interdependence in a relationship of stewardship called the Cooperative Program, and . . . we hereby declare this program of cooperation to be self-evident of our denominational unity and a manifestation of our vision for the future under the Lordship of Christ."

The Convention concluded with a thrust forward, a note of anticipation, and a commitment among messengers that is basic in the Scriptures. It is true that there were clouds which were "no larger than a man's hand" that were little perceived, but this "Southwestern" Convention was great and memorable.

Convention Center • Miami Beach, Florida

Robert Taylor

JUNE 10-12
1975

"LET CHRIST'S FREEDOM RING" HAD BEEN CHOSEN FOR THE THEME OF THE 118TH SESSION OF THE SOUTHERN Baptist Convention, meeting in its 130th year in Miami Beach, Florida. The theme was in recognition of the beginning of the bicentennial year of our nation. The liberty that we celebrated was religious liberty, and the Program Committee had arranged a fifteen-minute sermon in each session of the Convention that underlined this theme. The emphases were "Let Christ's Freedom Ring Through Church Ministry" by James T. Draper of Texas; "Through Denominational Involvement" by Schneider Groten of Connecticut; "Through Church Outreach" by Richard A. Jackson of Arizona; "Through Mission Action and Giving" by Verlin Kruschwitz of Kentucky; and finally, "Through Mass Evangelism" by Angel Martinez of Arkansas. These moments were highly inspirational and representative of the special emphasis of the Convention.

President Jaroy Weber of Texas called the Convention to order on Tuesday, June 10, 1975, at 9:30 A.M., in the Convention Center in Miami Beach, Florida. Under the direction of William J. Reynolds of Tennessee, we sang "All Hail the Power of Jesus' Name."

The motion to constitute the Convention indicated that 12,485 messengers had been accredited and that all later accredited messengers would be recognized as members of the Convention when they were enrolled. The final number of messengers was 16,421. Miami Beach was a city highly approved by our Southern Baptist Convention hosts as a convention city.

Searcy S. Garrison, the chairman of the Committee on Business, presented the Program Committee's report, calling our attention to the fact that the program underlined two special events. As already indicated, this was the beginning of our bicentennial year. For Southern Baptists, this year was the fiftieth anniversary of the beginning of our Cooperative Program. No history will adequately measure the impact of this togetherness. Along with our national celebration, it was indeed proper for us not to forget that this program had been highly blessed by God, and that it was of greatest significance to all of us.

Soon President Weber recognized Jerry Clower of Mississippi to emphasize features about the Convention Program. I do not recall this ever being done before. Those who were there would not forget that Clower, a Baptist deacon, faithful layman, and professional humorist, had also nominated Owen Cooper for president of the Convention in a speech that was unforgettable. He did as well with these features.

Vice-president Stuart Sims was asked to take the chair. He recognized Joe T. Odle of Mississippi, who was to introduce the special feature relating to the Liberty Bell. This bell, an exact replica of the original Liberty Bell which hangs in Independence Hall in Philadelphia, was made available by the State of Mississippi. Beginning May 12, 1975, it was transported to Nashville, then to Philadelphia, and on to the White House and other historical points for appropriate celebrations while enroute to Miami Beach. Placed in the Convention Hall, it stood as a fitting symbol of the heritage of freedom which is enjoyed by this nation and of the commitment of Baptists to religious freedom for all people. The bell served as an impressive compliment to the theme of the Convention, "Let Christ's Freedom Ring."

Following this presentation, Nettie Beth Weber, President Weber's daughter, sang a solo. Her father then presented the presidential address, speaking on the subject, "Let the Bell Ring." At the conclusion of the address, the Liberty Bell was rung while messengers stood in appreciation and prolonged applause. The messengers then sang "My Country, Tis of Thee."

Each of the following sessions of the Convention began with the ringing of the bell. For me, these were moving experiences. I noted that the attendance at the opening of each session was greatly improved. At this point, the Executive Committee presented its report and recommendations. This committee acts for the

Convention between sessions; but it must report its actions to the Convention in session, and those actions must be approved. Their recommendations would represent the work of the year.

The first recommendation concerned the Cooperative Program allocation budget of $51,000,000 for 1975-1976, which was up from the $40,000,000 budget for 1974-1975. Our funds were now advancing dramatically. The appropriation for Southwestern Seminary was $2,379,827. In 1958, when my leadership responsibility there began, the seminary received $225,000 from the Cooperative Program after much struggle. This challenging budget was adopted without discussion. In less than five minutes, the Convention had set out on its most ambitious year.

Other approved recommendations called for small changes in the bylaws, i.e., moving from the state where one has been elected terminates board membership; and after the termination of a term, a trustee or director is not eligible for another appointment until after one year. The composition of general boards was also addressed. Other actions included a requirement that bylaw changes must have the approval of two successive annual sessions. Program statements that had been adopted by previous Conventions and had been refined and changed came up again for amendment and change. In almost every case, changes represented a development of the area of activity of a particular board, institution, or agency. The program concerning evangelism became three programs. The program statement for the Sunday School Board was amended to allow conference center operations. The Christian Life Commission and the Public Affairs Committee programs were both amended.

Albert McClellan presented the recommendation concerning "emphasis plans for the years 1979-1986." These plans were approved without discussion.

There was much miscellaneous business which reflected the concerns of the members of the Convention. There was one motion that the money that was being used by the Sunday School Board, in its program for cooperative education promotion work with the state conventions, be given to the Cooperative Program. Of course, these motions were referred to the Sunday School Board.

There was another motion to change the name of the Southern Baptist Convention. There was even the suggestion that the name be given a trial period of one year. All of this was resolved by the report by the special committee, which had been appointed the previous year to study the work of the Executive Committee, and also to measure the sentiment concerning the name change. The committee had concluded that the vast majority of Southern Baptists did not want the name changed, and it was so voted by the Convention. This largely put to rest a recurrent theme.

On Tuesday afternoon, following the ringing of the Liberty Bell, we were led in singing "God of Grace and God of Glory." After the theme emphasis, it was time for the election of officers. Jaroy Weber of Texas was nominated for a second term for president. Since there were no other nominations, he was elected by acclamation.

There were three nominations for first vice-president. Those nominated were Hunter Riggins of Virginia, James Monroe of Florida, and James Sells of Missouri. The ballots were cast and Riggins was chosen.

The seminaries had been given thirty minutes for their presentation in the early session of the Convention. W. Randall Lolley of North Carolina, chairman of the president's group, presented the report. Landrum Leavell was presented as the recently elected president of the New Orleans Baptist Theological Seminary. The combined report was a visual presentation to the Convention.

According to the bylaws of the Convention, resolutions were presented and referred to the Committee on Order of Business for a time of discussion. To say that the resolutions were presented this afternoon would indicate that they occupied a large portion of time in future sessions of the Convention. The subjects of the resolutions presented were as interesting as were all of the motions in miscellaneous business. They included religious freedom, strengthening the Royal Ambassador work, bio-medical issues, the economic crisis, peace, and broadcasting and religious freedom. There was also a resolution concerning prayer for persecuted Baptists.

At this point, a recurring problem of this Convention surfaced. A motion to extend time for the order lost. Again and again, this matter of not enough time appeared. We were late in coming to the end of the Wednesday morning session. A messenger asked permission to make a point of personal privilege; he expressed the hope that the Convention might adjourn. The time for adjournment had passed. There were seminary luncheons and other commitments. That was what was required to close the session. Finally on Thursday, it was necessary to set aside special time for miscellaneous business at 4:40 P.M.

There were many resolutions, even resolutions on violence. One resolution expressed appreciation to those who had made the Liberty Bell possible. Appreciation was expressed to the Ford Motor Company which had made the transportation possible. There were resolutions concerning religious freedom, family relationships, and religious broadcasting and religious freedom.

There was an attempt to amend a resolution concerning the Holy Spirit by adding the words "Southern Baptists are not charismatic." The amendment lost and the original resolution was adopted. There was a resolution on "Freedom '76" which concerned the public school curriculum and expressed appreciation to our host city.

Tuesday evening, the second special emphasis was introduced. President Weber presented Mike Speer of Tennessee to lead in the presentation of this special feature—the celebration of the fiftieth anniversary of the Cooperative Program. The intention was to impress upon all in attendance the historical background of the Cooperative Program, and to point out its contribution to Southern Baptist life and work for the past fifty years. This emphasis was also meant to challenge Southern Baptists to a more meaningful involvement in its support. Many people shared in this presentation.

The Convention joined in singing "To God Be the Glory." The most dramatic presentation was by Glendon McCullough of Tennessee as he told of the involvement of the Royal Ambassadors who ran from Memphis to Miami Beach to bring a lighted torch celebrating the light made possible by the Cooperative Program. His presentation was climaxed by the entrance into the Convention Hall of the last runner, who was greeted with applause by the messengers. There were 2,153 boys who shared in running to bring the torch to Miami Beach.

The executive secretaries of the state conventions and the stewardship secretaries were invited to sign the Declaration of Cooperation, relative to the Cooperative Program. To symbolize their commitment, 1,029,663 signatures had already been gathered. The wonderful hour was concluded by singing "Send the Light."

Wednesday night featured the work of the Home Mission Board; and Russell H. Dilday, Jr., of Georgia, who was chairman of the board, spoke on "The Gospel Response." We joined in singing "America the Beautiful," and Arthur Rutledge led in the conclusion of the program.

The final session on Thursday evening had been left for the Foreign Mission Board. It somehow seemed especially appropriate to me that at Miami Beach, we should conclude the Convention by reaching out to a world that seemed within the touch of our hands. Angel Martinez was to have spoken at the beginning of the session, but missed his plane and was not in attendance. Russell Newport of Missouri sang a number of songs which was certainly a blessing. Under the leadership of Baker James Cauthen, we recognized the emeritus missionaries present. Reports from the field reflected the needs of the world and, in many areas, an openness to the gospel. Cauthen ended the session with a challenge, "Let the Fire Fall." At the end, all of the people in the auditorium stood quietly for the ringing of the Liberty Bell. A concluding prayer sent us out. Miami Beach, June 1975, remains a high-water mark in the Conventions.

Scope Convention Center • Norfolk, Virginia

[signature]

JUNE 15-17
1976

THE MEETING OF THE SOUTHERN
BAPTIST CONVENTION IN VIRGINIA
WOULD BE OF GREAT PERSONAL INTEREST
to us. Virginia was Goldia's home state; she was born in the heart of
the Blue Ridge Mountains. It is the most beautiful country I have
seen in this world. All of these years we had faithfully returned to
Virginia with the children. "The Old Dominion" was to touch a
heartstring with us. Now the Convention we loved would meet in
Virginia in the bicentennial year of the life of our nation.

Normally, we would have said that Norfolk, Virginia, was out on
the edge of Convention territory, which would be reflected in the
decreased attendance of the Convention. However, in this case it
would be far different. We had met in Richmond in 1938, but this was
the first time we had met in Norfolk. It was a smaller city and the
accommodations were somewhat scarce. People were staying in
accommodations all the way from Williamsburg to Virginia Beach;
but the people came, more than eighteen thousand of them, for this
special Convention in the country's bicentennial year.

There were two or three special attractions about this meeting. It
would be the first time that a sitting President of the United States
would address the Convention. President Gerald Ford had accepted
our invitation. Of course, anyone of us looked forward to this special
occasion. For all Americans who cherish and love their liberty and
history, this had to be a part of its cradling experience. Just up the
road was Jamestown which was basic to the fundamental principles
of our republic. It was in Williamsburg that Patrick Henry had
defended two Baptist preachers indicted for "preaching the Gospel

of Jesus Christ." Only a few miles south was Virginia Beach and the ocean with its endless attraction for young and old.

As a girl, Goldia had gone to Virginia Beach for the State Baptist Encampment. It was here that she heard, met, and loved Dr. and Mrs. Marshall Craig, who were later to become our family friends for life. It was also in Virginia Beach in 1939 that I saw the ocean for the second time. On the same trip, following a meeting of the Baptist World Alliance in Atlanta, we had come to Myrtle Beach with our boys. There I reveled in an ocean that has always held a charm for me. You can sense, even in this distance of time, the excitement that was mine and ours as we approached the meeting of the Convention.

The first day of the Convention was different because of the presence of the President of the United States. The messengers streamed into the Convention Hall early. We passed through metal detectors and, under the sharp eyes of heavy security, into an auditorium that had been searched by specially trained dogs and made secure for the President. All of this was an experience in itself. You can imagine that it took a while for all of us to get into the auditorium, and a longer while for us to settle down to the routine matters of the Convention. The President was not to speak until 3:00 that afternoon, but everyone stayed because of the security arrangements. I remember that Goldia and Mrs. Duke McCall left about 11:30 A.M. and bought hot dogs for some hungry seminary presidents sitting near the front. It was quite an atmosphere.

President Jaroy Weber of Texas called the Convention to order at 9:30 A.M., June 15, 1976, in the Scope Convention Center in Norfolk, Virginia. An unfading thrill was the singing of the hymn "All Hail the Power of Jesus' Name." Fred Kendall, the Convention secretary, reported even at that hour that there was a registration of 14,107 messengers; and he made the motion constituting the Convention. The number would reach 18,637. The Convention then moved with its normal routine of business. The program for the Convention had been published for weeks in our denominational papers and was formally adopted. Committees were announced that likewise had been published in the papers. Then, President Weber brought his address on the Convention theme, "Let the Church Stand Up." The Convention responded to the singing of the president's daughter, Nettie Beth Weber, who sang "Grace So Amazing."

From that point on the Convention was occupied with business. The Executive Committee began its report. As usual, the first item was the adoption of a Cooperative Program allocation budget for the years 1976-1977, in the amount of $55,000,000. It was a unanimous adoption. I noted in my margin that the allocations for the six Southern Baptist seminaries was $11,037,682. Marvelous!

The Convention procedure called for the presentation of resolutions and motions. These were presented without discussion and were referred to the Committee on Program which would suggest an hour or time for the discussion of the items presented. In reflecting on the Convention, I thought that it would be remembered for certain major indications of interest and concern. It was a changing time in the Convention.

At 3:00 in the afternoon, President Weber escorted Gerald Ford, President of the United States, to the platform while the Convention messengers stood to greet him with applause. Religious liberty was the theme of the Convention. After all, Baptists had written a good chapter in the fight for such liberty in our country. At the end of the address, our president again escorted President Ford from the Convention while the messengers stood and applauded as an expression of their appreciation. The Convention then joined in singing "Blessed Be the Name." The President's coming to address the Convention was a recognition of the historic significance of the bicentennial year of our nation. At this point, the messengers sought to pick up the normal business of the Convention and discussed those things, many of which were not normal.

Early Tuesday evening was the time for the election of officers, and the nominations for President were received. There were six nominations. The names were familiar to the Convention: Kenneth Chafin, Clift Brannon, and Jack Taylor of Texas; Adrian Rogers of Tennessee; Stewart Simms of South Carolina; and James L. Sullivan of Tennessee. Adrian Rogers asked that his name be withdrawn from consideration. Dr. Sullivan was elected.

After the election of the president, the six Southern Baptist seminaries brought their report. It was my year to be chairman of the group, and therefore, it was my privilege to present all of the presidents to the Convention. I gave them an opportunity to say a brief word and then concluded the period with an address on theological education. There is a line in the minutes which I would not want to omit: "A solo by Mrs. Virginia Seelig of Texas concluded the presentation." How often she had blessed my ministry and our home with a gift that was truly hers, and a friendship I will always cherish. The seminary reports were optimistic. Attendances were increasing.

Southwestern, the largest seminary in the world, had again reached a new high in attendance with 2,906 enrolled. The evening session concluded with a report on the Cooperative Program.

Here, I think it would be worthwhile to call attention to some unusual resolutions. There were the usual resolutions that we always considered, but there was a new thrust at this Convention. The issue of abortion had suddenly become a major issue. The many resolutions made suggested that suddenly this was to become a major issue. The Convention spoke with such conviction on the matter of homosexuality, in my memory the first time it had been presented formally to the Convention. The Convention affirmed their opposition overwhelmingly. There was a resolution on transcendental meditation. There was one on religious liberty and taxation. The messengers had begun to feel that the government was seeking to intrude upon the separation of church and state. There was an expression of continued uneasiness with the Christian Life Commission. There were motions that suggested that the stance taken on social issues by the commission should not be represented as that of the total sentiment of the Convention.

In the year previous, a committee of seven had been appointed by the Convention to study the Executive Committee, its authority, parameters of power, and its responsibilities. Before the Convention was finished, another responsibility had been added to this same committee, the task of studying the request for a new name for the Southern Baptist Convention. The report of this committee was one of the major items of the Convention.

It is understandable that there would be concern about the power of the Executive Committee. All of the other agencies would be very sensitive to any suggestion that the Executive Committee controlled their actions. With independent boards of trustees under the authority of the Convention, this would not be acceptable. The new committee had done a thorough work under the leadership of Chauncy Daley of Kentucky. They very carefully outlined the limitations of the Executive Committee, the tremendous scope of the work which had been accumulated for the committee, the ultimate authority of the Convention itself, and the independence of other agencies in any authoritative action.

When it came to the question of changing the name of the Convention, it was evident again that the committee had done its work. They reported that a survey of churches in thirty states "showed 16 percent in favor of a name change and 84 percent against." The surveys made by state papers also resulted in an overwhelming rejection of a name change for Southern Baptists. The committee said, "We reach this decision on a name change after careful study of all of the known reasons for and against a name change. . . . In light of its findings, it is the committee's considered judgment that the name of the Southern Baptist Convention should not be changed at this time." This settled the question for a generation of whether the name of the Southern Baptist Convention should be changed.

It was at this Convention that the phrase "Bold Mission Thrust" had its acceptance. A committee appointed in a previous Convention, under the chairmanship of Warren C. Hultgren of Oklahoma, had been given this forward-looking responsibility. The committee began its report "that the Convention set as its primary mission challenge that every person in the world shall have the opportunity to hear the Gospel within the next twenty five years." The report included, among other things, that "the two mission boards be requested to develop as many ways as possible for long and short term involvement for persons in direct mission work." It also urged "that the Convention request the six seminaries in cooperation with the two mission boards to review and strengthen the academic and clinical programs for the training of those dedicated to mission service." The theme, "Let the Church Reach Out," would continue to appear in Convention programs.

In the meantime, the first vice-president had been chosen after three nominations. Dotson Nelson was elected. Likewise, in the election for second vice-president, there were four nominations; and Mrs. Carl Bates of North Carolina was chosen. Historically with us, elections can be the brotherly determination of a people united.

It was a great year for the Convention and a great year for our nation. Its total appeal was reflected in the attendance. Every state in the union was represented by messengers except for three— Wyoming, Montana, and Vermont. As we came to the closing moments of the Convention, as had been planned by the Program Committee, W. O. Vaught of Arkansas spoke about the Liberty Bell, made available by the State of Mississippi and brought to the Convention as a symbol of freedom, the heritage of our nation, and a reminder to Baptists of their freedom in Christ and their commitment to religious liberty. The Liberty Bell was rung while the messengers stood with applause and gratitude, thus closing the 119th session of the Southern Baptist Convention.

Bartle Convention Center • Kansas City, Missouri

JUNE 14-16

1977

THE SOUTHERN BAPTIST CONVENTION MEETING IN KANSAS CITY, MISSOURI, IN 1963 HAD PROVED TO BE THE BAPTIST Faith and Message session, and it is remembered as such. It was not the first time we had met in Kansas City. The first Kansas City Convention had met in 1905. I looked at the attendance record of 816 and wondered about the things that took place at the meeting. My own first attendance at the Convention here was in 1956. In 1963, as I have indicated, there was a reaffirmation of the Baptist Faith and Message. This was the result of continuing agitation about the things that we most surely believe. A committee had worked a year on the statement only to discover that we still believed the things we believed in 1925.

Kansas City had proved to be a delightful Convention City. The hotels were close by and adequate, and the auditorium had proved to be excellent. I think that the fellowship of a western city is actually different and a little warmer. One of our Southern Baptist institutions is located there—Midwestern Baptist Theological Seminary. Because of all of these factors, the atmosphere at the outset was one of fellowship and of being at home.

There was also a personal side to this Convention. Dr. Don Wideman, pastor of the First Baptist Church in North Kansas City, had invited me to preach to his people on Sunday morning prior to the Convention. Don and his wife were perfect hosts. The church was delightfully warm, responsive, and Baptist. I remember that we were taken to a lovely restaurant on the outskirts of the city. It was an old home that had been converted to a beautiful restaurant. I saw something there that I had not seen before anywhere. It was a sign that said, "Children Not Allowed." We laughed about the sign and remarked about the quietness. It was a great fellowship and a great way to begin the Convention.

President James L. Sullivan called the Convention to order at 9:00 A.M., June 14, 1977, in the Bartle Convention Center in Kansas City, Missouri. William J. Reynolds from Tennessee led us in "All Hail the Power of Jesus' Name." The Convention was in session.

W. Fred Kendall of Tennessee, the registration secretary, reported an opening registration of 12,189 messengers, and made the motion that constituted the Convention. The ultimate attendance was 16,271, as compared to 12,971 at the last Convention held here in 1963.

When the Program Committee was called to present its Order of Business, they presented what had previously been printed with certain changes. At the very beginning they called for an extension of time for the election of officers on Tuesday afternoon. They had also fixed a night session on Tuesday to begin at 6:40. With the theme, "Let the Church Reach Out," we were under way.

It was a departure from the usual, when after naming the committees, the program called for a miscellaneous business order as the first order of business. The Convention procedure called for motions to be made and read but not discussed, except at the time determined by the Committee on Order of Business. Resolutions followed with subjects indicated but not read. Both the resolutions and motions were brought to the secretary's desk to be discussed at a time determined by the committee. As indicated, there were four motions and fifteen resolutions presented. Though the procedure is limited, it takes time. This completed the first session.

Following the presentation of motions and resolutions, the Executive Committee's report was received. Eleven of the twenty-four recommendations were presented and discussed at the first morning session. Before making specific reference to these recommendations, I would like to underline the fact that each time of worship was made a preferred order of business. When the time arrived, we simply set our business aside and prepared ourselves for worship and the message. At the first session we came to the hour for the president's address. President Sullivan spoke on "Let the Church Reach Out." His message was preceded by a solo by Dean Wilder entitled "Great Is Thy Faithfulness."

The number one recommendation of the Executive Committee was the budget for the new year. A recommendation was made for

$63,500,000. This amount included $3,427,050 for Southwestern Seminary. It seems incredible even now. How quickly we went from $225,000 to this amount. As in most of the previous Conventions, these recommendations largely had to do with the structure or the revision of our bylaws about the constitution of trustee bodies. The president's office term was limited to two years. An outgoing president would not be eligible for re-election for one year. Likewise, there were limitations put on the terms for trustees and commissioners.

On Tuesday afternoon, the first order of business was the election of the President. President Sullivan had announced prior to the Convention that he would not be available for reelection. Those nominated were Jimmy Allen of Texas, Clifton W. Brannon of Texas, Dotson M. Nelson of Alabama, Warren C. Hultgren of Oklahoma, Richard Jackson of Arizona, and Jerry Vines of Alabama. Allen and Vines were in a run-off, with Allen being elected. I always gave attention to the election in the Convention because it was gradually becoming apparent that politics was becoming a major element.

The Executive Committee continued its report and gave its recommendations. An interesting trend surfaced here. Recommendation 18 called for a reporting of the actual vote on any balloted matter, principally the election of officers. Not only the outcome but the size of the vote would become a matter of Convention record. There were other recommendations that underlined the sense that a part of the Convention was being shut out of the actual results.

A recommendation concerning government regulation was interesting. The underlying premise was that "since Southern Baptist Convention agencies exist to serve the churches in keeping with their theological position, all Convention agencies are 'integrated auxiliaries' of the churches."

The longest recommendation called for a development of Convention emphasis promotion previously planned by our Bold Mission Committee. The concluding paragraph said it well, "that the Southern Baptist Convention ask its Executive Committee to adopt a single, over-arching, prominent theme to promote the Convention's world mission goals, and that each Southern Baptist Convention agency adapt its promotional plans to this common theme."

The Tuesday evening session, under the direction of Baker James Cauthen, included a great mission emphasis. He explained the agreements that had been reached by the executives of five agencies: the

Woman's Missionary Union, the Brotherhood Commission, the Sunday School Board, the Home Mission Board, and the Foreign Mission Board. All of these agreements related to missions education strategy. There was a larger call for volunteer missions than the Convention had previously heard.

It was now time to discuss the motions and resolutions made and presented at the first session. The first motion presented had to do with homosexuality as promoted by the media. Although this motion was not discussed until Thursday afternoon, it should be noted here that it led off.

The fourth motion requested that "trustees of all boards, seminaries, commissions, and committees which received support from the Southern Baptist Convention . . . include in their annual report to the Convention specific information concerning the salary and fringe benefits provided for the Senior Executive Director." This motion was discussed Wednesday morning until time expired and Thursday morning until a ballot was necessary. It was amazing to discover the resistance to giving this kind of specific information. The resistance was couched in the fact that our bylaws already made that information available to any Southern Baptist who requested it. However, making the information easier to access was strongly resisted. Even though I was personally involved as an executive of an agency, I had very strong feelings that all information should be made available to the whole body. Even in our churches at this present hour it is a rare thing for the congregation to be made aware of the exact salaries and the fringe benefits of its staff members. This one motion took all of these sessions to resolve and was finally adopted with amendments which changed very little.

The first resolution presented was on "religious liberty and employment practices." This was not just another resolution for us. It had to do specifically with Southwestern Baptist Theological Seminary. The federal government had sued Southwestern through its EEOC for failure to sign and present certain reports on employment personnel. It is too long a story for these minutes, but I had refused to sign those documents, feeling they were not applicable to a religious institution. I will explain how this situation was finally settled in court in another document. We spent hours on the witness stand. One of our staff members insisted that even though he was responsible for the physical plant, he was a minister of the gospel. It was very inspirational really. This first resolution was the

Convention's support of the seminary position in strong and unmistakable terms.

The subjects usually found in these resolutions included the Equal Rights Amendment, the American Bible Society, one "on a call for hunger convocation," the separation of church and state, and higher education.

There was the continuing resolution concerning abortion and the emphatic position of the Convention. It was unusual for us to have a resolution on "torture," but this simply recognized the violation of human rights that takes place in the world.

When the Resolutions Committee brought its first report on Wednesday, the report was concluded by a special committee chaired by Dr. Baker James Cauthen. It had to do with the opening of Canada to our mission responsibility. This was not a new problem. We had some wonderful Canadian churches established that were affiliated with our Northwest Convention. It was actually a question of polity concerning our relationship with Canadian Baptists. The report was carefully worded, and it called for cultivating fraternal and cordial relations with all Canadian Baptists.

The Convention sermon by William L. Self of Georgia, speaking on the subject "For Such A Time As This," concluded the Wednesday morning session.

The Southwestern Theological Seminary luncheon on Wednesday was not just another luncheon for us. Goldia was to receive the Distinguished Alumnus Award from the seminary. In presenting the award, Dr. James Coggin had prepared a beautiful, wonderful, well-deserved resolution. He began by indicating that Goldia was "demonstration 'A'" as to why such a reward is given. All of this was very personal to me because it has always been a wonder to me all of these years that she loves the seminary just like I do. She did not grow to love it through me, but she learned to love it for herself, having come to the seminary which was so far from her home. When God brought us together, there was a common sense of debt and appreciation for the institution. The fellowship was wonderful there, and we were having another record attendance year. There was every evidence of God's continued blessing upon the institution.

The reports of the seminaries were for Thursday morning. Duke McCall was our chairman, and he presented the reports from the six seminaries. He called special attention to the approaching retirement of Harold K. Graves of California, who had been president of Golden Gate Seminary for the past twenty-five years. There was a Convention expression of appreciation for his ministry as he was greeted by each of us.

In the Thursday morning session, there was a motion that called for a Statement of Purpose by the agencies of the Convention that included the following criteria: "(1) That the Bible be respected as being the inspired Word of God and that its teachings be accepted as the criteria and defining lines by which educational policy, conduct codes, and administration decisions affecting the institution and its witness will be formed." Our semantic debate about the inspiration of Scriptures, with us at every Convention since 1959, often presents a sad cover for other designs. Southern Baptists are committed to the authority, inspiration, and the infallibility of Scriptures.

Thursday afternoon the Resolutions Committee continued the report on "permissiveness in family planning," abortion, and Christian morality. The Christian Life Commission report paid special attention to the challenge, danger, and the moral quality (or lack of it) of modern television, warning us about a day that was already here. William Pinson closed that Thursday afternoon session speaking on "Our World and the Gospel."

The closing session of the Convention on Thursday evening was aimed at challenge, commitment, and consecration. Billy Graham preached and concluded his message by leading the congregation to join him in a responsive affirmation of a "Covenant of Salt," a commitment of the people to be the salt of the earth.

This was the kind of Convention that reminded us that the Southern Baptist Convention session is autonomous. All of the resolutions adopted were the sentiments of that particular Convention. They were binding on no church and represented no others. It is a remarkable New Testament concept which, among others, needs to be constantly set before our Southern Baptist people.

Georgia World Congress Center • Atlanta, Georgia

Robert Naylor

JUNE 13-15

1978

THIS ATLANTA CONVENTION WAS TO HAVE GREAT PERSONAL SIGNIFICANCE. IT WOULD BE THE LAST CONVENTION that I would attend as an agency executive. For months, my retirement had been the occasion for many wonderful things. It (the Convention) represented a major event in my life. For twenty years I had been going to Conventions as the president of Southwestern Baptist Theological Seminary. This meant an early fellowship with other seminary presidents. It also called for special responsibilities in the actual workings of the Convention. Suddenly all of this was to change, and I had accepted that with no personal problem.

As any reader of this would know, I had been attending Southern Baptist Conventions much longer than I had been president of the seminary. Southern Baptist Conventions were a part of my lifeblood and certainly the center of a very personal commitment and a life-long sense of obligation. Because of our church polity, the meeting of the Convention, in its total freedom, bears an unusual relationship to all of the rest.

It was pleasant to anticipate Atlanta. Strangely enough, the Convention had not met there since 1944—our "War Convention." But, the city had been significant in ministry, and I had often been there and been blessed there. We liked Atlanta and anticipated the Convention. It was a plus that we were meeting within walking distance of the Convention Hall.

President Jimmy R. Allen of Texas called to order the 121st session of the Southern Baptist Convention in the 133rd year of its history, at 9:30 A.M., on June 13, 1978, in the Georgia World Congress Center in Atlanta, Georgia. Reference was made to the organization of the Convention in 1845 in Georgia. The messengers began by singing "All Hail the Power of Jesus' Name."

Secretary Lee Porter reported 17,833 messengers at 9:40 A.M., and made the motion that constituted the Convention. The final tally was to be 22,872, one of our largest Conventions to date.

In the presentation of the Committee on Order of Business (one of the first things that we always did), there was a change. Winston Crawley and R. Keith Parks were to replace Baker James Cauthen on the Wednesday evening program. This was to underline the changing guard, the generational change that was to have its birth at this Convention. More will be said about this subject later.

After the naming of the committees, President Allen delivered the president's address on the subject, "Where There Is a Vision—the People Flourish," calling attention to the theme, "Let the Church Be Bold in Mission Thrust."

The Convention proceeded to hear the report of the Executive Committee and its opening recommendations. As usual, the first motion was to approve the Southern Baptist Convention Cooperative Program allocation budget for 1978-1979. The total challenge of the budget was $75 million, and was adopted without a single dissenting voice. All of this speaks to our commitment to work together. The seminary total was $13,409,000, of which Southwestern was to receive twenty-eight percent, $3,779,574. When we say twenty-eight percent, we need to remember that at this point, Southwestern had more than forty percent of the total student enrollment in the six seminaries. It also underlines the unity at the base of all else.

Recommendation 2, which was also adopted, presented a five-year capital needs distribution to the seminaries, Brotherhood Commission, and Radio and Television Commission. Following this, the Executive Committee presented changes in Convention procedure which were worked out during the year. These are seldom debated, but even now are significant in the way we proceed.

There was one requirement that had to do with the presentation of outside causes. I do not recall a time when it was used but it gave the officers authority to present a cause outside the run of our normal business.

Recommendation 5 was a lengthy presentation by the committee on the consolidation of bylaws and Convention procedure. A major section had to do with the election of officers. There was a full listing of the agencies which are auxiliary and the commissions. Like the office of president of the Convention, trustees and commissioners of the agencies were to be limited to two terms. The fine-tuning process would not cease. All of this was done before the scheduled election of officers.

The Convention voted to adopt a paragraph which concerned fraternal messengers. We would be sending a fraternal messenger to the American Baptist churches and the National Baptist conventions. This messenger was to be our president, or if he could not attend, someone he appointed.

We defined "layperson" and "non-layperson" in terms of employment by the agencies of the Convention. The Executive Committee, which had grown multi-fold in the years, was given full outline of its responsibilities and powers. Since I had been a part of it, I was particularly interested in the Interagency Council. This council involved the leadership of the agencies in an organization that had no power to legislate. It was apart from any authority of the Executive Committee or any other agency. It had proved to be simply a conference in which meeting together we discovered our fellowship. All of this is to say that that which was simply "nuts and bolts" becomes really important.

With that accomplished the Convention was open for the presentation of resolutions. At this time I will say that this was the busiest Convention in point of the number of actual resolutions and motions that were offered. Even on this first morning there were resolutions presented on temperance, world hunger, nuclear arms control, inflation, amendments to the U.S. Constitution, conditions in Uganda, and the desired release of Georgi Vins, whose name would be recognized.

The presentations continued with resolutions on Social Security, the handicapped, the J. P. Stevens Manufacturing Company, soil conservation, national security, lobbying legislation, the mentally ill, and abortion. All of these could be presented only in name and then carried to the secretary's desk. The Committee on Order of Business would set a time for discussion or recommend the reference of a particular resolution to an agency for further consideration.

It is worth noting here that in that first session, Jack Gritz of Oklahoma moved "that the Southern Baptist Convention request its Executive Committee to study the feasibility of establishing a seventh theological seminary, and report to the next annual meeting of the Convention." Gritz was the editor of the *Baptist Messenger* in Oklahoma. He was a personal friend, but I surely felt then and now that we did not need another seminary.

The election of officers came on Tuesday afternoon. Jimmy Allen was elected to a second term by acclamation. Nominations for first vice-president followed with the nomination of Anita Bryant Green of Florida and Douglas Waterson of Tennessee. Waterson was elected.

In the afternoon session, a motion was made that underlines another significant element of the Convention previously referred to. Brooks Wester of Mississippi, chairman of the Search Committee to recommend a successor to Porter Routh, asked for prayer in behalf of the committee. Not only were we to have a new president for Southwestern Baptist Theological Seminary, but Porter Routh, who had become an establishment as the executive secretary of the Executive Committee of the Southern Baptist Convention, was also to change. In addition, it had already been reported to the Convention that Baker James Cauthen was ill and that the Foreign Mission Board was to change. The Education Commission Chairman, Ben Fisher, was also ill, and the commission would need a new Chairman. Suddenly twenty-five percent of the agencies had changed leadership. Most of the other agencies soon followed.

Transition in the leadership of an organization as large as the Southern Baptist Convention is inevitably traumatic. This does not speak at all to the quality of the leadership that is to follow, nor does it pass judgement upon the leadership that has preceded. It does say that many of the problems with which we have dealt in these years are actually to be expected from change. We would spare ourselves much agony if we would but remember that such change inevitably has its turbulence. The measure of our response is the steadfastness of our forward march.

The report of our Bold Mission Thrust Emphasis was encouraging. The one who brought the report from the Education Commission, prepared by Ben Fisher, contained a strong statement about ownership of schools and seminaries. This was in response to a question that had been raised by a messenger from Mississippi concerning the relationship of the Convention to its institutions, and whether restrictions are imposed consistent with the Baptist Faith and Message statement.

Does that sound familiar to you? It could have been "present tense" in the fifteen years that were to follow. The statement said, "The Southern Baptist Convention does have responsibility, with reference to its six seminaries, in the election of trustees and the allocation of funds. The Southern Baptist Convention owns no colleges and schools other than the six seminaries. The Education Commission has no jurisdiction over the Southern Baptist Seminaries and their involvement with the Baptist Faith and Message statement is a matter for the seminaries to address."

Tuesday evening was the election of a second vice-president. Three were nominated and in the run-off, and Bill Self of Georgia was elected. Each evening session was devoted to our Bold Mission Thrust, making evenings of inspiration.

By Wednesday morning we had begun to sort out and adopt the resolutions. Resolutions adopted in that session concerned the host city, appreciation of Convention officers, and support for the American Bible Society. There followed resolutions concerning child abuse, arms control, world hunger, the handicapped, and lobbying legislation. It could be worthwhile to point out here that I underlined this one because it said that our efforts to influence legislation could very well destroy our church freedom under government. This was a word of warning.

The Convention sermon was preached on Wednesday morning on the subject "The City of God—The Hope of His Calling," by Jesse Fletcher of Texas.

Now I need to recall the very personal part of the Convention. First of all, there was the Convention action itself which would be expected. The proceedings read like this, "Landrum Leavell of Louisiana led in the presentation of the report from the six Convention seminaries. Robert E. Naylor of Texas, retiring President of Southwestern Baptist Theological Seminary, was presented and warmly greeted in appreciation by the messengers. Russell Dilday (Texas), the President-elect of Southwestern, was introduced, followed by William Pinson (California), Milton Ferguson (Missouri), Randall Lolley (North Carolina), Landrum Leavell (Louisiana), Duke K. McCall (Kentucky), and by Naylor, who briefly addressed the Convention. Leavell moved in behalf of his colleagues, that the reports of the six seminaries as printed in the *Book of Reports*, be adopted."

The printed word cannot portray the moving emotions that were mine. The expression of the Convention and the colleagues was so warm, full, and undeserved that I felt that I could have only lasting appreciation that God had granted me the privilege.

More personally was the Southwestern Seminary Alumni Luncheon on Wednesday. It was designed, as you would guess, to honor us, the family, and to give testimony of their love. It was a grand occasion. In the first place it brought our family together, Robert, Richard, and Rebekah, who were all present, all supportive, and all cherished. The grandchildren, Robert III, Richard, and Melodee were also present. There were friends from nearby Columbia, South Carolina, whom I had pastored. The attendance itself was heartwarming. This is all to say that there was absolutely nothing missing in those things that were said and done for us. Surely God had blessed full measure, beyond all deserving, and it remains to this day a very moving and present memory.

The Summit • Houston, Texas

JUNE 12-14
1979

HOUSTON SEEMS TO HAVE PLAYED A LARGE PART IN OUR CONVENTION PILGRIMAGE. IN WRITING ABOUT THE 1968 Convention, I reflected upon those significant events that had been determinative for us. In our attendance in 1953, the concerns for the seminary were so overwhelming. We had a new president and I had become chairman of the trustees. The actions of the Convention would be crucial for Southwestern. The 1958 Convention would have to be a life-changing time for me, for I was then acting president of the seminary. It was mine to represent Southwestern on the occasion of their Fiftieth Anniversary. The Convention had chosen me to bring the Convention sermon that year. Suddenly, I was confronted with the knowledge that God had chosen me for Southwestern.

Ten years later in 1968, we were rejoicing in God's confirmations. The growth of the student body had been great. The support of the Convention had continued on an ever-increasing level. At this Convention, however, I was retired. It would be my first Southern Baptist Convention after turning away from the position of denominational leadership. The concern for the seminary and the details of its operations was not any less. It would, however, be a time of discovery for me as to the future relationship to the meetings of our Southern Baptist Convention.

President Jimmy R. Allen called to order the 122nd session of the Southern Baptist Convention in the 134th year of its history, at 9:30 A.M., in The Summit in Houston, Texas. We were led in singing "O for a Thousand Tongues to Sing." The opening prayer was led by T. B. Maston of Texas. Dr. Maston had been a member of the Southwestern Seminary faculty while I was a student there in 1928.

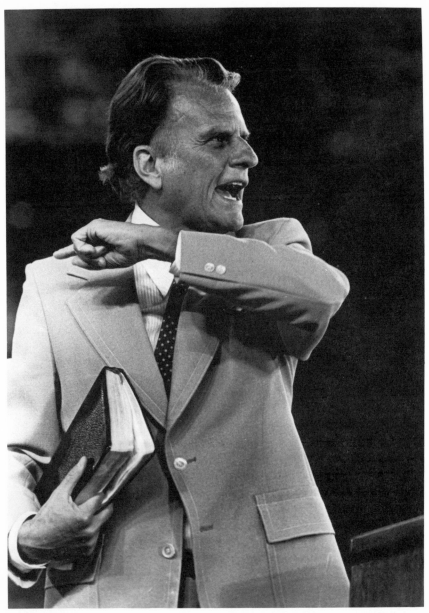

Billy Graham preaches at a Bold Mission Thrust rally at the Houston Astrodome during the 1979 Southern Baptist Convention meeting. Courtesy—Southern Baptist Historical Library and Archives.

He was both young and popular. Through the productivity of his seminary years, he had real stature among Southern Baptists. He not only led the opening prayer, but he, along with William Pinson, was recognized for a new book, *An Approach to Christian Ethics*.

The registration secretary announced an opening attendance of 12,514, and made the motion that duly constituted the Convention. The ultimate attendance was 15,760, which was much less than the previous year in Atlanta.

The Committee on Order of Business presented a program to be approved which was to be the structure of our session. For reasons I shall presently indicate, the election of officers on Tuesday afternoon had unusual significance. There had been great pre-convention political activity concerning that moment.

The seminaries were scheduled to report on Tuesday evening. There was also the Convention sermon on Wednesday. Wednesday evening was "Great Mission Night," which would be concluded with a message by Billy Graham of Montreat, North Carolina, who emphasized the enforcing of our Bold Mission Thrust. Baker James Cauthen, who was retiring, was to bring the closing message on Thursday morning. We were set for another busy Convention.

The report of the Executive Committee was our first major structural procedure. As always in that first morning session, it should be noted that the Executive Committee in its multiple recommendations dealt largely with structure, reporting the activities of a year in which the committee had held two meetings and required constant staff and committee activity. The concerns of the members of the Convention present were expressed in motions and resolutions that together constituted a major part of our business. The Executive Committee began the report with a recommendation for the Cooperative Program allocation budget for 1979-1980. The final total was $83,000,000. The motion to adopt it was unanimous and was not even discussed by the messengers present. I noted that Southwestern Seminary would receive $4,182,888 for its operation. At the other end of my service as president, the appropriation had been $225,000. For most of those twenty years, the money for seminary education was divided on the basis of a formula conceived in the early months of my service.

In passing, I want to make note of the appropriation calling for a Southern Baptist Convention operating budget for 1979-1980 in the amount of $1,164,000; $627,020 of this appropriation was for the work of the Executive Committee itself. Convention expenses amounted to $244,640. The percentage of growth was great.

This time there was even a recommendation for a total Cooperative Program goal of $226,001,938 for 1979-1980. This amount included all contributions from the churches. It was in line with a goal of doubling the Cooperative Program in five years.

A constitutional amendment was presented for its second year dealing with the terms of service on the boards of agencies which are subject to their charters.

A restated charter for the Sunday School Board, of great importance legally and operationally, was approved without discussion.

Of particular importance for the seminaries was the adoption of a program statement that came in the second session of the Executive Committee report on Tuesday afternoon. I have always liked the statement of objective, "The objective of the six Southern Baptist theological seminaries is to provide theological education, with the Bible as the center of the curriculum, for God-called men and women to meet the needs for trained leadership in the work of the churches." The programs of the seminaries included the different degree levels. The relationships which the seminaries bore towards each other, toward other agencies, and toward the accrediting agencies were fully outlined. This statement remains virtually unchanged even now.

The result of a year's study, the report concluded with a recommendation that there be no seventh seminary. There were procedures for auditing. There was an action undergirding Bold Mission Thrust. The retirement of Paul Stevens from the Radio and Television Commission, Baker James Cauthen from the Foreign Mission Board, and Porter Routh from the Executive Committee were noted with appreciation.

While this covered the recommendations of the Executive Committee and a summary of their activities during the preceding year, the concerns of the messengers had already been expressed in the Tuesday morning session. These concerns would become the basis of the discussions in the days that were to follow.

Motions that became resolutions would detail these concerns. Those resolutions spoke about the American Bible Society, student missions, domestic violence, peacemaking, energy, beverage alcohol, poverty among migrant farm workers, and concern for family farms. The people who made the motions that became resolutions are names that would often be recognized; they were a relatively small number compared with the total number of messengers. It is always interesting to notice the recurring disposition to speak.

Continuing with the concerns, Wayne Dehoney, former president of the Convention, made the motion that reaffirmed the 1963 Baptist Faith and Message as it had to do with the statement on Scriptures. I have called attention before to the fact that since the middle 1950s, there has been a constant address to what we believe about Scriptures. Much of it was in a context that left doubts about the Scriptural integrity of others.

Owen Cooper offered a motion concerning "evaluating television programs." The IRS and church-related schools were a subject. There was also a resolution on the crisis in education.

Larry Lewis of Missouri had a motion on doctrinal integrity as it related to the seminaries. It was not very constructive in its framing. This man would become the executive director of our Home Mission Board. There were motions concerning the Lord's Day, church mission teams, beverage alcohol, and disavowing political activity in selecting Convention officers (a motion which was not adopted).

One messenger made the motion that a statement of itemized beliefs must be signed by any nominees for Convention office. There were motions that had to do with our temperance lessons.

Special notice should be given to a resolution offered in appreciation for the seminaries and their staff and faculty. The pros and cons were discussed, and it was later fully adopted by the Convention. There was a motion which asked for television time in advertising during the Super Bowl. Family worship, Christian day schools, appreciation for Convention arrangements, second-class postage rates, abortion, pornography, and inflation were all subjects brought to the Convention by motion in a single morning. The Tuesday morning session that would become our continuing agenda was concluded with the President's Address by Jimmy Allen on the Convention theme, "Bold Mission Thrust: While It Is Yet Day. . . ."

This report has referred to special concern for the election of officers. Some weeks before the Convention, Larry Baker of Missouri asked that I consent to being nominated as president of the Convention. I told him that I thought it was not for me. When I became an agency employee, I put aside any thought of Convention office. It has always been my feeling that a pastor or a layperson should be our president. It should be a position of honor, trust, and of course, performance; but primarily it should be a leadership in spirit. Therefore, I refused.

This call was not the last of the matter. It continued day by day. In the midst of all of this, there were those who were actively seeking the office. This I could never agree with. We once had a President of the United States that refused to leave his front porch during the entire campaign. I felt anything less than that would be improper in Southern Baptist life. Having said that, some very fine men have made a point of "running for the office," which I deplore.

I felt that the Convention had acted improperly in requiring the consent of the nominee. I liked the old system where if nominated, and not desiring to serve, a man asked that his name be withdrawn. To presume the nomination in advance was difficult for me to understand.

On the evening of the election and under great persuasion, (weakness of the flesh, I suppose), when I was already present at the Convention, I finally consented that my name be presented with the others. The election of president came on Tuesday afternoon. Ray Roberts of Ohio nominated C. E. Price of Pennsylvania. Welton Gaddy of Texas nominated A. Douglas Waterson of Tennessee. Homer Lindsey, Sr., of Florida nominated Adrian Rogers of Tennessee. John Sullivan of Louisiana nominated Robert E. Naylor of Texas. Frank Pollard of Mississippi nominated William Self of Georgia. William Hinson of Louisiana nominated Abner V. McCall of Texas. The ballots were cast. I remember that during the process, there was a moment when I thought, "What if I should actually be elected?" But then, I dismissed that as a remote possibility.

When the ballot return was announced just before the close of the afternoon session, Ed Price received 223 votes (1.87%), Douglas Watterson 474 (3.97%), Abner McCall 643 (5.39%), William Self 1,673 (14.02%), Robert E. Naylor 2,791 (23.39%), and Adrian Rogers received 6,129 (51.36%). Rogers was elected in that first ballot. My chief gain in all of this was the nomination by my good friend John Sullivan. It is rare indeed for anyone to have things like that said about them, whether it is deserved or undeserved. It was a great nominating speech for which I am grateful. I have always felt honored just for being considered for such a high office.

Nominations were then received for first vice-president, resulting in the run-off ballot between T. A. Patterson of Texas and Abner McCall of Texas. McCall was elected.

The six seminaries made their report at the evening session on Tuesday. William Pinson was acting as chairman. Each of the seminary presidents was presented to briefly address the Convention.

Nominations were received for second vice-president, which resulted in the election of Don Touchton of Florida.

The evening session concluded with an address by Charles Colson. There was an interesting sentence in the proceedings, "messengers responded with prolonged applause of appreciation while standing."

Some of the resolutions brought on discussion. I thought that a longer look at those concerns reflected that they were not born with this Convention. The actions of this Convention belong only to this Convention by our Baptist polity. Many of these concerns had previously surfaced. Motions made reflected long shadows that would be cast over our fellowship.

Wednesday was indeed a great inspirational mission night. Cliff Barrows of South Carolina directed the eight-thousand-member Baptist choir singing "The Lord's Prayer." William Tanner of Georgia, executive director and treasurer for the Home Mission Board, brought their report, which was accompanied by testimonies.

Baker James Cauthen was recognized to introduce the report of the Foreign Mission Board. He concluded the report with a message that presented the mandate facing the current generation to reach the world for Christ. Cliff Barrows then led in the singing of "To God Be the Glory." President Allen introduced Billy Graham, who confronted Southern Baptists with the imperative in this day of "Turning the World Upside Down for Christ." At the conclusion of his message an invitation was given, and over 1,200 persons responded and registered decisions. The mission rally in the Astrodome ended with praise as the congregation sang "To God Be the Glory."

Woman's Missionary Union always receives an honored place in the proceedings of our Convention. They are an auxiliary, yet they are in every sense cooperative and a mission pulse for our Convention.

Resolutions which began the day before were continued. Resolution 16 was entitled "On Gratitude for Our Seminaries." In the Thursday morning session, Paul Pressler of Texas, whose name was to become familiar in our politics, was granted personal privilege to respond to comments that had been made concerning him during the discussion of a resolution. Much of the political activity of the session and preceding it is not reflected in the proceedings.

On Thursday afternoon, one of the emotional moments in the Convention was a farewell to Porter Routh as the executive secretary of the Executive Committee. He had indeed wrought well.

This is the moment to call attention again to an item that had been major in the 1978 Convention proceedings. With all of the turmoil and the politics, the thing that should be remembered is that a great organization was undergoing a tremendous generational change. This says nothing concerning their successors, but it indicates that the leadership of the largest agencies in the Convention was changing immediately. Southwestern is our largest seminary by a good margin. The Foreign Mission Board, Executive Committee, Radio and Television Commission, and the Education Commission were all involved in change. Two of the seminaries had already changed leadership. A generational change does not occur in an organization of this size without that which amounts to a convulsion in its life.

Thursday evening, the Convention would close with an address by Jerry Clower on Christian life and influence. Manuel Scott of Los Angeles preached on the subject, "Mandate to Togetherness." President Adrian Rogers insisted that he intended to serve all Southern Baptists.

Even though my position had changed, I had not changed. The meeting of the Southern Baptist Convention remains a miracle in Baptist polity. Every Southern Baptist pastor should be faithful in his presence. I eagerly awaited the next Convention.

Cervantes Convention Center • St. Louis, Missouri

Robert Taylor

JUNE 10-12
1980

ST. LOUIS, MISSOURI, WAS A GOOD CONVENTION CITY. THOUGH IT WAS CONSIDERED A BIT OFF-CENTER IN 1980, the frequency with which our Convention had gone there testified that we liked the city. For those of us reared west of the River, the towering arch alongside the Mississippi River had a certain glory. Across these waters came our forefathers, founding churches, preaching the gospel, and populating the West. Baptists had taken root there early. The Southern Baptist Convention meeting here in 1936 was the only Convention that Goldia had missed since we began attending in 1933. In those other Convention years in St. Louis, she was right there with me.

President Adrian P. Rogers of Tennessee called to order the 123rd session of the Southern Baptist Convention in the 135th year of its history on June 10, at 9:30 A.M., in the Cervantes Convention Center in St. Louis, Missouri. The opening gavel always had with it an aura of excitement. For those who came early to the session, the pre-session music was an inspiration. In this Convention, the sanctuary and youth choirs of the Bellevue Baptist Church in Memphis brought the music. With the opening of the session, we sang "All Hail the Power of Jesus' Name." Through succeeding sessions, the congregational singing was very inspiring and encouraging.

Our secretary announced that at 9:40 A.M., 10,537 messengers had been registered. The figure would reach 13,844, only 128 more than the 1971 Convention in St. Louis. The secretary moved that these messengers constitute the Convention along with those who would be enrolled later. According to our Constitution, the Southern Baptist Convention was now in session. The Program Committee then presented their recommendation for the approval of the Convention which would be the timetable under which the Convention would function. Following this was a welcome from the Lieutenant Governor of Missouri, with a response made by Morris Chapman of Texas.

That morning our president presented an unusual number of fraternal messengers. Without the names the Conventions represented were the National Baptist Convention, USA, Inc.; European Baptist Convention (English language); American Baptist Churches in the USA; Brazilian Baptist Convention; Seventh Day Baptists; North American Baptist Conference; General Association of General Baptists; and the National Baptist Convention of America. Greetings were read from the archbishop of the Roman Catholics in the St. Louis area. As always we affirmed a fellowship of faith with those who believed in Christ Jesus.

Committees were announced. Our president was right on schedule as he presented the Executive Committee for their report and recommendations. The first item was the budget. This budget would be our 1980-1981 Southern Baptist Convention Cooperative Program Allocation Budget. It consisted of the total basic operating budget, a capital needs budget, Bold Mission Thrust challenge budget, and a fourth step with further challenge. All of this became a budget of $90,000,000. Southwestern Seminary would receive $4,606,303. When it came to the challenge budget, the seminaries percentage was fifteen percent compared with twenty-one percent of the operating budget. The vote, which was upbeat, was unanimous.

The Executive Committee had been given forty minutes for an introduction to its business. Part of this time was used to survey those in attendance that would describe us in age, ethnics, churches, etc. A picture was also taken of the Convention assembled.

President Rogers then opened the floor for the introduction of miscellaneous business and resolutions. In a fifteen-minute period, these items were introduced simply by name. A multitude of resolutions were referred to the Resolutions Committee to be discussed later by the Convention. In this period two motions were presented, each of which would have changed our Constitution. The first one would have denied all employees of Southern Baptist agencies, receiving at least half of their salary from such an agency, of the privilege of being eligible for election as a messenger to the Convention. I was horrified that it reflected little understanding of our

Baptist polity. On Wednesday morning when this resolution came up for discussion, the messengers moved the previous question almost immediately and voted "no."

The second matter was of a different character. It was a motion to amend the Constitution by making the sessions of the Southern Baptist Convention quadrennial sessions. In the periods between, there would be sectional meetings. This, too, when it came up Wednesday morning, received short discussion and immediate rejection.

Almost with a sigh of relief, we stood and sang "Stand Up, Stand Up for Jesus." President Rogers was introduced for the president's address entitled "The Decade of Decision and the Doors of Destiny." It seemed an appropriate title to introduce a new decade.

Beginning Tuesday afternoon, each of the sessions would have a fifteen-minute interpretation of the theme for that session. The general theme for the Convention was "That We May Boldly Say" (Heb. 13:6-7). The Tuesday afternoon theme was "Boldness in Convention Advance." Harold C. Bennett of Tennessee, our new executive secretary of the Executive Committee, brought the address.

It was time for the election of the president. The politics of the year had already intensified the interest. Milton Cunningham of Texas nominated Frank Pollard of Texas. David Lay of Tennessee nominated Jimmy Stroud of Tennessee. Ed Perry of Texas nominated Hal Boone of Texas. Ralph Langley of Alabama nominated James L. Pleitz of Texas. Jimmy Draper of Texas nominated Bailey Smith of Oklahoma. John Sullivan of Louisiana nominated Richard Jackson of Arizona. Suddenly, we had a host of nominees. At the close of the Tuesday afternoon session when they announced the results of our ballot, 13,336 had registered and 11,106 had voted. Bailey Smith of Oklahoma had received 51.67 percent of the votes and was declared president. Pollard had 21.45 percent and Pleitz had 13.65 percent. There will be a comment about this later.

A period for business and presentations of resolutions followed. The chair then called upon the Executive Committee for the second part of their report. There was a recommendation for the Southern Baptist Convention operating budget. Charter changes for the Annuity Board and the Education Commission were presented. Three amendments to the bylaws of the Convention were presented. These recommendations were passed almost without discussion.

A section called "Program of Black Church Relations" was added to the Home Mission Board Program Statement. Bold Mission Thrust was given full time for a report. Finally, there was a fine resolution of appreciation for the service of Albert McClellan. He had served as a member of the staff of the Executive Committee of the Southern Baptist Convention since August 1, 1949. He was a very personal friend, and I had a genuine appreciation for the quality of his service, as well as his faithfulness. I enjoyed the appreciation shown him and stood with the rest of the congregation to express my best wishes. Note in passing that the generational change was becoming a reality. All that I have described was passed almost without question.

After the announcement of the election results for the president, nominations were received for first vice-president. Whereas more than eleven thousand had voted for the president, there were only 8,100 present to vote at the end of the session for first vice-president. Those nominated included Dennis L. Ireland of Alabama, Nelson Duke of Missouri, Jack Taylor of Texas, C. Wade Freeman, Sr., of Texas, Ralph Langley of Alabama, Brian Harbour of Florida, and Sam Cathey of Arkansas. The run-off ballot on Tuesday evening had only 5,661 voting. Jack Taylor was elected. Where were the rest of the people in the Tuesday evening session? The six seminaries were given fifteen minutes to report. Each of the presidents spoke very briefly.

The Foreign Mission Board report, which was brought by its new President, R. Keith Parks, was given thirty-five minutes. There was a fine conclusion to this mission emphasis when Doctors Giles and Wanda Ann Fort, medical missionaries to Zimbabwe (Rhodesia), spoke in conclusion. Landrum P. Leavell II of Louisiana had brought the theme interpretation on "Boldness in Reaching a Lost World" in that evening session.

We began Wednesday morning with singing "Blessed Assurance" and "God of Grace and God of Glory." It almost prepared one for the day. At 10:00 the chair opened the floor for nominations for second vice-president. Even at this choice hour, there were 7,335 messengers who voted. The nominees included Kenneth Story of Tennessee, E. Harmon Moore of Indiana, Bill Sherman of Tennessee, John Hollingsworth of Alabama, Fred Powell of Missouri, Russell Newport of Missouri, George Bagley of Alabama, and C. Wade Freeman of Texas. When time was extended, others added included J. D. Rush, Jr., of South Carolina, Gordon Dorian of Kansas, Tom Clayton, Jr., of New Mexico, and Robert Walker of Tennessee. Out of such a number, it was no surprise that the run-off had to include three instead of two in order to have a majority total. There were

6,409 messengers who voted in the run-off ballot. In fact, a run-off ballot before that Wednesday morning session closed found 3,503 voting. C. Wade Freeman of Texas was elected.

The Committee on Resolutions began their report in that Wednesday morning session. Resolutions on the American Bible Society, the crisis in Cambodia, marriage tax, and overseas earned income tax were passed with little discussion. This was also true of resolutions on world hunger and prayer for the nation.

Without a Wednesday afternoon session, Wednesday evening contained the Home Mission Board report and the closing message by Stephen Olford of Wheaton, Illinois.

On Thursday morning the Resolutions Committee continued their report, reflecting matters that had been introduced at the opening session. Such resolutions as "taxing unrelated business enterprises" and "appreciation for the hospitality given us" attracted little discussion. Then the resolution concerning abortion was presented, and it became apparent that this had become a national flame. There was a substitute resolution offered that would have referred simply to the action of the Houston Convention of 1979. This was debated and the 1979 Convention action was read by request. When a vote was finally taken, the substitute resolution failed. Other amendments were offered. Finally, the original resolution was passed. It reaffirmed the view of the Scriptures concerning the sacredness and dignity of all human life. It rejected "abortion on demand"; it abhorred the use of tax money for such purposes. Finally, it called for legislation that would recognize only "the life of the mother" as sufficient reason for abortion.

A resolution was passed concerning William R. Tolbert, Jr., President of Liberia, who had been slain in a military coup. He was a Baptist preacher, and as a friend, there was an immediate emotional response in me.

The resolution which evoked the greatest discussion and controversy was one under the title of "On Doctrinal Integrity." In the original resolution there was language such as:

> Whereas, We acknowledge not only the right but the responsibility of this Convention to give explicit guidelines to the governing bodies of our various institutions. Therefore, be it Resolved, That the Southern Baptist Convention express its

profound appreciation to the staff and faculty members of
our seminaries and other institutions. . . . Be it further
Resolved, That we exhort the trustees of seminaries and
other institutions affiliated with or supported by the
Southern Baptist Convention to faithfully discharge their
responsibility to carefully preserve the doctrinal integrity of
our institutions and to assure that seminaries and other institutions receiving our support only employ, and continue the
employment of, faculty members and the professional staff
who believe in the divine inspiration of the whole Bible,
infallibility of the original manuscripts, and that the Bible is
truth without any error.

It is my opinion that ninety-nine percent of Southern Baptists
would have responded to such sentiments with the warmest affirmation. Yet basic in the resolution was the fear and suspicion sown that
we had among our seminary teachers, faculty, administration, and
denominational employees those who betrayed our basic belief in the
Scriptures. Individuals spoke for and against the resolution. There
was one person who would have amended the resolution by removing the last phrase, "infallibility of the original manuscripts, and that
the Bible is truth without any error." The amendment failed, to be
sure.

Herschel Hobbs offered an amendment by striking the last paragraph which read "assure that" and adding "trustees and administration of Southern Baptist seminaries and other institutions be
strongly urged to see that teaching is done within the framework of
the Abstract of Principles and/or the Baptist Faith and Message
Statement of 1963." Even this amendment by a respected leader in
our Convention was rejected.

The proceedings in our Convention documents are very careful
in their wording. But here lies the framework for all of the division
that was to follow.

On Thursday afternoon other agencies made reports. The
Resolutions Committee was presented for a final report. Resolutions
were presented on "Permissiveness and Family Planning." There
were those for and against this resolution also. It was passed in its
original form. The resolution resolved against "sexual information
and devices." It lamented the violation of the rights of family to provide

information or medication for unmarried minor-age children. Finally, it asked that our churches speak out against the permissiveness of the new morality.

The resolution on "Women" recognized the contributions of women in all avenues of service. It called for fair compensation and advancement. It stressed their biblical role. It did not endorse the Equal Rights Amendment. We passed resolutions on "pornography" and "homosexuality." There was one resolution which offered prayer for our fifty-three hostages in Iran. Those other matters not contained in the resolutions offered by the committee were detailed in that which had become of them. Some had been offered by more than one motion. Others simply duplicated actions already taken. Still others were referred to various agencies of the Convention.

We came to the final session to sing "Victory in Jesus" and "The Solid Rock." Grady and Eleanor Nutt presented the theme interpretation, "Boldness in Christian Living." After a concert of gospel music by Russell Newport, Carl E. Bates of North Carolina brought the closing message of the Convention.

The vote on the election of a president had been made the peak of the Convention. This pattern would grow in the next decade. Its chief problem lies in a misunderstanding of the basic Baptist polity involved in the organization called the Southern Baptist Convention. We press on asking God to do for us what He did for Simon Peter, "come to an understanding that God is no respecter of persons."

Los Angeles Convention Center • Los Angeles, California

JUNE 9-11

1981

A HOME MISSION FIELD IS WHERE GOLDEN GATE BAPTIST THEOLOGICAL SEMINARY IS SITUATED—THIS REGION of the nation has the highest percent of unchurched persons. Mission field indeed! It had been that from the first struggling witness of Southern Baptists forty years previously. For a Southern Baptist Convention to meet in California was to invite our host to participate in a mission journey. We had already been to San Francisco twice. We had been to Portland, Oregon, in 1973. Now in 1981, we were going to Los Angeles. I had always found a particular satisfaction in the way in which Southwestern Seminary men and women had been the pioneers of the far West with the gospel.

In these Convention reflections, I have suggested in very bare outline that "going to the Convention" was a family affair. We report the number of messengers that attended. We talk about the number of visitors, but basically, those visitors constitute members of the family who have not been elected messengers. We had begun to meet in June to allow families with children, who had children in school, to make the trips to the Convention.

There is always a bit of tourism involved. Often it is somewhere we have not been. In going to Southern California, most of the families remembered that Disney Land was located here. As far as we were concerned, we planned to see it. I will not give you a detailed report, but be sure that we did see it and we enjoyed it thoroughly, as did many other messengers.

President Bailey E. Smith called the Convention to order, the 136th year of its history, on June 6, at 9:30 A.M., in the Los Angeles

219

Convention Center. The Convention theme was "Our Bold Response
. . . Now!" In a moving moment of fellowship, we sang "Amazing
Grace." The Scriptures were read, and we were led in prayer.

Lee Porter, our secretary, reported an opening registration of
9,521 messengers. The count would reach 13,529. This number was
within 315 of the total attendance in St. Louis the past year. We were
then presented with the report of the Committee on Order of
Business, whose program had been printed in our denominational
press. There were two or three innovations in the program, there was
more time given to business. Wednesday morning after we heard the
Convention sermon and Thursday morning, the sessions were closed
with time given for business and resolutions. This allotted time
underlined the importance politically of "what we do here," as did
also many of the discussions that followed.

The welcome address and response, the introduction of fraternal
messengers, and the Convention photograph were standard items of
beginning. Committees were announced which also had appeared in
our denominational press.

By 10:30 A.M., we were ready for the initial report of our
Executive Committee. Executive Secretary Harold Bennett outlined
the work and the achievements of the committee that had taken
place in the past year. Then he used various members of his committee to present their recommendations.

It seemed that in every one of these reports, I wanted to give
major attention to the adoption of the Cooperative Program
allocation budget. Almost without exception, year by year, it is
adopted without discussion or question; however, undoubtedly
the budget was meant to be the focus of the Convention. The
1981-82 budget was in four parts totaling $93,000,000. The actual
Operating Budget was $83,400,000. Of this amount, $18,118,900
was to be allocated to the seminaries. This amounted to a little
more than twenty percent, and had changed only by a point in the
past twenty-five years.

There was a capital needs section of the budget. There was also a
Bold Mission Thrust section of the budget which was in two phases.
Together, these last two sections constituted less than $7,000,000. The
statement made in presenting the budget was that after the opera-
tional budget, in the order suggested above, the monies received

would be disbursed. The importance of this was in the fact that people who gave across our Convention could know in advance the direction of our cooperation.

It was most interesting to all of us, though not a matter of objection, that Recommendation 3 presented a program of pioneer missions for the Home Mission Board. The Historical Commission had been made the depository for the Convention for its archives. There was an amendment to the charter of Midwestern Seminary that changed the name of the "President" of the Board of Trustees to "Chairman." This did not seem earthshaking to me.

You never know where the major attention will fall. This time it was Recommendation 9, which concerned Southern Baptist Convention Bylaw 21 that had to do with the Committee on Committees. It was discussed, amended, and the amendment was rejected. It was spoken for and against, and finally it failed, due to a lack of a two-thirds vote as required. That ended the first Executive Committee report which lasted forty minutes, and brought us to a time for business and resolutions. Two things about this time stand out in my memory. In the fifteen or twenty minutes allowed, there were ten resolutions presented simply by name. Our concern was that which we finally discussed and adopted or rejected. One of these resolutions, however, reaffirmed the Baptist Faith and Message Statement of 1963. This was something we started doing every year.

The morning session concluded with the president's address by Bailey Smith entitled "The Worth of the Work."

The music for inspiration which began the afternoon session was presented by a group of musicians in the field of evangelism. After a survey of the messengers directed by Martin Bradley, we proceeded to the election of the president. As we had been well informed previously, Bailey Smith was nominated for a second term. Abner McCall, president of Baylor University, was nominated by Ralph Langley of Alabama. The votes were cast and the ballots were taken. Before the afternoon session concluded, the ballot report was given. There were 12,952 messengers who registered and 11,458 who voted. Bailey Smith was elected to a second term. After the announcement of the results in the afternoon session, five nominations were received for first vice-president. When the report was given Tuesday evening, a run-off was called for between Stan Coffey and Mrs. Harrison

Gregory. Between the time that we voted for president in the afternoon and then voted for first vice-president before the same session
concluded, we had lost four thousand voters.

The afternoon session began with resolutions and business. First
of all, Herschel Hobbs moved a rather lengthy motion reaffirming
our historical Baptist position about the Scriptures. In retrospect, we
see that this had been made the basis of our divisions and of our politics.

Twenty-two resolutions were presented within a twenty-minute
period of time. The chairman of the Executive Committee was then
recognized to present the rest of their report. Much of the time was
occupied in discussing the amendment to Convention Bylaw 22 for
the structure of the Committee on Resolutions. How would this committee be appointed?

Recommendation 11 provoked no discussion, and yet was one of
the lengthiest and most forward-looking of them all. It concerned the
Bold Mission Thrust report. The Executive Committee even had a
recommendation about world hunger. The report was concluded in
the afternoon.

The evening session began with a run-off ballot between Mrs.
Gregory and Coffey in which 5,900 messengers voted. Mrs. Gregory
was elected. Reports were heard from the Annuity Board and the
Sunday School Board. We sang "Standing On the Promises" and
came to what is always a high point of our Convention, the report of
our Foreign Mission Board.

R. Keith Parks of Virginia was now president of the Foreign
Mission Board. The original handwritten book of minutes of the
Convention dating from 1845 to 1863 was given to the Southern
Baptist Convention Historical Commission. It is a treasured document. The Foreign Mission Board hour consisted of emphases presented by missionaries Charles Bryan, board vice-president; James
Crane of Mexico; Aldo Broada, a layman mission leader in Argentina;
and Tom Elliff, a newly appointed missionary to Zimbabwe. (His service there was made very short.) The session ended as we stood to
sing "All Hail the Power of Jesus' Name."

We began the Wednesday morning session with the Committee
on Committees report, and the report of the Committee on Boards.
For one of the few times that I can remember, the Committee on
Board's report was amended twice by the substitution of one name
for another. Usually the Convention refused to amend that report.

The Brotherhood Commission and the Education Commission brought their reports, and at the prescribed hour, we came to the Convention sermon. We always interrupted what we were doing for this particular hour. James Monroe of Florida was the preacher and his subject was "Great Is Thy Faithfulness." When the sermon was concluded, we turned back again to business and resolutions.

The first report of the Resolutions Committee included Bold Mission Thrust, evangelism at the Southern Baptist Convention in New Orleans, strengthening families, alcohol awareness, changing the National Election Law, and appreciation for our officers and leadership. Wednesday evening had been given in its focus to the Home Mission Board.

This time the report of the seminaries was a part of that evening. It was unusual that forty minutes had been given to this report. Wayne Dehoney announced that President Duke McCall of Southern Seminary was retiring; this emphasizes "the generation change" that I have discussed. The president of Southeastern Seminary then recognized McCall's contribution, and the Convention stood in appreciation for Dr. and Mrs. McCall.

The chairman of the Home Mission Board presented their president, William G. Tanner of Georgia, who closed the Wednesday evening session as he spoke.

You will note that I have missed Wednesday afternoon. We did not have an afternoon session, as was customary on Wednesday in order that all of the seminaries could have their alumni luncheons and meetings. Our luncheon was very fine. A member of the faculty, Curtis Vaughn, had been presented the Outstanding Alumnus Award. Before the Convention, Dr. John Seelig, vice-president at the seminary, and Edwin Crawford had met us when we arrived at the airport. The fellowship of the Southwestern family was a big part of every Convention. All of the seminaries reported larger enrollments, financial needs, and optimistic predictions concerning the future.

When the Convention met on Thursday morning, there were two items that I suppose were not serious, but they were different. First, the chairman of the Credentials Committee recommended that "Mr. and Mrs. D. Wade Armstrong, whose credentials are not in order, be disqualified and unseated as messengers of this Convention." I was Wade Armstrong's pastor in his college days. In point of worthiness, none could have been more deserving of messenger status. The point was that we had begun to be very careful and particular about the constitutional requirements for messengers.

Only a little while later, the same chairman recommended the disqualification of Olivia Johnson and Marilyn Chrisman of the Cliff Temple Baptist Church in Dallas, one of whom I knew. They had just messed up their credentials statement a little. I thought about this situation recently while I was attending a Texas Baptist Convention meeting. We were asked to present proof of identity when we registered. Can you imagine that happening at a Baptist convention?

The Committee on Resolutions continued their report. The subjects about which they were resolving were subjects about which we resolved almost every Convention. There was a different resolution on "the role of women." The last phrase in the report said, "does not endorse the Equal Rights Amendment." You can be sure that someone stood and offered an amendment to eliminate the last clause. There were those for and those against, but finally the last clause prevailed and the amendment was adopted. There was a resolution on "violence in the cities." The resolution on "family planning" provoked no end of discussion.

Routine business was a part of Thursday afternoon. Singing "When We All Get To Heaven" is never routine. The Convention concluded on Thursday evening with Perry Sanders of Louisiana preaching on the subject, "What Chance to Turn the World Upside Down," based on a text in Acts 17.

The work of various agencies, which are Southern Baptists witnessing, are matters of printed record. I have not sought to make the reports in these reflections. Instead, I have presented the pulse beat of a people that are children of grace who have difficulty being graceful; and I think underneath they are always mindful that God has called us to missions. The proceedings in our minutes have been carefully written. The depth of our division has not been probed. The direction of our mission remains unchanged.

Louisiana Superdome • New Orleans, Louisiana

JUNE 15-17
1982

FOR THOSE OF US WHO ARE SENSITIVE TO AMERICAN HISTORY, NEW ORLEANS, LOUISIANA, WILL ALWAYS BE A SPECIAL place to visit. For Southern Baptists who have remained alert to the changes in Southern Baptist life, New Orleans would offer a special invitation. Conventions meeting here previously had set attendance records. In the course of those years, the city had changed from a predominantly Catholic city to a majority Southern Baptist position. God had blessed us in the city, and New Orleans Baptist Theological Seminary situated there was a part of that blessing. The sense of blessing would belie the storm signals that were in the Convention.

President Bailey E. Smith called the Convention to order, the 125th session in the 137th year of the Southern Baptist Convention, at 9:30 A.M., in the Louisiana Superdome on Tuesday, June 15. The Convention theme was "Affirming Christ's Bold Commands." Our opening hymns were "Victory in Jesus" and "Blessed Assurance." This was a bit of a break from tradition, but it was surely acceptable. The secretary reported that 14,803 had already registered, and made a motion that these messengers constitute the Convention, along with those who would register later in accordance with our Constitution. The final number of messengers for the Convention would be 20,456. This was 6,927 more than our previous Convention.

My friend, Charles G. Fuller of Virginia, presented the report for the Committee on Order of Business. For the first time in my memory, there was even a motion made to amend this report. It was quickly rejected, but the amendment itself was a prophecy.

Actually, the order of business was traditional enough. Tuesday morning, there would be the address of welcome and response. At

10:30 A.M. the Executive Committee would come with its first report, followed by a business and resolutions session lasting fifteen minutes. The president's address would close the morning session.

As a personal note, my lifetime friend, J. D. Grey, a remarkable Southern Baptist, welcomed us. The Executive Committee recommendations began as always with the Cooperative Program goal. In 1982-1983 the goal, being $106 million, was beyond the $100 million mark for the first time. Even the operating budget itself was $96,635,000. I made note that the seminary appropriation was $20,520,600, over twenty-one percent of the total budget. Of this amount, Southwestern would receive 27.736 percent. Southwestern would report to the Convention more than forty percent of the students in our six seminaries.

Recommendation 4 would have required that one of the officers of the Convention be a layperson. There was a speech in favor, a speech in opposition, and finally the motion was voted down by the Convention.

With the introduction of business and resolutions, it was evident that the messengers were just waiting for their opportunity. There were nineteen resolutions named in the first fifteen-minute session. Along with that were proposed changes in Bylaws 21 and 16. That they were later referred does not obscure the fact that it was all under review.

Bailey Smith, in closing the session with his address, spoke on the subject, "Southern Baptist's Most Serious Question."

In the Tuesday afternoon session, after Scriptures, prayer, and an information survey of the messengers, the Convention was ready for the election of the president. There were four nominations, John Sullivan and Perry Sanders of Louisiana; Duke K. McCall of Kentucky; and James T. Draper of Texas. The results reported toward the close of the session indicated that with 19,555 registered, 17,555 had voted. It makes one wonder about the other two thousand. In the runoff at the close of the session, James Draper was elected with 56.97 percent of the vote.

Because this seemed to cap the divisive interests of the messengers, we might as well continue with the elections. Nominations for first vice-president were made on Tuesday evening with 9,688 voting. John Sullivan of Louisiana was elected.

On Wednesday there were eight nominations for second vice-president. The number voting was 15,242. The run-off included three names, which was unusual. When the vote was finally taken, however, Gene Garrison of Oklahoma was elected, with 7,659 voting.

In this Convention report I have given more space to the elections for two significant trends. First, and most serious, was the evident division which was organized and deepening in its distrust. There was a ruling by the chair that no negative comments could be made about nominees. You could only say positive things about a person that you were nominating.

The second concern was the vanishing attendance as the Convention continued. I do not know the answer, but I have wondered if it would not be a better magnet for attendance to elect the president on Thursday afternoon.

The large period for introduction of business and resolutions was a part of the Tuesday afternoon session, using most of the time. There was a motion to amend Bylaw 21. There were twenty-seven resolutions offered and named in this session. The few new names that appeared included the Ku Klux Klan, the Lebanese crisis, the Stalnecker open house, and even a resolution on resolutions. All of them had to be scheduled later for discussion, and would be pointed up in the report on the Committee on Resolutions.

The Executive Committee proceeded with the second session of their report. One of the first of the recommendations passed concerned the Executive Committee contingency reserve fund. What a day to which we were coming! There was likewise a resolution for the Education Commission contingency reserve fund. There were suggested charter changes for the Brotherhood Commission and for New Orleans Seminary which passed without discussion. I heartily approved a resolution of appreciation for Duke Kimbrough McCall. We had come to understand one another and to establish a deep friendship and appreciation for one another.

Bold Mission Thrust received a major approval and report from the Executive Committee when the goals and emphases before us were given. One can certainly understand that these matters filled the afternoon session. Tuesday evening overall was recognized as the time for the Home Mission Board report. We still could give major attention to the report of our mission boards. The WMU report and the report of the Sunday School Board both preceded the Home Mission Board report.

When the results of the ballot for first vice-president were given and it was discovered that a runoff ballot was necessary, the chair ruled that since it was not previously scheduled, the run-off ballot would be handled the next day. Immediately there was a motion that we take the ballot now. The motion passed and the ballot was taken.

The Home Mission Board report was presented through a program called "See How Love Works." William G. Tanner, board president, brought a challenging message entitled "Love Is Reaching Out to People."

The Wednesday morning session began with the chair's statement about no "negative talk." Immediately, the Committee on Boards brought their report and it became a battleground. In previous Convention reports I have mentioned the motions to amend the Board Committee's report. This time it was far larger and indicative of the deep division in the Convention. It was interesting to me that the same people offered amendments.

Kenneth Chafin moved to substitute two names for those named from Texas. It was earnestly debated and yet the amendment prevailed and the new names were established. By the time the second set of amendments had been offered, it was necessary for Chairman Charles Fuller to move an extension of time of twenty minutes, which the messengers passed. It was also necessary to cast a ballot to determine the fate of these amendments to the Committee on Boards. Later, it was announced that the amendments prevailed.

Much time had been involved in these debates. The Brotherhood Commission, Baptist World Alliance, Education Commission, and the Baptist Foundation all brought reports to the Convention rather quickly.

Suddenly, it was moved that the entire report of the Committee on Boards as amended be referred back to the committee for further action. The people who spoke for and the people who spoke against represented the basic personality division that settled into two groups. A ballot was necessary, and the motion to refer was defeated. All motions to change, or refer to change bylaws or the constitution were finally referred after debate.

The Wednesday morning session closed with an inspirational hour that included the Convention sermon by William Hull of Louisiana. His subject, too, was prophetic and entitled "Who Are Southern Baptists?"

There was no afternoon session, to allow for the luncheons of the seminaries. Even with the divisions that had come into the alumni, our gathering was always inspirational. The attendance was excellent, the spirit was manifestly good, and I always took a little bit of hope from that spirit.

Wednesday evening was foreign mission night. It was hopeful in itself that the messengers were always in one spirit in looking forward to our mission reports. There was a visual feature called "Global Strategy—Now." There were missionary testimonies. Finally, there was a stirring address by Keith Parks, the board's president.

It was obvious that Thursday morning had to be filled with business that remained. The seminaries had made their report on Wednesday evening. It was really a prime time in the program, and each of the seminary presidents spoke of accomplishments and unfolding plans for the seminaries.

The music was inspirational. Claude Rhea led us in singing "At Calvary."

The Credentials Committee was ready with a report of illegal but unintentional registrations. The names of certain people and churches were called as being disqualified. Some of these names I recognized and confess that I felt we were nit-picking with our requirements.

It was necessary that a motion be offered that we vote on the report of the Committee on Boards. Someone arose to a point of personal privilege but was soon ruled out of order. The report of the Committee on Boards, as previously amended, was adopted.

Then we began on the long list of resolutions from that Committee. Resolution 2 was called "Regrets to President Smith." A big deal had been made of the fact that the president's address had been released to the press six days early. Apparently, this release hurt the president, but full apology was offered in that resolution.

After three resolutions, Dotson Nelson of Alabama moved to table the remainder of the report of the Committee on Resolutions. The motion failed, but it was amazing. Even television programming had to be amended and adopted with the consent of the committee.

A major debate arose about a resolution on "release of nominations." First of all there was a motion to refer, which was debated and failed. Then, there were speeches opposed to the resolution. Finally, Owen Cooper of Mississippi moved that the original resolution be deleted and replaced by one that he presented. This, too, though debated, was finally adopted. There was a resolution on "prayer in schools." A substitute resolution offered simply said, "Therefore, be it *Resolved*, That we the messengers of the Southern Baptist Convention in session, June 1982, New Orleans, Louisiana, reaffirm the 1980 statement on school prayer." The substitute resolution failed and the motion was adopted.

There was another motion to table the remainder of the report of the Committee on Resolutions. The motion failed.

Remembering that none of these resolutions were binding upon any church or group, and that they were only the expression of this Convention, I realized that the long debates were not to our credit.

The afternoon session took up again the report of the Committee on Resolutions. The usual subjects were addressed. At least in the afternoon the pace had quickened, which meant that the messengers were nearly through. When we came to the resolution on "alcohol," there was an amendment offered which was ruled out of order. An amendment was offered to the resolution on the Ku Klux Klan. Last of all, the committee returned to Resolution 11 which had to be taken off the table. It was on "abortion and infanticide." Amendments that were offered failed. A reference to previous actions of the Convention called for a reading of the 1980 minutes on the subject. Finally, amendments were rejected and the resolution was adopted.

In closing, I need to note a motion to adjourn the business session which failed. In the last few minutes, someone moved that the business segment of the session be adjourned. This motion passed and we were nearly ready to adjourn.

It was my feeling that we had not done New Orleans justice. The attendance indicated fine family attendance. My own memory suggests that we enjoyed the pleasant atmosphere of the city again, but Southern Baptists were having problems with each other.

Civic Arena • Pittsburgh, Pennsylvania

[signature: Robert Taylor]

JUNE 14-16
1983

WE FLEW TO PITTSBURGH, PENNSYLVANIA, FOR THE 1983 MEETING OF THE SOUTHERN BAPTIST CONVENTION. I HAD been through the airport previously, but had never been downtown. An introductory moment set the tone of the Convention for me. As we drove into the city, we topped a hill. As we passed through a cut at the top of the hill, suddenly, there was the city, spread out before us. The rivers were in the distance; and contrary to my previous impression of the city, it was beautiful. Later, south of the city, we stood on an eminence and looked down upon Three Rivers Stadium. It was so named because at this very point, three rivers meet to make the Ohio River. It was beautiful. Our hotel was comfortable and was within a short walking distance of the auditorium. So, my rating for Pittsburgh as a Convention meeting place must be high.

President James T. Draper called to order the 126th session of the Southern Baptist Convention, in the 138th year of its history, on June 14, at 9:28 A.M., in the Civic Arena in Pittsburgh, Pennsylvania.

After we sang "God of Grace and God of Glory," Secretary Lee Porter announced the registration of 10,603 messengers, and made a motion that constituted the Convention. The final figure would be over 13,700. When the Program Committee presented the Order of Business for adoption by the Convention, there were some innovations. Of particular interest to me was the separation of the seminaries, one from the other. On Wednesday morning, three of the seminaries would report separately, and a report would be given by another agency. Southern Baptist Theological Seminary led off the list, followed by the Annuity Board, and others. This was something different, and I felt a contribution to the identity of the individual seminary, especially Southwestern, whose ministry I loved.

231

The Convention actually has four areas for transacting its business. First, there is the report of the Executive Committee which gives a summary of its year's work. Second, there is an opportunity to give notice of resolutions to be offered, which is a major area for the Convention. Alongside this is what is called business, meaning individual motions that can be offered for discussion and disposition. Finally, there are the reports from the agencies of the Convention. Within this framework, the Convention moves forward.

The theme of the Convention was "Unity of the Spirit in the Bond of Peace" (Eph. 4:3). Dr. Joel Gregory had been invited to take five fifteen-minute periods and interpret this theme in the sessions of the Convention. This included Tuesday morning and Tuesday afternoon, Wednesday morning, and Thursday morning and afternoon. Dr. Gregory was professor of preaching at Southwestern Seminary, and his interpretive messages were well received.

On Tuesday morning, part one of the Executive Committee report was given fifty-five minutes. Recommendation 1 had to do with the 1983-1984 Southern Baptist Convention Cooperative Program allocation budget. Representing a major challenge, it passed without question or discussion. We had set for ourselves the goal of $125,000,000. Of this amount, $114,500,000 constituted the operating budget for the coming year. Fifty percent of this budget went directly to our foreign mission enterprise. About twenty percent was appropriated for the seminaries. Southwestern would receive $6,574,425. I marvelled at this figure.

A second section of the budget was called the "capital needs" budget. The third section, called the "challenge budget," had two phases. Phase 1, in the amount of $1,075,000 (or sixty-three percent), went to the six seminaries. Phase 2, in the amount of $5,884,615, was divided according to the percentages in the budget. The order in which these amounts would be paid would be dictated by the amount received, with the "operating budget" being first.

Recommendation 2 was a detailed capital needs appropriation schedule. There was an immediate motion that the amount in the budget of $8,000,000 that would go to the building of a new Executive Committee Building be separated from the consideration of the rest of the budget. This provoked much discussion, and finally called for a ballot. Later, when the ballot results were announced, the amendment passed and the $8,000,000 for the Executive Committee Building was left for separate consideration. The amount had been divided into the various agencies as all of them were to be beneficiaries of a new facility. When the amount finally came to a vote, it was approved.

Recommendation 4 was a lengthy report called the Bold Mission Thrust report. Goals were detailed, achievements were cited, and the goals for tomorrow were established. All of this was moved and adopted without opposition.

The Executive Committee also recommended contingency reserve fund limits for the Christian Life Commission, Home Mission Board, and for the six individual seminaries. The idea was astonishing to me that we had come to a day when we could discuss how much contingency reserve each agency should set aside. Southwestern was limited to a ninety-day portion of the budget.

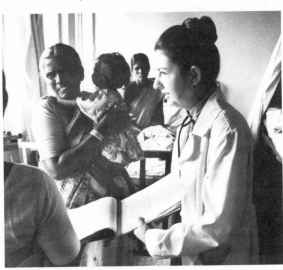

Rebekah Naylor, daughter of Dr. and Mrs. Robert Naylor, ministers in 1983 as the only missionary surgeon on the staff of Bangladore (India) Baptist Hospital. Courtesy—Southern Baptist Historical Library and Archives.

It was time now to offer resolutions and present motions. Overall, forty-five resolutions were presented by name Tuesday morning and Tuesday afternoon. These resolutions became the business of the Resolutions Committee to bring to the Convention for discussion. This was supposed to be done in a ten-minute time frame. Of course, it did not work like that. Two motions were immediately made to amend the bylaws. One would have required a three-fourths majority to pass a resolution. The other would have required that there be a five-year interim between services on any of the boards or agencies. Both of these motions were referred for later study.

In reflection upon these Conventions, I have often commented upon the thinning numbers as the Convention proceeds. Looking at all of these subjects that were presented for the Convention consideration, I began to feel a little tired and understood why. The morning session closed with these resolutions.

The afternoon session contained the election of officers. Contrary to the preceding three years, it was of small moment to the messengers. James T. Draper was elected to a second term by acclamation. John Sullivan of Louisiana was elected to serve as first vice-president for a second term by acclamation. There were three nominations for second vice-president. These resulted in making necessary a run-off ballot between Fred H. Wolfe of Alabama and C. Edward Price of Pennsylvania. Later, it was announced that as a result of the run-off, Price was elected. I was pleased that for whatever reason, there had been no "running for office" to occupy the month preceeding.

Business and resolutions were continued, fifteen of them in the afternoon session. There was a motion to "study the possibility of changing our name from the Southern Baptist Convention to the United Baptist Churches." As fate would have it, about this time we sang "I Know Whom I Have Believed."

Recommendation 5 from the Executive Committee was called "Southern Baptist Convention Cooperative Program Study Committee Report and Recommendations." It began, "During the meeting of the Executive Committee of the Southern Baptist Convention, September 22-24, 1980 . . . , the following motion was adopted: 'That a committee be appointed to study Cooperative Program promotion and stewardship emphasis in the Southern Baptist Convention.'" The Committee was appointed. The study was launched, and at this point was brought to the Southern Baptist Convention. There were no recommendations that stirred opposition or required lengthy discussion. But the report itself, though lengthy, was a very sound analysis of the Cooperative Program as practiced by Southern Baptists.

The 1983 minutes should be kept by the individual Southern Baptist for the value they offer at this point. In their divisions, there was one called "principles of cooperation." There was an emphasis upon the voluntary. There was a statement about the equality of Baptist bodies. There was a statement of common purpose in the Cooperative Program. Along with the historical analysis of the Cooperative Program, the minutes also presented a great challenge to cooperation and planned growth in giving.

The chairman of the Sunday School Board introduced Lloyd Elder of Tennessee as president-elect of the board. Grady Cothen was introduced to present the report, and the Convention expressed appreciation for his long service. The "changing of the guard" had become nearly complete.

There were further resolutions presented, since the afternoon session would be the last opportunity.

Then we heard the Committee on Boards bring its report. In the two previous years there had been amendments offered that changed a name here and there, and presented someone in their place. The amendments had been successful. However, there was something new about this report. Even though amendments were offered, in each case, the proceedings said, "the motion failed."

In fact, in this connection the most often repeated phrase in the 1983 report of our Southern Baptist Convention was "a motion called for the question, and messengers concurred." Though it happened almost dozens of times during the Convention, never once did the messengers refuse to concur in shutting off debate and getting on with the business. That was noteworthy.

The Tuesday evening session began with an hour devoted to the Foreign Mission Board's report. A special program on the theme, "People," began with a presentation of the flags of the countries where there was a Southern Baptist mission witness. This presentation is exciting and moving and is often repeated in our churches. President Keith Parks brought a key message emphasizing "People of Prayer, Who Are Aware, Care." The Tuesday evening session and the first day concluded with Harold Bennett presenting the Bold Mission Thrust report and the messengers singing "To God Be the Glory."

The Wednesday morning session began with a continuance of the Executive Committee report. Bylaw 8 of the Southern Baptist Convention was amended in the first motion. The recommendation had to do with the enrollment of messengers, how and when; and it was accepted. Then there was a motion to amend Southern Baptist Convention Bylaw 16, regarding the election of board members, etc. Board members would be required to be members of churches for a year within the state from which they were elected, prior to election to a board. Then one after another, one brother moved to refer, someone spoke against referral. Someone supported referral. Others spoke against, and in favor and finally the motion to refer failed. There was an amendment offered to change a single word. Discussion followed and the amendment failed. Time was extended by the Convention. Another substitution was offered. When the smoke cleared away, the recommendation was adopted. This was the tempo of the remainder of the Convention.

The time for the Executive Committee having expired, we moved on to the reports from the agencies. Three of the seminaries reported, as I have suggested, in the morning session. Roy Honeycutt, from Southern Seminary, was asked a question about personal witnessing efforts and the results, to which he made adequate response. Southwestern and New Orleans made their reports, but neither president was asked any questions about his institution.

A major matter in the afternoon was introduced that would cover two or three Conventions. It had to do with Southern Baptist work in Canada. The motion, as a successful substitute indicated, was to establish a Canada Study Committee of twenty-one persons to report back to the 1984 Southern Baptist Convention. For those who might not know, our work in Canada had grown. Many churches in Western Canada had identified with our Northwest Convention. A question of polity and of relationship to the Canadian Baptist Convention was involved.

In the Wednesday evening session there was a special recognition of Grady C. Cothen for his thirty-eight years of denominational service, with special emphasis on contributions made while serving as president of the Sunday School Board since 1975.

Southern Baptist Convention site and housing guidelines were recommended by the Executive Committee, after information was requested and given as to the number of cities that could meet those guidelines adopted by the Convention. Finally, the Committee recommended the sites for the meetings in 1989 and 1990. The recommendation that the Convention meet in Las Vegas, Nevada, in 1989 drew major discussion. Amendments were offered and failed. The phrase returned to earlier, "moved the previous question; messengers concurred," was repeated many times in this single discussion. Finally, on the premise of a great evangelistic opportunity, the meeting in Las Vegas was adopted.

Thursday morning we began with the three other seminaries, separated by different agency reports. Then Tal Bonham of Ohio, chairman of the Committee on Resolutions, began their report. Even for Resolution 1 concerning "support of the Bold Mission Thrust," there was an offered amendment. Churches would be encouraged to increase their giving to the Cooperative Program by a greater percentage than they increased pastor and church salaries. The amendment failed, and the resolution was adopted.

A major discussion ensued on freedom and responsibility in Southern Baptist seminaries. There were some who wanted to use the words "abstract of principles," but they were overruled because the term did not apply to all the seminaries. Substitute wording, paragraph by paragraph, was finally rejected after debate had been shut off by the messengers. Finally, the resolution was adopted which set forth basic requirements of the seminaries in acceptable language.

Even the resolution on "religious liberty" drew major debate. There was a desire to change the wording. There were amendments offered which failed. There was even a motion to postpone. All of these finally ended, however, when the messengers cut off the debate and the resolution was adopted.

A resolution on "alcohol" drew a messenger's statement asking for the rationale for recommending a resolution on alcohol. The person presenting the resolution talked about drunken driving and its perils. The resolution was adopted.

In the afternoon, there were reports from the Christian Life Commission and the Baptist Joint Committee, both of which drew questions and discussion from the messengers. The Baptist World Alliance representative gave a report, as did the Stewardship Commission. Joel Gregory brought the fifth and last of his interpretations of the Convention theme. The Resolutions Committee Chairman presented a resolution on "women." This provoked a long discussion. Someone offered an amendment that would make it clear that they were not referring to the ordination of women. One amendment was ruled out of order. The statement was finally adopted.

There was a resolution which was not debated on "the forced termination of ministers." Even the resolution on "the *Reader's Digest Bible*" received discussion. Amendments were offered, debate was cut off, and finally it was adopted. A resolution was offered on the "Year of the Bible." Someone spoke against it, the previous question was called, and adoption followed. Then the Chairman of the Resolutions Committee gave the rationale for all of the offered resolutions that were not finally presented to the Convention. Many were repetitive, and some were referred by reason of the constitution or bylaw.

Thursday night was not used for business, but was for inspiration. Committees were introduced, and a report from the WMU was heard and responded to. Russell Newport sang "He Is Alive." Finally, Charles Colson of Virginia, president of Prison Fellowship, brought a closing message on "Unity of the Spirit—In Ministry."

In summary, the Pittsburgh Convention showed little disposition to accept things without question. Those things which we most surely believed could be debated, amended, and substituted. *For* and *Against* had become familiar words in these Convention proceedings. There were more special recognitions of people, more exchanges of flowery appreciation, more presenting of books to authors, more exchanging of gavels, etc., none of which affected those deep underlying feelings of the Convention.

With this, it was evident that God was still using Southern Baptists in world witness. We went away grateful that we still knew His will, our fellowship of witness, and our desire for reconciliation.

Roe Bartle Hall • Kansas City, Missouri

JUNE 12-14
1984

WE WERE VERY COMFORTABLE WITH THE THOUGHT THAT THE SOUTHERN BAPTIST CONVENTION WAS MEETING IN Kansas City, Missouri. The auditorium was comfortable. The hotels were within easy reach of the place of meeting. We had quoted the Baptist Faith and Message since 1963. We had been back to the city once since then. Now with a theme that called for the repentance of the people, we thought the climate had improved.

President James T. Draper called the Convention to order in its 139th year, on June 12, at 9:32 A.M., in the Roe Bartle Hall in Kansas City, Missouri. John Sullivan of Louisiana announced the place of prayer rooms and encouraged us to pray. We were led in singing "All Hail the Power of Jesus' Name." We had honored our traditions.

The registration secretary reported that at the time of beginning 13,013 messengers had registered. The final figure was 17,101. The motion was made that constituted the Convention and set us on course.

The Committee on Order of Business presented the program previously printed, and suddenly there was a motion to amend. The amendment was to change the time for the report of the Committee on Boards to the Wednesday morning session rather than on Tuesday afternoon. The battle lines were drawn. It was necessary to cast a ballot. Without final approval of the program, we began doing the things that the program called for.

Again this year, the Program Committee had made plans for a fifteen-minute theme interpretation for five of the sessions. Lewis Drummond of Louisville, Kentucky, had been asked to bring these messages. The theme, "If My People . . . I Will" (2 Chron. 7:14), was appropriate and the messages were good.

239

The Committees were announced and Harold C. Bennett, executive secretary-treasurer of the Executive Committee, presented W. Dewey Presley of Texas with the report of the committee. As the first item of our business, the motion was made to adopt the Cooperative Program Budget Goal for 1984-1985. It was immediately challenged with a motion to amend by temporarily setting aside the funds allocated for the Public Affairs Committee, the operating budget, and the challenge budget. Some spoke for and some spoke against. The time was extended by vote. Finally, we had to cast a ballot and the Executive Committee report had used its time for only one item of business. Not until Tuesday afternoon did we know that the budget goal had been adopted and that the amendment had failed. This was a division right down the middle.

The president then opened the floor for the announcement of resolutions and for the presentation of motions. In this first session, already twenty-four resolutions had been left on the table and were named with their authors for the Convention. The list seemed exhaustive. Then the chair offered opportunity for motions and other business matters. Immediately one man presented three motions, the substance of which was to require of all people nominated to office to indicate the percent of their church income given to the Cooperative Program. He concluded by suggesting a minimum of six percent (it should be ten percent.)

There followed a motion "that we reaffirm our abiding and unchanging objection to the dissemination of theological views in any of our Southern Baptist agencies which would undermine faith in the historical accuracy and doctrinal integrity of the Bible, and that we courteously request the trustees and administrative officers to take such steps as shall be necessary to remedy at once those situations where such views now threaten our historic position."

Then there was a motion "that the Convention prevent distribution of secular, humanist, un-biblical pamphlets." The seeds of suspicion were readily apparent.

One man asked the Convention for the privilege of counting our personal Convention expenses as part of our Cooperative Program giving. Someone else wanted to change the name of the Cooperative Program to that of Cooperative Ministries.

Finally, the president's address focused on the subject, "Debtors to the World." Mrs. Draper led the closing prayer.

Tuesday afternoon, it was announced first that the amendment to the Committee on Order of Business had failed. We adopted the program as presented.

With that, the amendment offered to the Cooperative Program budget goal likewise failed, and the budget was adopted. Until we registered that action, the Cooperative Program had not been discussed here. The goal was to be $130,000,000. The total of $118,000,000 was to be the Operating Budget of which the seminaries were to receive $24,264,703. Southwestern was to receive $6,788,529.

The capital needs budget largely reflected the cost of the Executive Committee's new building. The challenge budget was only about $5,000,000. In the midst of our problems we needed to pause and remember that God was still in business, that our people still loved the Lord and sought a lost world. The budget did represent some very faithful stewardship.

Full time was given to the discussion of the Bold Mission Thrust report. The new work was underlined. Strengthening of families had entered into the report. There was no disposition to question it.

Two motions would have amended Bylaws 16 and 21, in effect to require one-year church resident membership in the state they represented by people nominated to boards or commissions. Amendments were offered to each that would have required at least four percent of the annual budget for the past two years for such nominees. The amendments failed and the change of bylaws was approved.

The election of officers had followed the announcement of ballot results from the morning. Ninety-one percent of those registered voted in the presidential election. The nominees included John Sullivan of Louisiana, Grady Cothen of Mississippi, and Charles Stanley of Georgia. Stanley was elected with fifty-two percent of the vote.

There followed the nominations for first vice-president which included Don Wideman of Missouri, Russell Bennett of Kentucky, and Zig Ziglar and Fred Roach of Texas. In a run-off ballot, Ziglar was elected.

Not until Wednesday morning did we have nominations for second vice-president. These included Harold Friend of Arizona, T. L. McSwain of Kentucky, Don Wideman of Missouri, Jerry Sheridan of Missouri, and Robert Click of Kansas. I thought it strange that in the report of the runoff, the minutes indicate that just 10,369 votes were cast. Wideman was elected with seventy-two percent of the votes totaling 7,467. In the earlier election he had received forty-six percent, totaling 3,187 votes. Where were the messengers?

In reflection, I believe the elections reveal best the division that is among us. Good people were nominated, but it seemed evident that the vote was predetermined. The matter of *who* was secondary to the company they represented. This is still true among us and is a sad note on our Baptist polity.

In that Tuesday afternoon session, Charles Fuller, chairman of the Committee on Boards, presented their report that had been printed in the *Daily Bulletin*. As in the previous three Conventions, there were immediate motions to replace one name with another. One amendment offered would have changed the name of Paul Pressler of Texas, chosen by the committee, to that of Bruce McIver of Texas. Pressler's name had become synonymous with our politics. By the fifty-three percent that was found in the election votes, Pressler's name prevailed and remained in the report.

We began Tuesday evening with business again. I was interested in a motion that we "instruct the Foreign Mission Board to review its policy of rejecting mission volunteers because they have teenage children." The full time assigned to the Home Mission Board was given under the leadership of William G. Tanner of Georgia. After testimonies as to the work of the board, Tanner concluded the period with a message "Why Evangelize?" Full time was given to the announcement of a new Communications Network and its dedication.

The seminary reports had been distributed among the periods of the Convention. Wednesday morning these were the reports of Southern, Southwestern, and New Orleans. The Southwestern report included an audiovisual presentation depicting some students and professors giving their testimonies during a worship period.

It was also during this period that Goldia and I were recognized for fifty years of unbroken attendance at Southern Baptist Convention sessions. In Columbia, South Carolina, I had been the pastor and friend of Ira Edens, a man the age of our older son. The friendship had been steadfast, and he was so impressed with fifty years Convention attendance that I think he promoted the recognition a bit. In either case, President Draper very graciously presented a plaque to us and commented upon that attendance.

While the recognition was given during the seminary report, it represented a commitment even beyond that, and not contrary to, the basic commitment at the seminary. My preacher father had taught me that every gathering of the people was significant to any man or woman whom God had called. We had been wonderfully blessed in those fifty years, and I have sought many times to convey to my fellow pastors the privileges of the Convention.

The report of the Executive Committee continued with bylaw changes that were structural. There was a program of Bible publishing approved for our Sunday School Board. There was a fine resolution of appreciation for Grady Coulter Cothen.

I had been the pastor of Everett Anthony of Illinois when he was a seminary student. He and his wife had been faithful members of our church. He brought a motion to the Convention that I thought was appropriate and fine, even if a bit hopeless. It reflected the ache in the hearts of our faithful that we were having trouble being a fellowship. The motion read, "That this Convention hereby constitute a committee of ten persons to meet at least three times before the 1985 Southern Baptist Convention to discuss, pray about, and plan how to effectively implement an awareness and understanding of and commitment to reconciliation among Southern Baptist people. . . ." The motion goes on to indicate personnel. Later the motion was rejected. We had to learn, and have to learn, that Christian fellowship cannot be initiated by a committee.

Fred Roach of Texas presented a report with reference to our Canada participation that I thought was very worthwhile.

The time for the Convention sermon had arrived. The Men's Chorus from Southwestern Baptist Theological Seminary presented the special music. The sermon was preached by Russell H. Dilday, Jr., on the theme, "On Higher Ground."

On Wednesday evening after hearing the Stewardship Commission report, Harold R. Cushing of Alabama, chairman of the directors of the Foreign Mission Board, was presented for that report. The theme was "Christ: Light to the Nations, Light for the Journey." Always inspirational, it was a high hour in which Keith Parks, the president of the board, shared the notes of victory around the world.

A business session concluded the evening. It developed into continuous debate. There were motions to refer, and there were those who opposed. It was necessary to extend the time thirty minutes. Some of the motions I have mentioned were brought up for discussion and division. Would you be surprised that someone made a motion "that the Resolutions Committee acknowledge resolutions honoring all Southern Baptists who have excelled instead of just recognizing denominational workers." They called for more time for business in the 1985 Convention. Finally, they sought to change the commitment of the Convention to a Las Vegas meeting.

We began Thursday morning by singing "God of Grace and God of Glory." President Draper repeated the time limits for discussions, motions, and speeches. Finally, we began to deal with the Resolutions Committee. Resolution 3 almost brought the Convention to a halt. It had to do with the "Ordination and the Role of Women in Ministry." There were many contrary opinions. There was even an attempt to require a ballot, a motion for which failed. Finally, the motion to adopt the resolution itself had to be determined by ballot. It was adopted 4,793 to 3,466. It is therefore concluded "that we not decide concerns of Christian doctrine and practice by modern cultural, sociological and ecclesiastical trends . . . and that we encourage the service of women in all aspects of church life and work other than pastoral functions and leadership roles entailing ordination."

The resolution on Civil Rights was debated but adopted. For the first time we had one on "cigarette smoking." A resolution on "abortion" was debated, and yet the Convention position reaffirmed.

Thursday afternoon and evening were largely made up of concluding the business. Many of the matters about which motions had been made were simply referred to different agencies for consideration. Lewis Drummond brought the last in his series of theme interpretations. Reports from the Historical Commission and the Southern Baptist Foundation were heard. Zig Ziglar was recognized for the final message Thursday evening.

At one point in the Convention, President Draper had reminded the messengers that what they did concerned only this Convention. We could not speak for others. It was timeless. It was also indicative of our divided fellowship. Many plaques were presented. Many important people were introduced. Many fine words were said, but when it was all said and done, the written record was not our best.

$\mathcal{S}$outhern $\mathcal{B}$aptist $\mathcal{C}$onvention

Dallas Convention Center • Dallas, Texas

[signature: Robert Taylor]

JUNE 11-13
1985

HOME AGAIN! IT HAD BEEN ELEVEN YEARS SINCE THE SOUTHERN BAPTIST CONVENTION HAD MET IN DALLAS when the Convention enrolled more than eighteen thousand messengers. It was often prophesied that the attendance at this Convention would be a record. For months the Convention had been embroiled in open, unashamed, enthusiastic, accepted political activity. That which had been long portended was to come to pass. The divisions among us now came into sharp focus. The sitting president was to be challenged in his bid for a second term. Both in the churches and in other public meetings, both sides had been presenting their candidate. It had to be a sad day for Southern Baptists.

President Charles F. Stanley of Georgia called to order the 128th session of the Southern Baptist Convention, in the 140th year of its history, on June 11, at 9:04 A.M., in the Dallas Convention Center in Dallas, Texas. The Convention theme was "Pray Ye Therefore (Matt. 9:38)." There was only room for the messengers in the Convention hall. Visitors who were unable to be certified as messengers by their churches had to sit in the overflow auditoriums because of quotas.

We were led in singing "All Hail the Power of Jesus Name." We were then led in prayer. Harold Bennett presented the Broadus gavel to the president.

Lee Porter, the registration secretary, announced an already record enrollment of 40,723. The final count would be 45,519. These were declared to be the Convention by motion and action of the Convention in session. The Committee on Order of Business presented the program outlined and unchallenged, having called attention to two fixed items according to Convention bylaws: the president's address and the Convention sermon.

245

There were a few unusual things. There was only one theme interpretation, and that was scheduled for Tuesday evening. The seminaries were given ten minutes each for their report, required to leave a third of their time for questions from the floor. The Foreign Mission Board time was forty minutes on Tuesday evening. The Home Mission Board report was also forty minutes and would be given on Wednesday evening.

The welcome address by William Pinson included a telegram from the Governor of Texas. Committees were announced, and as was traditional, we came to the report and recommendations of the Executive Committee.

Items 1, 2, and 3 had to do with the Cooperative Program budget, capital needs, and the challenge section. It was noteworthy that capital needs led the way. This had the unique idea of extending the total of the 1984-1988 capital needs budget to a five-year plan without altering the agency totals. The strain evident in the capital needs budget was the building of the new Executive Committee building.

The Cooperative Program basic operating budget for 1985-1986 was the challenging figure of $120,600,000. The seminaries were to have $24,709,000 of this budget. Southwestern Seminary topped the $7,000,000 figure for the first time. The Capital Needs Program unpaid in 1983-84 was carried over into 1985-1986 budget. All of this was adopted without question.

Recommendation 4 covered the Bold Mission Thrust report, year number two. When presented, a messenger asked the chairman to respond to the apparent fact that ten of the twelve goals for Bold Mission Thrust covered in the report were not reached. The proceedings simply say, "Wilson replied." It is too bad that the reply is not indicated. These were worthy goals.

As in previous Conventions, several recommendations covered changes, read for the first time, in the constitution. A change in Bylaw 20 followed. All changes were undiscussed. Within a few years, we had made major changes in Convention structures. These would influence the fashion of doing business in the years to come.

The Executive Committee recommended the Sunday School Board Program Statement. It began by listing the Sunday School Board programs, which numbered seventeen. In a scope of twenty pages in the proceedings, it developed in detail the seventeen programs. Of course, the presentation was a very simple, brief statement as to what we could expect. Two or three minutes were enough.

Most messengers who regularly attended would know that the Sunday School Board was a cash return asset of the Southern Baptist Convention. A recommendation was adopted that outlined the rules under which these contributions were made out of the profits of the board to the work of the Convention. Following this Sunday School Board Program Statement, there was a new statement for the Home Mission Board on the Program of Chaplaincy Ministries.

New Orleans Seminary received a contingency reserve figure. Golden Gate Seminary had a charter revision, changing the trustee representations of the institution. This closed the first Executive Committee period.

There followed the opportunity for miscellaneous business and resolutions which, if anything, constituted more narrowly the structure of the Convention than the program itself. In a thirty-minute period, thirty-six resolutions were named and the persons who made them. These had been solicited prior to the Convention.

Item 57 would cast a long shadow. Bill Hickam of Florida and Franklin Paschall of Tennessee jointly submitted a motion as follows: "That a Special Committee be authorized by this Convention, in session, in Dallas, June, 1985 . . . to determine the sources of the controversies in our Convention, and make findings and recommendations regarding these controversies, so that Southern Baptists might effect reconciliation and effectively discharge their responsibilities to God by cooperating together to accomplish evangelism, missions, Christian education and other causes authorized by our Constitution, all to the glory of God. 'By this shall all men know that ye are my disciples, if ye have love one to another.'"

Following the introduction of substance, the motion reflected the fashion in which the membership of this committee should be determined, the rules concerning expenses, the matter of open and closed sessions, the way to fill vacancies, and a final admonition to all Southern Baptists to exercise restraint. It was a remarkable motion, both in size, substance and hope. You will recognize that this was the birth of the SBC Peace Committee.

When you read the names of the people who were included in the motion to be members of the committee, you realize at once that these are mostly familiar names. There are people in whom I would have personal confidence. They were charged with a responsibility that I personally regarded as outside our Baptist polity and history. We do not make peace with committees. We shall be hearing more in the reports from this committee, but it has been long enough now to observe that nothing really changed.

There followed twenty-eight motions which were still within this thirty minutes. They covered many subjects. I was personally touched by the fact that there were five or six motions that simply affirmed Southwestern Seminary. I appreciated the sentiment, but I felt no need for affirmation. It was true that following President Dilday's Convention sermon of the year before, "On Higher Ground," there had been a flame of controversy which I am sure he did not intend. Inevitably the seminary comes under attack in these situations, and there seemed to be a great host of the family that wanted to say, "Southwestern is alright."

I noticed one motion that was offered: "That we discontinue the entertaining of resolutions in the sessions of our Convention beginning in 1986, and that we take the necessary steps in regard to the Constitution and bylaws to put into practice this intent." I could be sympathetic with growing tired of this resolution process. None of these were allowed to be discussed. This period was simply intended to place before the Convention, and in the hands of the proper committee, the time for discussion of the various items. If we had discussed all of them, we would still be in session.

There were the continuation motions from the previous year. There were many attempts to discover the Cooperative Program support amount for people nominated to boards. There was a desire to fix quotas by which a person became eligible from one of those churches.

Before the period was done, nine additional resolutions had been presented. Finally, and fortunately, we came to the constitutionally fixed hour for the president's address. Charles Stanley, president, spoke to us on the subject, "Healing Hurts in the Family of God."

Just after the beginning of the afternoon session, we came to that for which I believe most of the messengers had come. What world missions, evangelism, and south-wide institutions could not do, Southern Baptists in politics had done. We had a record attendance to elect a president. Charles Stanley was nominated for a second term. Winford Moore was nominated in opposition. Exactly 44,248 people cast ballots in this presidential election. Charles Stanley was elected with 24,453 (55.3 percent) of the votes. Through all the things of the morning, the messengers were obviously just waiting for this moment.

An hour later, in the same session nominations were received for first vice-president. Zig Ziglar of Texas was nominated for a second term. Henry Huff of Kentucky and Winford Moore of Texas were also nominated. Exactly 34,049 had voted. Within the hour we had lost nearly ten thousand messengers. Moore was elected.

Not until Tuesday evening did we have the run-off ballot for second vice-president involving W. O. Vaught of Arkansas and Henry Huff. Huff was elected. The total vote in that evening session was 16,636.

After the presidential election, the chairman announced that fifteen additional resolutions had been received. Again they covered a wide range of subjects. Announcement was made as to the hour in which we would begin discussing these many motions and resolutions.

At this point the Executive Committee began its final report. The committee introduced the launching of the 1985-1990 Bold Mission Thrust emphases. Joel Gregory of Texas, by way of videotape, spoke to those emphases. Martin Bradley then led the Convention in an information survey describing the demographics of the Convention.

President Stanley announced the time for introduction of business motions. Fourteen of these were presented in the next few minutes. The first one wanted to add the following sentence to Bylaw 10. "When an incumbent President is eligible for re-election, the Committee on Order of Business must schedule the first balloting for President to take place prior to the President's address." This was a diehard sentiment.

Someone wanted to vote by mail. Others wanted any messenger to be from a church that had baptized at least one person. There were the financial restrictions proposed in these motions. There was finally one "that we pledge our support to the President elected by this Convention." When this one came up for discussion, it was quietly passed with nothing said.

More than once in all this business, a messenger would object to the fact that the motion he made had been referred to a committee. To refer was, of course, the principal device in such a multiplicity of motions and resolutions. When the motion "that the motion be discussed" came, it was defeated by the Convention.

Finally in the afternoon, there was the report of the Committee on Boards. Immediately a motion to amend would have changed one name in the report for another. There were speeches for and against the report. The nominee of the committee prevailed. The committee chairman moved to extend the time fifteen minutes, which passed. There was a call for another substitution, names of trustees of Southern Baptist Theological Seminary. Again spoken for and spoken against, the motion to amend lost. Time was extended again. There was a call for a ballot on two amendments. The motion that we have a ballot failed. Messengers concurred in the call for previous question. Finally, the Committee on Boards' report was passed, so we closed the session singing "Glory To His Name."

The Tuesday evening session began with ten more resolutions, the final time that such could be presented. We heard the report of the Sunday School Board in a thirty-minute period.

R. Keith Parks, president of the Foreign Mission Board, was recognized. He began by affirming his support of the president and inviting him to attend a summer meeting of the Foreign Mission Board at Glorieta. Harold Cushing, the trustees' chairman, introduced a video memorial for the late Baker James Cauthen, former executive secretary of the board. Mrs. Cauthen was then presented with a greeting by the messengers. A video report was then introduced indicating missions challenge and selected results of the board's work. Missionary representatives from Guatemala, Japan, and Tanzania offered testimonies as did the president of the board.

Beginning on Wednesday morning, the Convention began to hear the reports from other agencies. Three of the seminaries, Southern, Southwestern and New Orleans, all brought reports as indicated in ten-minute periods. In each case there were two people who asked questions to which the president made response. Likewise, Golden Gate Seminary gave their report and responded to questions.

We began the discussion of the motions previously presented. The Committee on Order of Business had scheduled the one that concerned the Peace Committee for first discussion. Edward Drake of Texas spoke against the motion. Bill Hickam, one of the makers, spoke for it. Questions were asked and answered. The report was amended by adding certain names to the group. At last, Wayne Dehoney moved the previous question, and messengers concurred. The Peace Committee had come into existence.

Next, the motion calling for an offering for world hunger was discussed and passed, and the offering taken in the amount of $77,000. Allen Schmidt was presented to speak to the SBC-Canada

Planning Group report. Schmidt, coordinator of Southern Baptist work in Canada, described the forming of a new Convention of Southern Baptists in Canada.

George T. Schroeder of Arkansas was presented for the report of the Committee on Committees. He began with a motion to amend the committee's report by substituting present state convention presidents and WMU presidents, with the exception of New Mexico, that they be added to the report. The chair ruled that the nominations must be dealt with on a state-by-state basis. The amendment was spoken against. The ruling of the chair was appealed on a point of order, a motion, and a ballot taken, and ruled that the chairman's ruling was not sustained.

At this point the time for the Convention sermon had arrived. The choir of the First Baptist Church, Roanoke, Virginia, presented special music. Charles D. Fuller of Virginia preached the Convention sermon on the subject, "Too Much to Lose."

There were no meetings scheduled for Wednesday afternoon to allow the seminaries to have their alumni luncheons. For us it was that rare opportunity to bring the Southwestern Seminary family back to the campus. Buses were provided for many. Already a host of alumni with precious memories had visited the campus. It was a good afternoon for Southwestern.

Wednesday evening the Committee on Order of Business announced the referring of one motion to the Sunday School Board and of ten others to the Executive Committee. There were a few motions declared out of order because of conflict with a Convention bylaws. One of the motions required a two-thirds vote and was defeated.

The Committee on Resolutions offered their resolutions. Resolution 1, "On Appreciation," was amended by a new paragraph commending the heads of our Southern Baptist Convention agencies. This resolution was adopted. There was an amendment offered that would have added prayer and fasting to that which had been called for. The amendment was defeated and the original resolution adopted.

The Home Mission Board was given its forty minutes at the conclusion of the evening. William G. Tanner, president of the board, presented the report under the theme, "Spreading God's Love Through Ministry."

The Convention was concluded with the Thursday afternoon session. The morning was largely devoted to the resolutions previously prepared. At this point, let me comment on one extra feature of the

Convention. Almost at the beginning, our Convention president was calling for prayer periods. He wanted to do this in groups of four so that we could have prayer meetings simultaneously. This method is widely used, but I must confess that it is a method I do not like. The confusion is incredible, but one thing about being a Baptist—you go along and participate.

A resolution affirming the Cooperative Program was adopted, as was one on "refugee resettlement." Interestingly enough, in the midst of it, John Sullivan of Florida, joined by Winfred Moore of Texas, moved "that the report of the Committee on Committees not be discussed further during this Convention." The motion passed. It might have been out of order, but it was certainly the sentiment of the Convention.

There were other resolutions adopted on "pornography" and "homosexuality." The longest item of the report simply listed a host of the motions and resolutions on which the committee took no action. Then there was a large number also named that were referred to various committees. The five motions read into the minutes on Wednesday evening were voted not to be discussed by the Convention. Even an attempt to suspend the rules and deal with a motion on abortion failed the vote of the Convention.

Thursday afternoon concluded the Convention. Actually the Convention was through much earlier. Reports from the WMU and the Historical Commission were offered. Even the Denominational Calendar report suffered an amendment which failed.

The final action of the Convention, as recorded in its proceedings, was ironic: "Charles Walton (TX), secretary for the Credentials Committee, reported that four persons had registered in error as messengers and moved 'that Mr. and Mrs. Gene Primm and Mr. and Mrs. Leon Jernigan, registered as messengers of the Liberty Baptist Church, Hampton, Virginia, be unseated as messengers to this Convention and that their badges and ballots be surrendered to the registration secretary.'" What a note to end a Convention that had just had its largest attendance in history.

We then sang "Praise God From Whom All Blessings Flow" and departed. In 1986 we would go to Atlanta, Georgia.

World Congress Center • Atlanta, Georgia

Robert Taylor

JUNE 10-12
1986

TRADITIONALLY, FOR MORE THAN TWENTY-FIVE YEARS, THE SOUTHERN BAPTIST CONVENTION BEGAN ITS formal sessions on Tuesday morning. We had always made it a practice to be present when the first session began. In fact, I could not recall that we had arrived later than Sunday afternoon in all the years. When we drove a long distance to the Convention, we would probably arrive on Saturday. The pre-sessions were always of vital interest to us. Goldia had often been a messenger to the Woman's Missionary Union meeting which preceded the regular Convention. I had been involved a long while in seminary sessions and discussions. This time, as we made preparation to go to Atlanta, Georgia, it was different.

Atlanta was certainly an anticipated place of meeting. We had always found the city itself interesting, our churches strong, and the sense of welcome very apparent. This time I had accepted an invitation to stop off in Birmingham and preach at the Dawson Memorial Baptist Church. This is a very fine church that was pastorless, and I had been privileged to participate in its ministry more than once.

Our hotel reservation was in the Omni Hotel just across the street from the Convention Center, and we were scheduled for Monday morning arrival. When we arrived, we were met with the news that the hotel had overbooked. There was no room for us. You can be sure I was quite unhappy about it. The hotel had made arrangements for us to stay at the Marriott downtown. They even made financial concessions intended to ease the matter. Actually, the hotel where we stayed turned out to be a plus place, but I thought it was an unhappy beginning for a Convention in a major city.

253

We were coming to Atlanta from that record-setting attendance in Dallas the year previous when we had over 45,000 in attendance. If anything, the year of political activity had exceeded that of the year before. There were to be just two nominations for president. The division among us, solidly established, entered into every consideration. It is no wonder that the attendance was to be exceeded only by the Dallas Convention.

In his hometown, President Charles F. Stanley called to order the 129th session of the Southern Baptist Convention, in the 141st year of its history, on June 10, at 9:00 A.M., in the World Congress Center in Atlanta, Georgia. We sang "All Hail the Power of Jesus' Name." This Baptist host singing that wonderful, old hymn was worth a trip to the Convention. The Convention focused on the theme "Love Never Fails" (1 Cor. 13:8).

We noted the presentation of the parliamentarians. The employment of a professional parliamentarian, C. Barry McCarty, was not a real popular thing with the Convention. He was not a Baptist. As far as professional performance, it seemed to be adequate, but many among the messengers felt that we could have used a Southern Baptist parliamentarian.

Secretary Lee Porter reported that 37,603 messengers had already been registered at 9:00 A.M., and then made the motion that constituted the Convention with these and others later registering as messengers of the churches.

Fred H. Wolfe of Alabama, chairman of the Committee on Order of Business, moved the adoption of the order of business previously printed in our programs. Even here there was a motion to amend, to allow each of the presidential nominees, Adrian Rogers of Tennessee and Winfred Moore of Texas, to be given a maximum of ten minutes to address the messengers before the presidential election. The president ruled the motion out of order. The program was adopted, and the Convention meeting moved forward.

I noted with personal interest that the seminaries each had ten minutes to make a report. Other agencies of the Convention were in the program to be sure, but in most cases they had a very limited time frame. Business sessions had been multiplied.

Our president, as he had done the year before, called for the small-group prayer procedure. I have already expressed my dissatisfaction with that. Committees were announced, and the Executive Committee was recognized, as traditionally, for its report and recommendations.

There was little disposition to debate these early recommendations. The focus of the Convention was upon an election soon to come that would represent victory or defeat for so many.

The first two recommendations had to do with our Cooperative Program goals and budget. This budget had an introductory statement that was new. It asked for increased personal giving. It urged the churches to increase the percentage given through the Cooperative Program. It called upon the states for a 50-50 division goal in their Cooperative Program receipts. It urged that they approve seventy-five percent to the Home and Foreign Mission Boards. All of this was to be the premise for a new growth strategy.

The budget goal itself was $136,000,000. The six seminaries were to receive $25,944,400, of which Southwestern would receive $7,533,242. Who would have dreamed of such an amount? These were adopted without discussion.

West Virginia was recognized and certified as having grown enough to be qualified for trustees on the boards and agencies of the Convention.

Constitutional amendments presented the previous year were read for the second time and approved. One of them, that simply called for the president to be named as treasurer, meaning the president of any agency, did have a motion to delay, which was ruled out of order.

There were new bylaws which would describe the fashion of election for board members, trustees, commissioners, or standing committees. Paul Pressler, on behalf of the committee, offered a new bylaw which would allow all registered members to participate in the discussions and activities. It was adopted, and, later, there was a request for reconsideration. The motion to reconsider failed.

Thirty minutes had been assigned by the committee to the Committee on Order of Business to announce resolutions, their authors, and their point of reference. In that brief period Chairman Fred Wolfe of Alabama presented twenty-three resolutions and the name of the person offering them. Following that, twenty-one motions were heard and given into the hands of the committee. As had become necessary previously, there were three dispositions which would be made of these. Many of them would be referred for consideration by various agencies of the Convention. There would be another number on which the committee would make no recommendation. Finally, there were those that were brought for discussion and either accepted or rejected by the Convention.

The time having arrived for the president's address, President Stanley spoke on "On the Brink of Blessing." This ended that first session.

Almost immediately in the afternoon, we came to the prime focus of the Convention, the election of a president. It surprised me a little that Winfred Moore would make a second run at the office. Pastor of a great church, with a record of fine ministry, it was almost too much. The year before, after having been defeated, he was on the platform when nominations were received for first vice-president. Someone arose and wanted to nominate him for that office. Our rule is that you cannot nominate a person without having their consent. I am sure he had no idea of being first vice-president. Engaged in conversations by people around him, someone sought to ask him for permission. Being agreeable and not really understanding the question, it was interpreted as assent, and immediately the Convention elected him. I have laughed with him about it since on several different occasions.

Nelson Price of Georgia nominated Adrian P. Rogers of Tennessee, and Richard Jackson of Arizona nominated Winfred Moore of Texas. The ballot results were announced. Of the 40,462 registered messengers, 39,099 had voted. Rogers received 21,201 (54.22 percent) votes. Moore received 17,898 votes (45.78 percent).

It was near the close of the afternoon session when the ballot was announced. Nominations were called for first vice-president. Jack Stanton of Missouri and Henry Huff of Kentucky were nominated. The results announced just before adjournment indicated that Stanton had been elected with 19,418 votes. As I have asked before and since, where were the other six thousand messengers not voting? The total vote for first vice-president was 33,369.

While discussing the elections, let me note that nominations for second vice-president were heard Wednesday evening. Nominated were Ray Roberts of North Carolina, Jay Truett Gannon of Georgia, Dan Ivins of Alabama, Darrell Robinson of Alabama, and Mike Johnson of Alabama. There was always something new. Mike Johnson nominated himself. We had not heard that before, and it was a light moment with the messengers. I guess one would be surprised that when the ballot was announced, though he did not win, 2,500 of the messengers had voted for him. We were getting tired of those nominating speeches. Fifteen thousand and seven hundred votes

Charles Fuller, chairman of the Southern Baptist Convention Peace Committee, reports during a news conference at the 1986 Southern Baptist Convention meeting. Courtesy—Southern Baptist Historical Library and Archives.

were cast, and Ray Roberts was elected on that first ballot.

Upon reflection it may seem that these elections received inordinate space in this report, but if so, it represented the focus of the Convention. This was that which had happened to us.

Eight other motions had been presented during the afternoon, with the makers, all to be discussed later. The Executive Committee returned for their report, the first being a report on the Bold Mission Thrust, year number three. Almost without discussion, the program was accepted. Likewise without discussion, the Foreign Mission Board Program Statement revisions, containing full discussion of their many areas of work, were adopted without adequate discussion.

Ten more motions were announced. Tuesday evening, we were to hear the report of the Peace Committee. There had been a year since their founding. By action of the committee, many of their meetings had been in relative privacy. Time was extended during the program. A motion to amend was defeated, and finally the chairman's motion to adopt was passed. The committee was well-meaning. Just a reference to all the motions and resolutions would have convinced me that this was not the way of peace for a Baptist body. Eighteen resolutions were added, and the day was concluded with the report of the Home Mission Board. William G. Tanner of Georgia, board president, climaxed the period with an address, "The Essentials of Bold Mission Thrust."

Continuing a pattern recently set, four of the seminaries reported Wednesday morning. They were separated, one from the other, by the report of an agency. Having made their reports, they were required to leave time for questions from the floor. The total amount of time assigned, as I have suggested, was ten minutes.

The Resolutions Committee began their report offering three resolutions. The first motion considered by the Convention was one that would have removed the Baptist Joint Committee from our Southern Baptist structure. Of the 40,806 registered messengers, there were just 21,557 present to vote; 52.08 percent of the vote referred the motion to the Executive Committee. This was to establish the pattern. It was time for the Convention sermon. Adrian Rogers of Tennessee spoke on "The Church Triumphant."

As usual, there was no afternoon session on Wednesday. The seminary luncheons and some smaller groups met. The fellowship of the family was always a fresh breath to me. On all the matters of division, there were members of the family on either side. But this was a time when we seemed to remember who we were and the debt that we owed.

Chairman Fred Wolfe in the evening session moved to refer many of the motions that had been made previously. This was also the last opportunity for new motions, and there were ten of these presented. The Foreign Mission Board was featured on Wednesday evening. William O'Brien of Virginia was warmly applauded as he paid tribute to foreign missionaries on the platform. Keith Parks, the president, inspired us with a reminder that the harvest waits.

The other two seminaries made their reports on Thursday morning. It was a personal note to me when President Stanley recognized the death during the past year of Louie D. Newton, Clifton J. Allen, and K. Owen White.

The business and the resolutions largely constituted the remainder of the Convention. The fourth resolution from the committee was on pornography. There was a motion to amend, to add items that the committee might have missed. The motion to amend passed. A second motion likewise passed and finally a resolution was adopted. A new subject, Resolution 5, on "prayer for farmers," was adopted. Resolution 6 was on the First Amendment and religious liberty. When it was offered, there was a motion to remove a paragraph, which was defeated. Three motions to amend did pass and a fine resolution finally adopted.

A resolution on "strengthening missions" surely would be routine. Not so. A messenger moved to amend the report by adding to it "an encouragement to messengers to attend the reports of the Home Mission Board and the Foreign Mission Board." Another amendment was offered which would have urged every Southern Baptist church to give at least a tithe of their undesignated gifts to the Cooperative Program, finally required a ballot. The resolution was adopted but total votes cast were less than ten thousand.

In summary, some of the old subjects were introduced. There was a call again for establishment of a new Southern Baptist seminary which was referred. Other subjects included "child abuse," "apartheid," "Nicaragua and Central America," "abortion," and "the status of women." There were motions that affirmed people. The question of "ordained women in missions," "the impact of divorce on children," and "a reaffirmation of Southwestern Seminary" also appeared in the list. Now and again time had to be extended. Most of the motions were referred. It does not mean that the subjects were unimportant. Most of them constituted individual expressions, and most of them simply reflected our troubled world and the sense of doing less than we should about it.

A last note in the proceedings suggested an atmosphere: "That the last statement of the gentleman from South Carolina who apologized regarding Dan Collins and stated that he wished he would resign from the Sunday School Board be considered inconsistent with the theme of the Convention and be stricken from the record." The motion passed.

The 129th session of the Southern Baptist Convention concluded with the messengers singing "Blessed Be the Tie That Binds."

suthern Baptist Convention

Cervantes Convention Center • St. Louis, Missouri

JUNE 16-18

1987

SINCE 1936, THIS MADE THE SEVENTH
SOUTHERN BAPTIST CONVENTION THAT
I HAD ATTENDED IN ST. LOUIS. THIS WAS
a commentary in itself upon the satisfaction of the messengers with
St. Louis as a meeting place. Usually the hotels had been close by,
sightseeing was always available, and the historical significance of
the area was worthwhile.

For my part, the trip to St. Louis for a Convention made a strange
mixed panoply of memories. The first one I remember very well
because Goldia could not go. It was the only one she had missed, and
much of the flavor of the Convention was gone. As an aside, that
ought to speak to every pastor that the Convention is a family affair,
if at all possible. Oh, to be sure, there were pastor friends. The sense
of being a part of something grand and wonderful was also present,
but it was different.

Aside from that there are memories of those other Conventions,
where we stayed, the friends we shared, and the excitement that
inheres in the Convention itself. During one of these we stayed in the
inner city at a nationally known hotel. Another Convention was in
progress and many of them stayed in this hotel. It was made up of
Jewish people. One evening when we were sitting up late, some of
these people came in from their meetings. As they looked at me, they
smiled as though they should know who I was. I laughed and told
my friends that they looked at me and thought I was one of their convention.

Just a few weeks ago, I saw a pastor in another state who said,
"Let me tell you when I first saw you. It was in 1947 at a ball game in
St. Louis, Missouri, where the St. Louis Browns played." I told him I
remembered the occasion very well. It had to be 1947 because I
remember that Lou Gehrig played in the game, and I could always

260

say afterwards that "I saw Lou Gehrig play."

This Convention was to be the largest of all the Conventions held in St. Louis. However, there were not as many as we had had in Dallas or in Atlanta. The tide was ebbing as over twenty-five thousand filled the facilities.

Adrian Rogers, our president, called the 130th session of the Southern Baptist Convention to order at 8:50 A.M. in the Cervantes Convention Center on Tuesday, June 16. The songs with which we began indicated a change of personnel. We sang "To Know Him and To Make Him Known," "Standing On the Promises," "No Never Alone," and "He Lives." Surely we did not sing every stanza.

There were the usual amenities. The registration secretary reported a beginning registration of 22,438 messengers. The final figure would be 25,607. He moved that these constitute the Convention, along with those later to be registered.

The theme of the Convention, according to the Program Committee, was "To Know Him . . . To Make Him Known," based on Philippians 3:10. This theme was interpreted for fifteen minutes each in three of the sessions under the themes "Know Him in Prayer," "Know Him Through the Word," and "Make Him Known."

With the report of the Program Committee, there were immediate motions to amend. One would have moved the report of the Foreign Mission Board before the election of officers. Another would have moved the report of the Peace Committee to Wednesday morning rather than Tuesday evening. The motions failed; the program was adopted as presented by the committee. The times for the president's address and the Convention sermon are, of course, sacred orders of business by the constitution. Other things would wait when those hours arrived.

The Governor of Missouri, John Ashcroft, welcomed messengers to the Convention and then concluded by singing "Thanks for Power."

After the announcement of committees, Manley Breasley of Texas presented the first of the theme interpretations. Then Harold Bennett, president of the Executive Committee, was recognized for its report and for the recommendations that were traditional at this point in our Conventions.

Here we had an interesting change. The first recommendation did not have to do with the Cooperative Program Budget Goal as usual, but immediately addressed itself to a matter of business. First,

there was a recommendation to recognize six new states as being
ready by reason of size and cooperation to have full representation
on the commissions and boards of the Convention.

Adopted without question, the second recommendation was
another Bylaw 16 amendment on the election of board members,
trustees, commissioners, or members of standing committees. At
every Convention we had been dealing with the machinery, trying to
fine tune our problems. This one dealt with such matters as serving
on only one board or one institution at a time. You could not nominate a fellow committee member or a member of the Committee on
Committees. No person could serve as a trustee who received part of
his salary directly or indirectly from one of the institutions and so on.
There was an amendment to change a single word. There was one to
remove certain words. These amendments were spoken to. One
amendment was declared out of order. All of this was to say that the
Convention finally adopted it as presented.

We had recommendations concerning standing committees and a
charter revision of the Executive Committee that expanded the possibility of its size. Finally, Recommendation 6 presented the Southern
Baptist Convention allocation budget. Without objection and without
amendment, it was adopted. It presented a goal of $140,000,000. The
seminaries were to receive $26,816,000. Southwestern Seminary was
to receive $7,855,949. This single appropriation represented 5.95
percent of the budget anticipated. We still could agree "to attempt
great things for God."

The report on our Bold Mission Thrust and Emphases for 1990-
2000 was a long document not read at this point but printed and in
the hands of the messengers. They were worthy goals. An amendment added "the call for each association to have a functioning network of intercessory prayer by 1995." It was adopted and the time
for the Executive Committee report had expired.

The time had come for introduction of business and resolutions.
As bylaws require, they could only be stated. Resolutions would be
read by the secretary as a name and the author of the resolution. For
example, he would say, "Mike Womack (TN)—"sex education in
schools." All of these motions and resolutions would outline the concerns of the messengers to the Convention, would often be offered by
the people whose names had previously appeared in minutes, and
had become a volume that no committee could have dealt with.

The Resolutions Committee and the Committee on Order of

Business would either recommend that they be referred to the appropriate agency, that they be ignored for reasons that the committees would assign, or that they would result in stated discussion periods in which the Convention could adopt. Three things were common to the procedure. There were too many instances in which a motion to extend the time had to be made. There were always motions to amend. There were always the motions to call the previous question, which was meant to cut off debate. In the midst of this, the Convention expressed itself and was often reminded that it could express only itself in the time of its decision. At the first opportunity there were ten individual motions and twenty-seven resolutions.

At exactly the time originally determined, Adrian Rogers delivered the president's address. Prior to the address Mrs. Rogers sang "The Carpenter Is Still Building Houses Today."

We began the afternoon session just where we left off in the morning, a period of business and resolutions. There were a dozen motions and an equal number of resolutions announced. The Committee on Boards was allowed to make its report. There were some amendments offered, but all were overruled. There was a sense of the Convention moving toward that for which they had come.

This means that we have arrived at the election of officers. Even though it was a second term for our president, all year long we had been aware that it would be another political contest. Edwin Young of Texas nominated Adrian Rogers of Tennessee. Charles Redmond of Texas nominated Richard Jackson of Arizona. The comment upon our politics is not intended to be an evaluation of the men. It is sad indeed that we had spent a year, as we had years previously, wrapped up in a political process costing money, requiring energies that could well be directed elsewhere. In any case, these two were nominated, and with 23,327 votes cast Rogers was elected with fifty-nine percent of the vote.

Let us complete the election process because even in reflection, this appears to be the main thrust of the gathering. Two hours later, when the result of the ballot for president was made known, only 16,733 voted for first vice-president. Jack Stanton of Missouri, Dan Ireland of Alabama, Wallace Jones of Missouri, and Victor Kaneubbe of Oklahoma were all nominated. When the results of the ballot were made known Tuesday evening, the number of messengers had shrunk to 11,721. Stanton was elected.

Nominations for second vice-president were received. There was an interesting little by-play in this election. The year before, Mike Johnson had nominated himself for one of the major offices. I said in recounting that Convention that we all laughed and had a real sense of sympathy for him. In fact 2,500 people voted for him. In this Convention, as we elected a second vice-president, he decided to try it again. He nominated himself and received 327 votes. We are tolerant only to a degree. Nominated for second vice-president were Ray Roberts of North Carolina, James Flamming of Virginia, Victor Kaneubbe of Oklahoma, and Jolene Rogers of Oklahoma. A run-off was necessary, and the minutes record that 7,075 voted, with Victor Kaneubbe becoming elected.

The preceding gives much attention to the elections. Yet the denomination had focused its attention on this process, and the attendance indicated that this was priority. The saddest thing about the whole matter to me was a misperception of the office of president of the Convention. It had become, in the minds of the messengers at least, a place of power. There is no such place in Baptist polity. Until we remember this we will not correct our problems.

Actually, the main business of the Convention is to hear reports from its agencies and to make known to those agencies and boards the desires and the goals of the Convention. Wednesday we were to hear from the seminaries. Again these were ten-minute periods from institutions involved in world evangelism. Roy L. Honeycutt, president, reported for Southern Baptist Theological Seminary. There followed the report of the Education Commission. Then Russell Dilday, president, reported for Southwestern Seminary. In every case time was left for questions to be asked, and in most cases there was a question or two, apparently answered satisfactorily.

The Christian Life Commission made its report. President Landrum Leavell of New Orleans Seminary presented its report. Somebody asked a question about Seminary Extension credit to which Dr. Leavell responded. President Crews of Golden Gate Seminary also made a report after other business had been transacted.

When the time for the Convention sermon arrived on Wednesday morning, Jerry Vines of Florida preached on "A Baptist and His Bible" (2 Tim. 3:14-4:13).

The first evenings of the Convention were usually designated for missions. Wednesday evening, the Home Mission Board presented its report. The board's recently elected President, Larry L. Lewis, of

Georgia, brought a message on "Winning America to Christ." The Sunday School Board had been given time earlier in the evening for its report. It was one that focused, as others, upon evangelism, reaching unsaved people for Christ and for Bible study.

The Resolutions Committee began to make their recommendations on Thursday morning. This included one on "integrity in Stewardship," another on "the 75th Anniversary of the Romanian Baptist Convention," and like resolutions. A very interesting motion on Thursday morning was to the effect "that the messengers vote on the remaining resolutions as a group." The motion failed, but it was evident that the messengers were pretty well tired of their activities.

Following that, however, there was much discussion and many amendments offered and rejected on a resolution on "honor for full-time homemakers." For the past several Conventions the place of woman in the home, in the church, in the denomination, and in the nation had been a subject of discussion. It was evident that this represented an increasingly sensitive nerve on the conscience of Southern Baptists.

The usual subjects for resolution were presented. Gambling, abortion, AIDS, sex education, and textbook censorship—all of these came into focus. Before he was through, Chairman Tom Melzoni of Tennessee had a long list of motions on which the committee had taken no action. While the previous motion on the matter had failed, Chairman Melzoni moved that all remaining resolutions be adopted. The motion passed. Ophelia Humphrey of Texas very properly raised a point of order with reference to the action, but her point was ruled not well taken. The Convention was well under control and through with its work.

In the morning session also, the Southeastern Seminary report was presented by President Randall Lolley. The minutes say that Lolley "spoke optimistically concerning reconciliation potentially growing out of the Peace Committee report." Midwestern Seminary reported through President Milton Ferguson.

My long-standing interest in Canadian Baptists was encouraged when a report spoke of the special opportunity and challenge in Eastern Canada and of the status of the new seminary in Western Canada. Bertha Smith, retired missionary now ninety-nine years of age, was greeted by messengers with warm applause and standing. The morning session was to be concluded by an address by the internationally renowned evangelist Billy Graham of North Carolina. We were at our best as we sang prior to the message "At The Cross," "At

Calvary," "The Old Rugged Cross," and "How Great Thou Art."

The Convention has not been adequately reported until we talk about the matters that were at the heart of the motions, representing the real interest of the messengers. A motion deplored the fact that we had been forced to divert hundreds of thousands of Cooperative Program mission dollars into the courts. You will recognize that this referred to a suit filed against the Convention and defended by us. Another motion asked that the Foreign Mission Board be directed to reinstate the policy "requiring all overseas missionary personnel to have received training at a Southern Baptist owned and operated Seminary."

Someone wanted the Convention to meet every other year rather than annually. Another wanted us to reconsider the basis on which the number of messengers from a church is determined.

A motion would have required a committee of ten persons to study the formula for the distribution of Cooperative Funds to our six seminaries in order to determine the most equitable and appropriate distribution. This motion was referred to the Executive Committee and, of course, had a very personal interest for me. The formula, when adopted many years earlier, had represented a great forward step in this matter. It also left the largest seminary out at the extreme. There was no Cooperative Program money for the last thousand of our students with the largest enrollment of any seminary anywhere.

There was a motion that no session of the Southern Baptist Convention be held without a display of an American flag and the Christian flag. There was a motion that our Southern Baptist seminaries and colleges charge full-tuition costs for all non-Southern Baptist students. There was one that the Executive Committee investigate the balance, integrity, honesty, and partisan politics of the Baptist Press, and so on. Someone even moved to request that the speakers on the program of the Convention refrain from comments and actions which demeaned persons of the black race. Of course, none of us would agree that such remarks were made.

Then what of this Convention? My interpretation of the Convention must be obvious in the reflections. Saddest of all, like the prophet of old, we cry "Peace, Peace," when there is no peace. Many nice things were said in introducing various people. We maintained the appearance of fellowship in Christ, yet our absorption in power and in politics could have no theological justification.

ℐouthern ℬaptist ℭonvention

JUNE 14-16

1988

SAN ANTONIO ALWAYS RANKED HIGH AS A PREFERRED CONVENTION CITY IN OUR FAMILY. WE HAD BEEN THERE many times as messengers to the Texas Baptist Convention, but this was only the second Southern Baptist Convention. In truth, I had wondered why we had not met earlier, aside from the fact the Convention facilities had been considered inadequate. It was one of those Conventions where you would surely want to bring your family, if possible. There was the Alamo which was always worth a visit. Not that it was only a sacred place for Texans, but actually it held a disturbing place in American history. There was the River Walk where you saw everybody, could eat most any kind of food, and in general pass some time as a tourist that perhaps you ought to be spending at the Convention.

There was a special touch to this Convention for us. Rebekah, our missionary daughter, who was on furlough, was with us. In fact, she was with us on business. The Foreign Mission Board was to meet and had invited her to appear in behalf of the new relationship that had been established with the Christian Medical College in Vellore, India. Under this arrangement the Vellore institution, Christian, historical, and successful, would provide hands-off management policies for the Bangalore Hospital. The Foreign Mission Board would continue to own the hospital. Rebekah, as the surviving missionary surgeon, would be there as a member of that board, and it was hoped that the contribution made by the Vellore Hospital would strengthen the program and the personnel of the institution.

Interestingly enough, when the other Southern Baptist Convention met in San Antonio in 1942, we had our two sons with us. They were just small boys and we stayed in the Saint Anthony

268   A MESSENGER'S MEMOIRS

Hotel, a magnificent institution in that year. I laughed to myself when I remembered that the room in the hotel cost us $8.00 a night in 1942 and that I thought that we were just about risking everything on that kind of luxury. So San Antonio had a family flavor as we met.

President Adrian Rogers called the Convention to order at 8:50 A.M., on Tuesday, June 14. Often in these Convention reflections, I have mentioned the special atmosphere that attends the formal opening of the Convention. The secretary of the Convention recognized 29,987 messengers as having presently enrolled, and made the formal motion that they constitute the Convention, together with those who would come with credentials and register later. With all of this, we were under way.

Tom Elliff of Oklahoma, who was serving as chairman of the Committee on Order of Business, presented the suggested program which was adopted. He also made the motion that the messengers be limited to three minutes in discussing any item of business.

After the announcement of committees, the welcome address by the mayor, and a response, the Executive Committee report was made the first order of business. In all of the time assigned to them, they succeeded in making three recommendations. The first of these recommended the Convention Cooperative Program allocation budget. For 1988-89, the recommended amount was $145,600,000. What a day of prosperity had come to us! Usually this particular recommendation was adopted without discussion, even though it proved always to be one of the most important things we did.

This time, however, when the motion to adopt the budget was made, there was a motion to amend that would have included the Baptist Joint Committee in the amount of $67,457; this was to be taken from money previously designated for a lawsuit contingency. At least the motion exposed what was at that moment the most tender nerve of our relationships. The Baptist Joint Committee had been excluded from our program because of certain positions taken in certain relationships to other denominations. This was intensely controversial and remains that to a great extent. The discussions for and against immediately followed, and much of the time was spent just at this point. The matter would recur in the course of the Convention. The motion was defeated, and the Cooperative Program allocation budget for the next year was adopted.

Another matter of dissatisfaction and concern among the messengers was found in the next motion, namely, to adopt a new

Southern Baptist Convention Bylaw 11, on "parliamentary authority and parliamentarians." Previously, this bylaw had simply stated that we would use *Robert's Rules of Order* (latest revised edition). This new bylaw would simply authorize that which was already taking place, the employment of a chief parliamentarian and the appointment of assistant parliamentarian as needed. In order to protect the present appointment, there was a final provision in the amendment that the chief parliamentarian must be certified by the American Institute of Parliamentarians. The man serving in that capacity even then, by presidential appointment, was not a Baptist. It is still a moot question whether the policy followed was worthwhile.

The time having expired for the Executive Committee, the president announced the time for introduction of business and resolutions. Sixty motions and resolutions were immediately presented to the Convention. All but ten of these were open motions. The provision was that they must be referred to the Committee on Order of Business and any resolutions to the Resolutions Committee.

As long as I have been going to Conventions, it is always amazing to me what the messengers have on their minds as evidenced by these motions. So many times, the motion does not really indicate the basic concern of the messenger. In this Convention, there were perhaps a hundred of these motions and resolutions, very few of which we will refer to. Ten of the initial sixty were simply mentioned on the closing day of the Convention as not acted on by the committees. There was a motion made, with some anger, that this Convention replace the eight members of the Public Affairs Committee who voted to dissolve ties with the Baptist Joint Committee on Public Affairs and so forth. The motion was defeated. An attempt was made to amend the Southern Baptist Convention bylaws to provide that a president should be elected for a two-year term and not allowed to succeed himself.

There was one motion to define a cooperating Baptist church in terms of amount given to the Cooperative Program over a given period. Sadly enough, many of the motions reflected the divisions and unhappiness that prevailed in the Convention. When that is said in this discussion, it ought also be remarked that the financial support of the Convention and its mission continued by the churches.

The president's address given by President Rogers to conclude that first morning session was filled to overflowing.

It should be noted just here that the theme of the Convention was

"Pour Out Revival . . . O Lord, Revive Thy Work" (Hab. 3:2). Messages, which interpreted the theme of the Convention, included "Pour Out Revival in My Heart" by Roy Fish; one called "Revival in My Home" by Ruffin Snow; "Revival on the Household of Faith" by O. D. Shook; and "Revival in My Homeland" by Bobby Welch. The messages were all good and encouraging.

The opening business session on Tuesday afternoon brought an additional flood of motions and individual concerns. Not for the first time, I observed there was one that instructed the Committee on Order of Business to place some women in the program. There were recurring motions aimed at the "Public Affairs Committee." There were the motions that amended bylaws, defined programs, and in general indicated attempts on the part of the agencies and of the Convention to adapt to the ever-increasing size. One lengthy adoption was a "Restated Charter of the Executive Committee of the Southern Baptist Convention."

There was the charter amendment adopted for the Annuity Board, the Southern Baptist Brotherhood Commission, Southern Baptist Foundation, the Stewardship Commission, and the Annuity Board. The Christian Life Commission program statement was revised. The Home Mission Board's programs were restated at length. Most of these could be regarded as housekeeping.

The messengers were, evidently, primarily interested in the election of officers. Early in the afternoon session, it was announced that nominating speeches for president should be made. Among the four nominated, it amused the Convention that Anis Shorrosh nominated himself, perfectly legal and quite in order, if a man so desired. In this first election with 32,436 messengers, 31,291 voted (96.47 percent). Jerry Vines was elected president with 15,804 votes (50.53 percent). Just at the close of the afternoon session, nominations for first vice-president were made. Interestingly, within two hours many of the messengers had left. There were 21,302 votes (65.56 percent) cast for first vice-president. Of this number, Darrell Robinson of Alabama was elected with 59.46 percent of the vote.

Tuesday evening Charles Fuller, my personal friend and pastor of the First Baptist Church, Roanoke, Virginia, reported for the Peace Committee. Among these members of the committee were those whom I had counted close friends through the years, yet from the first it was my conviction that Baptists do not make peace with a committee. This final report deserves some quotations:

"We deplore the divisive political activities and counter activities by all sides this past year. We would observe that the conscious disregard of the political recommendations of the Convention-adopted Peace Committee Report has contributed to the escalation of conflict among us.

"We recognize that many Southern Baptists have firmly held convictions on all sides of the spectrum that are not going to change.

"We believe that some things need to be corrected and that the momentum for such correction is underway."

The committee followed with a recommendation that it be discharged; this was passed and the committee commended. History cast its own verdict upon the process.

Tuesday evening was given to the report of the Home Mission Board, and Wednesday evening to the report of the Foreign Mission Board. These reports were printed but no printed page could quite give the inspiration that we always received from the mission hours. In the midst of our storms, the Convention stayed focused upon taking the gospel to the whole world. As reflected in these discussions, the marvel of the Cooperative Program finds its explanation in the inspiration of our Southern Baptist determination to be witnesses in this world.

As usual there was no Wednesday afternoon session in recognition of all of the seminary luncheons and other meetings. It was also an opportunity for the messengers to see San Antonio with its historical significance.

The seminaries reported on Thursday morning, each one of them being given ten minutes for report. The most that could be done by any one of them would be simply to reaffirm our commitment to those things which Southern Baptists believed, to the objectives which we had surely adopted, and to the assurance to the Convention that they were true in their stewardship. Of course, I am always present when the seminaries make their reports. The details with which they put the reports in the minutes are worth the reading of every Southern Baptist. It is to be observed that at this San Antonio Convention in 1988 the enrollment of the seminaries, which had been showing steady increase, finally peaked.

The seminary enrollments had two emphases. There was always the "head count." The enrollment of any educational institution is difficult to determine at that point. There was also the more accurate statement of enrollment that talked about the "full time equivalent,"

F.T.E., of each seminary. Whereas Southwestern reported over five thousand students during the year past, they reported that in terms of full-time students, this amounted to just under four thousand. Having said that, it should be added that Southern Baptist seminaries remain the wonder of the American theological seminary scene. Our smallest seminary would be almost equivalent to the largest of these. Our largest seminaries are, of course, the unlike. This means for us, in terms of our commitment, that God continues to call men and women to the ministries of our churches and of our mission causes.

When the Convention finally adjourned on Thursday afternoon, we had registered 32,727 messengers. This was a retreat from that 45,000-plus that we had registered in Dallas. Hopefully, it recognized that which the Peace Committee had affirmed, that "healing has begun."

On a personal note, the Convention remained within our family circle a very special time. The Foreign Mission Board, in its session, had so wonderfully affirmed the Bangalore Hospital and the commission in which Rebekah was spending her life.

Las Vegas Convention Center • Las Vegas, Nevada

Robert Taylor

JUNE 13-15

1989

IT SEEMED A LONG TIME AGO THAT WE HAD FIRST HEARD LAS VEGAS, NEVADA, PRESENTED AS A SITE FOR THE MEETING of the Southern Baptist Convention. In the years since the introduction, it was an item brought up again at every Convention asking whether or not Southern Baptists ought to go to a city which was most famous for its gambling. Here we were, getting ready to go.

Only a few days before, I awoke one morning with a strange feeling about the Convention. All of those that had been a kind of inner circle in the years of attending the Conventions were not going to be there. Most of them were in heaven, and others were in such ill health that they could not go. I said to myself, "What is the reason for your going?" There would surely be a loneliness about it, even in the midst of the crowds. As we prepared to board the plane on Sunday morning, June 11, I had my obvious answer. It was made up of people going to the Southern Baptist Convention. The plane that seated almost three hundred people was full of folks I knew; many of them I had known for a long time. The fellowship, which makes the Convention, had already begun its work.

The pilot asked us to fasten our seatbelts and prepare for a landing in Las Vegas. Sitting where I could look out the window, I realized that we were within a hundred feet of the runway. Suddenly, I felt the pilot give power to the motors, and I realized that he was trying to abort the landing. Gradually, we began to pull out of the landing pattern. The pilot came on the intercom to say, "A plane in front of us failed to clear the runway. We have pulled up and we must go around and land again." There was nervous laughter that followed. Most of us understood quite well, but it was a tight moment. It took twenty-five minutes for us to make a complete circle and then come in for landing. I wondered if this was a prophecy of the Convention.

Goldia and I attended the Woman's Missionary Union meeting on Sunday evening and then again on Monday evening. What fine programs the Woman's Missionary Union always presents! It was Carolyn Weatherford's last convention. She was retiring and was being married shortly. There were two noteworthy addresses. One was by Wanda Fort, as she described their missionary family and how God had wrought in the lives of their five sons. It was a thrilling story. The other address was by our friends Jack and Avah Shelby, telling of their work in Cooperative Services International, which brings a witness to countries otherwise not accessible.

The Convention itself was called to order on Tuesday morning at 9:00 by President Jerry Vines. It was reported that at 9:07 A.M., registration was 18,085. The newspaper had been predicting a limit of sixteen thousand in attendance. John McKay led the Convention in the opening singing. For a lifetime, I had been accustomed to the Convention beginning by singing "All hail the power of Jesus' name, Let angels prostrate fall." This time the Convention began with choruses: "This is the Day" and "I Have the Joy, Joy, Joy, Joy Down in My Heart." I must confess, it was a bit of a letdown.

The Convention had been prepared for an evangelistic effort in Las Vegas. It was a thrilling moment to report at the beginning that on the previous Saturday, fifty thousand homes had been visited and witness had been given, and that there had been almost four hundred professions of faith. Perhaps the impact really was there. The theme of the Convention was "Going, Weeping, Sowing, Reaping," taken from Psalm 126:6. This was the text from which Jerry Vines preached as he brought his presidential address at 11:25 A.M. It was a fine sermon.

It should be noted here that Vines had evidently asked the heads of the agencies, in bringing their report, to share with the Convention their latest personal soul-winning effort. That could have been a difficult assignment. Vines indicated that he kept his own personal record of witnessing, and he shared one or two of his experiences.

The election of officers at 2:30 P.M. had become the focal point of the Convention. It was in this that the great division in the Convention seemed to be most clearly seen. Danny Vestal of Georgia had made a determined bid for the presidency. Vines was being presented for a second term. The results should not have been a surprise. There were 10,700 votes for Vines and over 8,200 votes for Vestal. It was interesting that between 9:07 A.M. and 2:45 P.M. the registration had exceeded twenty thousand. Both the Sunday School Board and the Foreign Mission Board reports were given on Tuesday evening. Even though there had been many previous statements about declining receipts, the actual reports indicated a worthy stewardship for our Southern Baptist people.

Wednesday morning there were reports again from the agencies including two of the seminaries. The morning session concluded with the Convention sermon by Morris Chapman of Wichita Falls, Texas. Wednesday noon the seminaries were having their alumni luncheons. John Seelig was among six who was recognized as distinguished alumnus of the seminary. Very few could have been as deserving of this award as he.

I was rebuked for any thought that I might have had about being alone at the Convention. Goldia and I agreed that never had so many people offered so many wonderful expressions of involvement with us, or of appreciation for some ministry by which they had been blessed, and by a sense of sharing a multitude of people. It was really overwhelming.

I also attended the Home Mission Board/Foreign Mission Board reception on Wednesday afternoon. Half of the missionaries who were home on furlough and present for the occasion were graduates of Southwestern.

Thursday morning had been scheduled as a reporting time for four of the seminaries. There would also be an afternoon session, but it was determined it was a possibility that the Convention could be finished by noon, so the schedule was changed. The program was crowded, and in the midst of it, both Roy Honeycutt and Russell Dilday did a fine job. The change of schedule caused me to miss the New Orleans Seminary report.

In summary, the Convention revealed the depth of the division that was present. I was confirmed again in the judgment that it was a political division, a seeking after power and place. Asked for assessment by many, I simply said, "We have really lost nothing in this session. I meant by way of those of us so committed to the Convention, to the denomination, and its programs. The fact that the fundamentalist faction is in control is obvious. We pick up from here, believing that God will bring another day to our Baptist life."

Louisiana Superdome • New Orleans, Louisiana

JUNE 12-14

1990

THIS WAS TO BE OUR FOURTH SOUTHERN BAPTIST CONVENTION MEETING IN NEW ORLEANS. IN 1937, IN the early years of ministry, we had attended an exciting Convention there. We were accompanied by Mrs. W. G. Hodges, our WMU president, and I was pastor of the First Baptist Church in Malvern, Arkansas. In 1969, I had surely made the adjustments from being a pastor who was attending the Convention to being a denominational employee attending the Convention on business. This did not mean that the Convention had lost its luster, but that the perspective and the relationship was certainly different. In 1982, when we returned to New Orleans, Rebekah accompanied us, and that added to that Convention.

New Orleans has always been a fascinating city to visit. I still remember my amazement that people are buried above ground because the city is below sea level. As our plane swooped down on New Orleans, I saw the lock from Lake Pontchartrain that drains water from the city. I remembered an engagement with the First Baptist Church, a church long pastored by J. D. Grey, my seminary classmate and friend. Our New Orleans Baptist Theological Seminary is also located there. All of this added to our anticipation.

We travelled by plane this time, on Sunday morning. When my pastor had asked me about my travel plans, I explained to him that retired pastors could travel on Sunday morning. Without previous agreement, it turned out that Dr. and Mrs. James Coggin had the same plane schedule, both going and returning. Our friendship is so close that it resulted in attending the Convention together.

On a beautiful Sunday morning, we set out on the Convention journey. As in all of these years, there were Convention people all around us. This was true the other years and, in a sense, our plane became the "Convention plane." The Convention headquarters was in the Hyatt Regency Hotel, and our room on the sixteenth floor looked out over the city.

There was a difference about this Convention. It could have been the gathering of the Republicans and the Democrats. The controversy that had plagued this Convention for a dozen years seemed to be reaching its apex. The methods on both sides were largely the same. Played up by the media, it was Morris Chapman and the Fundamentalists and Daniel Vestal and the Moderates. That was certainly a tragedy to me.

We went to the WMU Convention on Sunday evening. It was a magnificent time, a real inspiration. The congregation was so reverent, the commitment was so evident, the music was so uplifting, that it became a high point in the Convention. Joanne Goetcher did well as she interpreted the sense of the Convention.

The Convention proper began Tuesday morning at 8:30 A.M. The Convention theme was "The Churches: Edified . . . Multiplied" (Acts 9:31). The crowds were enormous, but this time the place of meeting was large enough. The Superdome in New Orleans is said to seat seventy thousand people. The forty-five thousand Southern Baptists there could make a comfortable crowd.

There were two items of burning interest from the previous days' publicity. For two years now, there had been a determined effort to sever the ties of the Convention with the Baptist Joint Committee on Public Affairs. Our relationship to that committee, which is interdenominational, was through a Convention committee called the Public Affairs Committee. They were Southern Baptist representatives on the subject of religious liberty.

Almost immediately, the Executive Committee of the Convention recommended that we transfer the program of the Public Affairs Committee to the Christian Life Commission. Immediately there was an amendment offered that preserved the status quo. The ballot vote virtually settled the matter. By a vote of 14,788 to 12,629, the responsibility would be transferred and the appropriation to the Baptist Joint Committee would later be almost deleted.

All of this was a prelude. The afternoon session opened in feverish excitement. Phil Lineberger nominated Vestal. John Bisagno nominated Chapman. The election was expected to be very close. When the results of the ballot were announced, it showed Daniel Vestal with 15,753 votes and Morris Chapman with 21,471. It was decisive; the fundamentalists were in full control. The Convention was over, or was it?

If I were to describe this Convention in one paragraph, it would be with the subject, "The Death of a Convention." Notice that I did not say "The Death of the Southern Baptist Convention." In the opening moments of the Convention on Tuesday morning, the messengers registered totaled 31,856. By the time for the election of the president, the total votes cast were 37,224. An hour and a half later on Tuesday afternoon, with the nominations for first vice-president having been made, the ballot cast totalled 27,036. In less than two hours, we had lost ten thousand messengers. On Tuesday evening there was a ballot cast for second vice-president. The total ballots cast were 9,932. Where had the Convention gone? Wednesday morning was to conclude with the Convention sermon. At the peak of the morning, it also included the elections for recording secretary and registration secretary. Even then, there were 18,290 ballots cast, and more than half of the messengers had disappeared.

Thursday morning, I went to the session to hear the report of the New Orleans Seminary. I discovered that the report had been made more than an hour ahead of schedule, and that there were not enough messengers in attendance to transact business. In fact, it looked like there was just a hand full of people there, perhaps 1,500. It was the saddest moment for me in this Convention. What had happened to us, indeed?

There are more details that ought to be placed in this record of the Convention. The music had always been an anticipation for me. In this Convention, the old hymns were absent, reflecting the contemporary churches. We began with choruses which were largely sung throughout the Convention. I noted that the people around me knew them. Evidently they had been singing them in their churches.

The applause and the irreverence were almost unbearable against my background. There was a man behind us who whistled and screamed. He stomped his feet and groaned in response to nearly everything that was said. When his side prevailed, and it usually did, it was deafening. Applause was present on every motion.

The Wednesday morning session included the reports of four of our seminaries, including Southwestern. Of course, I was there. The crowd that was there responded warmly to Southern Seminary and also to Southwestern. These two had been in the headlines with their own problems. It seemed to me that most of the people had come to affirm the seminaries. However, there were questions from the critics.

There was a facet of the Convention that seemed to ever increase for Goldia and me. At every meal, and on every hand there were those who stopped us to tell us how much they loved the seminary, how grateful they were for us, and what a part in their ministry our relationship had been. It was overwhelming, humbling, and wonderfully gratifying. If it had only been that in the Convention, it would have been another wonderful experience for us.

The Southwestern luncheon is always a high point. This time there were more than a thousand people present. Jay Chance, the new director of development and vice-president, was introduced and was warmly received. He responded in the finest fashion and was entirely competent in it all.

On Tuesday evening Goldia and I had dinner with James and Carolyn Coggin in the revolving restaurant atop the Hyatt Regency. The view of the Mississippi River and the City of New Orleans in the gathering twilight was just breathtaking. Everything we had felt about New Orleans previously at the conventions came back to us fresh in those moments. How grateful we are for that inner circle of friends across the years that made the Convention a special person-to-person reward.

There must be a summary of the Convention. On every hand after the presidential election, there were notes of gloom and despair. "What do we do now?" they were saying. I think we have learned that we are not meant to "fight fire with fire." That is not God's way, and it is not our Baptist people's way. I am totally unchanged in the conviction that we must simply press on. This is our world witness, our doctrinal conviction as Southern Baptists, and our commitment to His proclamation.

Foreign Missions Night on Wednesday was inspirational. There was a poignant moment for us. It had been planned as an appointment service, and was begun with a parade of flags. Then, there was finally the march of the thirty-four missionaries who were being appointed. There was one single girl marching in line in the midst of all of the couples. You know what that did to us. We had attended another appointment service in which there was a lone single girl. Wonderful are the ways of God and His patience with His people.

In a postscript, in the contest for first vice-president, James Flamming nominated Carolyn Weatherford Crumpler and Tom Elliff nominated Douglas Knapp. The results were, Weatherford with 10,688 votes, and Douglas Knapp who was a retired missionary, with 16,348 votes, for a total of 27,036. For second vice-president, Fred Lowery of Louisiana was elected. The total votes cast were 9,932. On Wednesday, when the secretaries were elected, Martin Bradley, a longtime recording secretary, was suddenly defeated; and David Atchison of Tennessee was elected with a vote of 9,026 to 8,044. Lee Porter was continued as registration secretary.

Georgia World Congress Center • Atlanta, Georgia

[signature: Robert Taylor]

JUNE 4-6
1991

ATLANTA HAD ALWAYS BEEN CONSIDERED
A GOOD CONVENTION CITY BY ME.
REPLETE WITH HISTORY, GOOD HOTELS,
the business hub of the Southeastern United States, it offered conveniences to the messengers which were not always available in some other cities. In spite of that, there were cities where the Convention had met more often. Southern Baptists had been to Atlanta for their session eight times in the 146 years of their life. In 1879, Dr. James P. Boyce was president of the Convention, and with 313 delegates present, the Convention met for the first time in Atlanta.

When we were in attendance at the last Convention in 1986, I remember putting in my recollections about the Convention the fact that for the first time (and the last time) our hotel had overbooked and there was no room for us. We were sent to a place previously arranged.

This time, however, we were staying at the Omni Hotel right across the street from the Convention. This is always a plus in attending the Convention. You can come and go at your physical pleasure.

The theme of the Convention was "Jesus . . . There's Power in His Name." The Scripture was "Thou shalt call his name Jesus: for he shall save his people from their sins" (Matthew 1:21).

President Morris H. Chapman of Texas called the Convention to order on Tuesday morning, June 4, 1991, at 8:45 A.M., in the World Congress Center in Atlanta, Georgia. After the usual preliminaries, Lee Porter, registration secretary, was recognized. He reported that as of that hour, 17,536 messengers had been certified. He moved that these be recognized as the Convention in session together with those properly certified who are yet to come. The final enrollment would turn out to be 23,465. This was quite a contrast to the 40,900-plus of 1986.

All through the Convention, there was a phrase, "led the Convention in singing a medley of Gospel songs and choruses." Perhaps I am simply reflecting my failure to join the generation. For me the inspiration was missing. There were two exceptions. At one point in the Convention, we sang "Great Is Thy Faithfulness," and in the final moments of the Convention we sang "Amazing Grace." Hopefully we had made progress and arrived.

The Committee on Order of Business presented their report, and I noted that things had changed. Most of the agencies of the Convention had been given ten minutes for their report, three minutes of which had to be open to questions from the floor, if desired.

We heard the report of the Radio and Television Commission. Then on this first morning the report of our Home Mission Board was given ten minutes. With our mission orientation, this was a shock.

The Executive Committee was recognized for an hour of their report and recommendations. (According to our constitution, the actions of the Executive Committee in the year between must be reviewed by the Convention). Actually, most of their work and reporting had to do with structural changes which in most cases were minor. Recommendation 5 had to do with bylaw change of the Standing Committee. Recommendation 6 was the Christian Life Commission charter amendment. Not until Recommendation 1 did we receive the Cooperative Program Allocation Budget. It recommended $140,710,282 to our basic Cooperative Program operating budget.

Recommendation 2 was the one that messengers had been waiting for. An amendment was offered to reduce the amount designated for the Baptist Joint Committee on Public Affairs from $50,000 to nothing. There were amendments. There was heated discussion. It was obvious that at last, this problem that had been troubling previous Conventions was coming to a conclusion. The motion to amend prevailed and the reduction was adopted. The vote was 6,872 for deletion; 6,101 opposed. Here we were split almost down the middle.

The time for the Executive Committee having expired, business and resolutions became the order. I will not attempt to list the names or the concerns of the messengers. There were perhaps more than fifty motions made, some of them relatively frivolous. Later, when the Committee on Order of Business came back to report how they dealt with these motions, most of them were referred to agencies or institutions under constitutional bylaws.

There was one motion concerning Free-Masonry and a request that someone other than the Home Mission Board investigate it. Someone else had a motion concerning salary and benefits, that upon leaving the employment of Southern Baptist Convention agencies, our agencies should not provide more than six months' salary and benefits. Here, also, previous unhappiness surfaced.

When the time for election came on Tuesday afternoon, usually the crisis hour of our Conventions, there was little interest as manifested by the size of the vote. At least it was affirmative in that President Chapman was reelected by acclamation. Nelson Price was elected first vice-president by acclamation. Tuesday evening there were two nominations for second vice-president which resulted in Ed Harrison being elected with 2,633 votes (58.09 percent of the ballot.) Messengers cast a total of 4,533 votes in a Convention that was to be reported as the sixth largest in our history with 23,000-plus registered.

Tuesday afternoon had brought most of the concluding Executive Committee recommendations, which included charter amendments for the Foreign Mission Board, Home Mission Board, and Brotherhood Commission.

It at least sounded hopeful when they announced the meeting site of the Convention for 2000 would be Orlando, Florida.

There were program revisions for the Sunday School Board and for the Stewardship Commission. A rather lengthy charter change for New Orleans Seminary was approved by the Convention. The size of our operation was underlined when the Committee on Nominations presented their report, which included all of the trustees and directors for the agencies and institutions of the Convention. There seemed to be little disposition to seek to amend the report.

It should be noted that on Tuesday evening, a full report on Bold Mission Thrust was given. The evening was concluded with an hour for the Foreign Mission Board. It was a dramatic report made up of video presentations, a musical/dramatic interpretation of "People Need the Lord," missionary testimonies, and a closing message by Keith Parks.

In reporting Wednesday morning, the president simply said that the election of remaining officers must be delayed for lack of a quorum.

Then the morning was given to the six seminaries. There is a note to be added. When the election did take place that morning for the office of registration secretary, Lee Porter, who had long been the secretary, about whom there was some dissatisfaction, was nominated together with James W. Richards. A ballot was taken that resulted in Porter being reelected with 4,523 votes (50.09 percent), Richards having received 4,509 votes. Messengers totaled 9,032 on a Wednesday morning when we had registered 23,000 messengers.

The Resolutions Committee began their reports. Resolutions addressed the subjects of usual concern to messengers. Abortion, beverage alcohol, and immoral behavior all received the attention of the messengers.

This Convention, unlike others, had dedicated Wednesday evening as a period of "A Fresh Encounter with God." The president of the Convention had insisted that the evening be set aside with prayer for spiritual awakening during the Convention.

The Convention concluded on Thursday morning with the usual housekeeping items that needed attending to. There were resolutions still to be presented to the Convention. Finally, a motion was made that we adopt the remaining resolutions and the balance of time allotted for the business session be used for corporate worship, prayer, and praise to the Lord. The minutes record, "A vote was taken and the motion passed."

The Radio and Television Commission presented the "Baptist Hour" Fiftieth Anniversary. It was personal to me when Dr. Paul Stevens, president (1953-1979), was presented to the Convention. Before the closing prayer this is the recorded item: "The Honorable George Herbert Walker Bush, President of the United States who was welcomed by Harold C. Bennett and introduced by Morris H. Chapman, spoke to the Convention."

In summary, there was a lethargy about the Convention that disappointed. Perhaps it was only a personal reflection, but I felt that the Convention had settled into fixed positions. The few votes that had a division emphasis were almost exactly even. With all of that, for those of us who longest had seen God at work in the life of Southern Baptists, there were many evidences that He had not turned us loose. We enjoyed Atlanta and always enjoyed a fellowship with some of the finest people on this earth.

Hoosier Dome • Indianapolis, Indiana

JUNE 9-11
1992

EVEN THOUGH THE CONVENTION IN INDIANAPOLIS HAD BEEN LISTED AS A FUTURE CONVENTION SITE FOR FOUR or five years, it did seem a little strange to be on the way there for the Convention. Of course, place had never been primary in the decision. It was Convention time. Every pastor, denominational worker, layperson who could do so would find the Convention a privilege.

President Morris Chapman called the Convention to order on Tuesday morning, June 9, at 8:30. Even at the beginning, there were two things I counted noteworthy. According to the minutes, the associate music director "led messengers in singing a medley of Gospel songs and choruses." Where was "All Hail the Power of Jesus' Name?"

Morris Chapman reported that "no church that endorses homosexuality has asked to be seated at this Convention." That seemed a little strange for a way to begin.

The Convention registration secretary reported that 15,342 messengers had been certified as regularly approved by the churches, and moved that the Convention be constituted of these messengers and others who would be approved later. The final total would amount to 17,956. Not since Kansas City in 1984, with 17,101 present, had our attendance been that low. Reflections suggest that the change of leadership had been enough to finally establish itself.

The theme of the Convention was "Bold Believers in a Broken World." The scripture was "for the perfecting of the saints, for the work of the ministry, for the edifying of the body of Christ" (Eph. 4:12).

The order of business was adopted, and our president introduced the Honorable James Danforth Quayle, Vice-President of the United

285

States, who spoke on moral and family values. This was a special
moment. This was Quayle's home state, and the message he brought
was extremely worthwhile.

The Executive Committee was recognized and began its report
with a recommendation for the Cooperative Program allocation budget. The motion to adopt it was unopposed. The 1992-1993 budget of
$140,710,282 was approved. It represented a decrease of less than one
percent (0.36 percent). The basic allocation budget was established as
a priority. All Cooperative Program receipts over this basic budget
were to be allocated equally to the capital needs budget and program
advance. It should be said that the budget had been given promotion
and publicity in our denominational press, and the adoption without
objection was a statement that we were willing to work together in
the main thing.

Recommendation 3 was a bylaw amendment. It was to provide a
vehicle for removing from office for "excessive, unexcused absences"
any member of our boards, and to that degree was a first.
Recommendation 4 called for "amendments to and restatement of
the Articles of Incorporation of Southern Seminary." It was a long
document, not read and adopted without objection.

Recommendation 5, adopted without debate, simply said, "The
Executive Committee of the Southern Baptist Convention recom-
mends that the Southern Baptist Convention terminate the
Convention's participation in the Baptist Joint Committee on Public
Affairs, without restricting the right of the Christian Life
Commission of the Southern Baptist Convention to relate to the
Baptist Joint Committee on Public Affairs in any manner it may
deem appropriate." They followed this with a recommendation that
had to do with a capital needs item that was to be a continuing
debate for the next few Conventions. There was a motion to amend
Recommendation 6, which would have called for binding arbitration
on this matter, perhaps a very wise settlement, but the motion to
amend was rejected.

For several Conventions, the proceedings have reflected changes
of program statements for the various agencies and institutions of
the Convention. These were publicized in the denominational press,
printed in the materials for the day at the Convention, and, when
presented to the Convention, they were never read, just the attention
of the Convention called to them and a motion made to adopt. Most

Dan Quayle, Vice President of the United States, after speaking at the 1992 Southern Baptist Convention. Courtesy—Texas Baptist Historical Collection.

of us understood that these program statements were serious matters with the institutions and agencies themselves. The structure was changed. The areas of involvement were defined in each one of them.

In this Convention, at this first session the program statements for the Executive Committee, the Christian Life Commission, and Woman's Missionary Union were all made orders of business and adopted in less than ten minutes.

Information was received on the Bold Mission Thrust Directions 2000. This program, adopted in 1979, was supposed to keep the Convention focused upon our ultimate goal that every person in the world should hear about Jesus by the year 2000.

With the completion of these Executive Committee recommendations, the usual flood of motions were made representing the various interests of the messengers.

Of current interest were two motions on "limiting severance benefits." In the changes of leadership that had been taking place in the agencies, one of them had received a great deal of attention on generosity of the severance benefits.

There was a motion on Free-Masonry that was destined to be a matter of division and discussion for several years.

In the midst of this, Golden Gate Baptist Theological Seminary presented its report in the ten minutes assigned.

President Chapman closed the morning session with the president's address entitled "It's Time to Move."

In the afternoon session, the report of the Committee on Nominations was presented. There was a motion to amend by substituting one name for another, in this case, Eugene Rogers of Texas for Paul Pressler of Texas as a trustee of the Foreign Mission Board. Later, the motion was rejected.

There were resolutions of appreciation for Harold Bennett, Lloyd Elder, and Keith Parks.

Recommendation 17 introduced something new in Baptist polity. "The Southern Baptist Convention is a noncreedal association, whose standards are those embodied in God's Holy Scripture. The Scripture clearly and unequivocally declares that homosexuality is a sin against God." Two churches, the Pullen Memorial Baptist Church of Raleigh, North Carolina, and the Olin T. Binkley Memorial Church of Chapel Hill, North Carolina, were cited as teaching contrary to the Bible on human sexuality and were declared no longer in friendly cooperation with the Convention. There was no question about the seminary position on homosexual behavior, but the exclusion of churches from our Convention was a sober moment.

Early in the afternoon, nominations were received for president of the Convention. Four were nominated and when the ballot was announced, it was reported that 17,675 messengers voted, or ninety-one percent of the enrollment. Nelson Price of Georgia had 16.28 percent, Jess Moody of California had 21.66 percent, and Ed Young of Texas, 62.05 percent. Young was elected.

Nominations were received for first vice-president. Jay Strack of Texas was nominated and, without other nominations, was elected.

The president then proceeded to call for the election of second vice-president. Ballots were cast for Allen Spear of Illinois; Tom Moody of Tennessee; Joe Aulds of Louisiana; Benny King of Missouri; and Glenn Molette of Kentucky. The ballot was cast. When the results were announced on Tuesday evening, there was no clear majority. When they tried to have a run-off between Aulds and Molette, there was no quorum present, and the ballot could not be cast. When the session began on Wednesday morning, there was still no quorum, but by the middle of the morning the ballot was cast and Aulds was elected to serve during the year ahead.

The Committee on Resolutions reported on Wednesday morning. One resolution recognized the situation in Eastern Europe as favorable to the gospel. There were resolutions on "religion in public schools" and "maintaining trust with the Cooperative Program."

Wednesday afternoon was given to the messengers for seminary luncheons. The Committee on Order of Business had arranged for the seminaries to report separately, although the time was still a ten-minute slot on the program. God had continued to bless the institutions in their enrollment. The support of the Convention manifest in the Cooperative Program was an encouraging promise for the future.

Indianapolis proved to be a good place for the Convention in facilities and personal comfort. Baptist work in Indiana had achieved a vitality that all of us needed to be in contact with. Convention attendance was a disappointment, but as suggested in the outset, perhaps this reflected a more peaceful time in the Convention.

George R. Brown Convention Center • Houston, Texas

JUNE 15-17
1993

ANOTHER HOUSTON CONVENTION! AS INDICATED IN THE ACCOUNTS OF OTHER HOUSTON CONVENTIONS, THIS is a place of particular and personal involvement for me. The Convention first met in Houston in 1915. Of course, I was not there. The first Houston Convention I attended was in 1953, and we were seeking a president for the Southwestern Seminary. In 1958, I was the center of the eye of the storm, and I knew by that time that I was to be the president of Southwestern. Ten years later in 1968, we were back again. In 1979, there was a Convention which has been widely billed as a major turning-point to the right for our Convention. (I think the conclusion is inadequate.) Houston would not be just another Convention.

This time we flew to Houston instead of driving. The headquarters hotel was comfortable and adequate. A shuttle service had been established which ran every fifteen minutes directly to the auditorium. As far as the physical circumstances of the Convention, we were just fine.

The preliminaries were interesting. Sunday afternoon, I registered as a messenger. We heard Cal Thomas, a layman and columnist from Los Angeles, do a very fine work at the Pastor's Conference.

Monday, I visited the pre-Convention meeting of the Executive Committee. For so many years I had sat in on these sessions as an interested observer.

An anticipated privilege of this Convention happened on Monday evening. The six seminary presidents and their wives had invited all of the former presidents of the seminaries, and their wives, to be their guests for dinner. The dinner was presided over by Russell Dilday, the current chairman of the presidents' group. It was a delightful affair. Duke McCall and Harold Graves represented a longtime friendship and seminary tie. Frank Pollard and Bill Pinson, who came later as presidents, were also present. It was a special time.

President Edwin Young, pastor of the Second Baptist Church of Houston, called the 136th session to order on Tuesday morning at 8:30. I will note here that he did an excellent job in presiding over the Convention. Seeking to be fair, he moved the business right along. The registration secretary indicated that there were 13,502 messengers who were certified by the churches and already enrolled. The customary motion that these messengers constitute the Convention was passed. Final registration would be 17,768. In 1979, there had only been 15,760 messengers.

The president presented three welcome addresses. Mayor Bob Lanier of Houston was first. Then Mary Lou Retton Kelley, the olympic gymnast and gold medalist, and her husband gave a fine Christian testimony. These addresses were followed by John Bisagno, pastor of the First Baptist Church of Houston. All of the addresses were brief, but they set a good tone for the Convention.

The Program Committee had planned for the various sessions to have the theme "For Such a Time as This," with a different emphasis being given at each session. Each sermon was very inspirational and was about fifteen minutes long. In the opening session, Charles Fuller of the First Baptist Church in Roanoke, Virginia, spoke on the topic, "We Need the Church's Holy Priesthood." It was a very fine message about the "Priesthood of the Believer." Fuller has had one of the greatest pastorates in the Convention.

At this point, the president announced that the time had come for the introduction of the business and resolutions. Even now, it is amazing to me how many different things are on the minds of individuals. In our Baptist way, any messenger can make a motion about any matter that is in good taste. Among the subjects in this early introduction were vacancies and resignations on boards, Bylaw 17, homosexuality, abortion, the qualifications of the Convention parliamentarian, and the matter of Free-Masonry, which was already a controversy, and a time had been set for its discussion. There were many references to the President of the United States and his views; actions taken by the Convention on these matters will be discussed further along. At this point, motions must be in writing, brought to the table, and a time set up by the Committee on Order of Business in order to be discussed. Motions would be correlated, recommended for referral to various agencies, or declared out of order. All of this procedure was to establish the structure.

The report of the Executive Committee accounting for their year's work and recommending actions for the Convention came next. The first recommendation concerned the Southern Baptist Convention program allocation budget. Without a dissenting voice, we adopted a 1993 budget proposal of $138,234,735.

Recommendation 4 and its proposed amendments was the first recommendation to draw discussion. It concerned a change in Article 3 of our constitution regarding membership. The recommendation contained this phrase, "among churches not in cooperation with the Convention or churches which act to affirm, approve, or endorse homosexual behavior." This was the *first time* that we, for whatever cause, had officially put a rejection of churches in our constitution. After the discussion for and against, the constitutional change was approved.

The morning session concluded with the President's Address entitled "Side Streets."

The Tuesday afternoon session included a theme devotion called "The Church's Spirit of Cooperation," by Adrian Rogers of Tennessee.

The first election of officers was for the office of president. Ed Young was elected for a second term by acclamation. The remaining recommendations of the Executive Committee were considered. Motions made in the second session were committed to the care of the Committee on Order of Business.

The afternoon session concluded with the election of the first vice-president. Jay Strack was elected with 77.63 percent of the votes. Of the 17,444 messengers who were registered by this time, 47.29 percent voted in the election.

The seminaries, in reporting to the Convention, did so in two separate sessions. On Tuesday evening, there was a visual presentation by the six seminaries under the title, "Challenge to Biblical Preparation." It was highlighted by testimonies, music, and personal challenges. The president of Southeastern, Paige Patterson, who spoke on behalf of the six presidents, gave an invitation at the conclusion of the thirty-minute presentation. He invited those who were interested in responding to a call to volunteer service, or for theological training, to come forward.

Following this presentation, the Sunday School Board had more than a hour of visual presentations, drama, multi-media, and music.

This presentation was under the leadership of James Draper.

Wednesday morning, the theme was interpreted by Richard Land, as he spoke on "The Church's Freedom."

The seminaries' second report of forty-minutes majored on a recognition of Roy Honeycutt, who had served for several years as president of Southern Seminary. A visual presentation presented the accomplishments of a rich leadership. It focused, too, upon the introduction of their new President, Albert Mohler, Jr., of Kentucky. Following this, the other five seminaries gave a very brief statement of their institutions and their blessings.

It was at this session that the previously planned discussion of Free-Masonry was introduced. The year before, there had been an introduction of a motion calling for a study of Masonry as being anti-Christian. The study conducted by the Home Mission Board refused to condemn Free-Masonry. It became a major matter at the Convention; but after much discussion, the resolution, which was a sensible one presented by the Home Mission Board, was adopted, having said that Free-Masonry was not a religion or cult.

We began the report of the Resolutions Committee during the Wednesday morning session. Two major concerns surfaced during the Convention. In light of our national scene, it should have been expected. The Convention, in unmistakable terms, declared homosexuality a sin according to the Bible. The constitutional rejection of churches that openly approved homosexuality strained at our Baptist polity.

In this connection, there was what I regarded as an ugly chapter in the Convention. There was an attempt by some to blame Immanuel Baptist Church in Little Rock for the positions taken by the President of the United States concerning homosexuality and abortion. There had never been any suggestion that these positions were church-approved positions. Motions suggesting that the church should exclude the President seemed to be in very poor taste, and were contrary to any understanding of our Baptist way. The church is and has always been autonomous.

The pastor of the church, who is one of our finest, spent almost thirty minutes meeting with the Credentials Committee of the Convention to set forth the position of the church where President Clinton had been, and is, a faithful member. There was an organized demonstration of those who were against the church outside the Convention Hall one evening. In my mind that was wrong and was entirely out of the purview of our Baptist position.

One of the finest hours of the Convention was on Wednesday evening in the presentation of our home mission and foreign mission witness. This had been traditionally true; but in the past few years, there had been some change. The truly heartening, exciting, and promising moment of the Convention was the announcement that Jerry Rankin, who was an area missionary for Southeast Asia of the Foreign Mission Board, had been elected the board's president.

This meeting of that board took place on Monday afternoon and lasted four hours. Rankin had been accused of being charismatic and of speaking in tongues, which he stoutly denied. At the same time, he affirmed the validity of spiritual gifts in the Scriptures. Seventy-five percent of the vote of the board was required. He was elected with eighty percent of the votes. Judge Paul Pressler of Houston, who voted against him, then moved to make the election unanimous.

One of the fine messages of the Convention was given on Thursday morning when Frank Pollard, interpreting the theme, spoke on the topic, "We Need the Church's Moral Witness." It was a fine, fresh, and challenging message.

My overall evaluation of the Convention was upbeat. There was a positive note as they spoke about 250,000 baptisms in our foreign churches for the first time. By looking at the finances, it was hard to believe that people were talking about the same Convention. The largest ever home mission offering had been received.

Our seminary luncheon on Wednesday afternoon was, as always, a wonderful fellowship. More than eight hundred attended, and there was the mark of the Southwestern family everywhere.

Like the other Conventions, there were the entirely personal privileges. There were people who were present at the Convention who covered the period of sixty years. They came to us to say "thank you," and to extend Christian fellowship and love. Much of that love was rooted in the seminary. One man came to me and said that he was in Ouachita College in 1937 when I was called to the pastorate of the First Baptist Church in Arkadelphia. He was present at the meeting and voted for my call. Indeed, there had been long shadows cast.

New Testament churches are to be "meeting" churches. The miracle of grace is that we meet not as a hierarchy, but as a fellowship.

The Southern Baptist Convention adjourned its 136th session, having agreed to meet in Orlando, Florida, on June 14, 1994.

$\mathscr{S}$outhern $\mathscr{B}$aptist $\mathscr{C}$onvention

Orange County Convention Center • Orlando, Florida

JUNE 14-16

1994

SINCE MY FIRST ACQUAINTANCE WITH
FLORIDA, THAT STATE HAD ALWAYS
BEEN A PLACE WHICH I LOVED TO VISIT.
Its moderate and contrasting climate and its lush green beauty produced a mindset peculiar to its citizens. The amazing vitality of the churches had always made it a privilege. As far as the Southern Baptist Convention was concerned, it had always met in Miami or Miami Beach since 1946. This time we were going to Orlando. Orlando was said to have more hotel rooms than any other city in America. People thought of Disneyland, Epcot Center, MGM Studio, and a world of other attractions. It is also a vital Southern Baptist city.

We could go to a meeting of the Southern Baptist Convention anywhere, and I would be keenly interested. There was to be something different about this one. We were meeting in the context of denominational controversy and upset. There had been other Conventions when the denominational context had quickly determined the agenda, but this more than any that comes to memory. On March 9, the trustees of Southwestern Baptist Theological Seminary had abruptly and summarily dismissed President Russell Dilday. The fashion of it had caused a storm of protest within and without the seminary. The trustees had voted twenty-seven to six to terminate his presidency. They explained that the source of the conflict was long-standing.

In addition, the Cooperative Baptist Fellowship, referred to as the Moderates, had achieved a sharper identity. The question of receiving funds, that had been first sent to them and through them, was of prime concern. Apprehension was inevitable.

At every opportunity, I had urged our Southwestern family to remember that the seminary itself was more important than Naylor,

295

Dilday, or any seminary president. We needed to keep our eyes upon the charge given to Southwestern Seminary by God, and blessed of God through these eighty-six years.

There is an even more personal matter for us. Earlier in the year Rebekah had been notified that she had been named to receive the Distinguished Alumnus Award from the seminary at our Southwestern Seminary Luncheon in Orlando. The response of friends had been overwhelming, and Rebekah herself was with us to attend the Convention.

We decided to leave on Saturday, June 11. The airfare was so much less that way, and we would have an opportunity to spend some time in Orlando. Our plane moved out into a waiting position for takeoff just after 1:00 P.M. Almost three hours later, we were still sitting there. A violent thunderstorm had swept across the airport, and the authorities had refused to approve departures until that hour. So we arrived almost three hours late on Saturday evening. It proved to be a hospitable city, and from the first, we were well treated in our hotel just across the boulevard from the Convention Center.

Early Monday morning we registered. Registration had become something else in our Convention. They examined your credentials very carefully. You must have been elected formally by your church as a messenger, the church must have been in cooperation with the Convention, and so forth. Since ten was the maximum number of messengers allowed from a church, Goldia had not been a messenger for several years. But this time, both of us registered. We spent a good deal of time at our Southwestern Seminary booth and were greeted by hundreds of the Southwestern Seminary family to express appreciation for the seminary and for us. It had become a very humbling and awesome expression of privilege to have served the seminary and to still be a vital part of the family.

The Pastors' Conference with its long list of inspirational speakers was in session. The Woman's Missionary Union was also in session. There were other groups meeting through Monday.

The Convention itself was called to order Tuesday morning June 14, at 8:30. President H. Edwin Young, pastor of Second Baptist Church in Houston, Texas, called the 137th session to order. The Convention theme was "For I Know—He Is Able" (2 Tim. 1:12).

The formalities are always worth a paragraph. The secretary of the Convention reported 15,551 messengers already registered and made the motion that formally constituted this session of the Convention, together with those who were likewise certified as messengers. The final number would be 20,370. The Committee on Order of Business received formal approval of the established order. They had inserted at various times in the program periods for business, which meant the heart of the Convention's activities.

The first of these was in the middle of the Tuesday morning session, prior to the report of the Executive Committee. Messengers were allowed simply to introduce motions, no discussion, and offer resolutions, mostly unread, in order that the committee might set a time for the discussion of all of these. As might have been expected, the first three motions made had to do with our seminary hurt. There was one that called for the resignation of the three trustee officers of the seminary. There was another that simply called for disciplinary action. There was a third that called on the Convention to affirm the action of the trustees, and to recognize the courage of their decision. It was later announced that these motions would be those first considered at 7:40 on Tuesday evening.

There was also a motion in this first long session concerning "funds received from the Cooperative Baptist Fellowship or any deliberative body in competition with the Convention."

As usual there followed the report of the Executive Committee, reflecting their year's work, and making recommendations to the Convention. I still marvel at the fact that the first recommendation, one that presented the 1994-1995 Cooperative Program budget, was received and approved unanimously without a dissenting voice. It called for over $136 million dollars. When I thought of the lean days of the Convention, I simply marvelled at the grace of God, and thought how little fitting it was that we should be quarreling among ourselves when God had so abundantly blessed us.

The morning session concluded with a sermon by President H. Edwin Young. Let me say at this point that he did an excellent job of presiding at the Convention. His spirit was excellent, his presiding positive and affirmative.

In these last years, we had always pointed toward the election of a president. There was a little different twist to this one. Fred Wolfe of Mobile, Alabama, was a valid candidate of the Fundamental faction of the Convention. James Henry, pastor of the First Baptist Church, Orlando, likewise considered a Conservative, had suddenly

1994 Southern Baptist Convention meeting exhibit area. Courtesy—Texas Baptist Historical Collection.

become the candidate of those who felt that he would move in a more Moderate direction. In reporting the ballots that elected Henry, it was said that ninety percent of the 19,868 messengers voted in the election. Some wanted to call the election an upset, but personally I did not consider it that.

There was another business session shortly afterwards. A host of motions was introduced. One was nearby when Clyde Glazner, pastor of Gambrell Street Baptist Church in Fort Worth, Texas, introduced a motion concerning the amendment of Bylaw 21, which specifies the choice of the Committee on Committees. He thought each state should name its own representation. The Convention rejected that.

The result of the presidential election was delayed until the evening session so that the election of a first vice-president had to likewise be delayed. Let me dispose of the elections here by saying that results were a bit unusual. Simon Tsoi of Arizona was declared first vice-president without opposition. The second vice-president, Gary Frost, elected on a run-off ballot, was an African-American. The president referred to the "Rainbow Coalition" to which the people responded in good humor.

There followed Tuesday evening what I considered to be the most far-reaching decision made in the Convention. This could be my personal involvement. President Young called into consideration the three motions that had been made concerning the seminary hurt. In conjunction with one of these, he had come up with this motion, "That the newly elected Convention president will appoint a committee of seven to investigate the process used in dismissing Dr. Dilday of Southwestern Seminary with attention being given to the proper use of authority, due process, fairness, and any other significant facts. This committee will report and bring a recommendation to the 1995 annual meeting of the Convention."

The motion had the blessing of a popular and persuasive president and presiding officer. He sought to be fair, but it was obvious in the discussion that he highly approved this solution. From my perspective, the idea that the matter would linger for a year, continue to be a thorn in the side of the Convention, indicated that the well-being of the seminary, unintentionally, did not have priority. Under those circumstances, you would almost assume that the motion would pass.

It was supported by Adrian Rogers immediately. O. S. Hawkins, the new pastor of First Baptist Church, Dallas, very courageously spoke out against the motion, indicating that it was time to move in recognition of the basic vital strength of the seminary. After full and equal discussion, a vote was taken by hands and declared to be indecisive. We must cast a ballot.

Even at an evening session, there were 9,741 votes cast by ballot. By a thousand votes the Convention rejected the motion, thus indicating that they were ready to move on with the main business. Though the Convention later adopted a resolution commending the trustees of all our agencies and encouraging them to do those things required of them in the right spirit, there was never again a mention of our seminary difficulty. God had delivered us and caused us to set our eyes again upon that which lay before us.

The matter of funds was the major consideration of Wednesday morning. There were those who believed this to be the most significant action of the Convention. The motion as discussed was, "I move that the Southern Baptist Convention direct agencies and institutions to maintain fidelity to the Convention, to avoid compromising the integrity of the Cooperative Program, and to decline to receive funds channeled through the Cooperative Baptist Fellowship."

When the Convention finally acted on Thursday morning, it was to approve the motion. It was important, as I listened to the discussion, that we understand that this was money channeled *through* the Cooperative Baptist Fellowship. Any Southern Baptist church seeking to give to a recognized Southern Baptist cause could do so directly and have it regarded as a designated gift. There was no problem at this point.

The basic thought was that money channeled through the Cooperative Baptist Fellowship, in being received, recognized the validity of a competitive organization to the Cooperative Program. It does undoubtedly sharpen the outline of the new structure. There will be churches that will decide to be only Cooperative Baptist Fellowship churches. I agreed with those who said we should treat these with respect, recognize them as a people separated by their own choice, and stay in our Southern Baptist Convention mainstream of a witness to a lost world.

Though I have saved it for almost a final consideration, I would want to mention the Southwestern Baptist Theological Seminary Alumni Luncheon on Wednesday at noon. This time of meeting was customary. The fashion of the meeting for us was extraordinary. There are three doctors in Orlando that have been a part of the work of Bangalore Baptist Hospital, and also very personal friends. Dr. and Mrs. Hellinger had actually been members of the staff in that first year of the hospital when Rebekah first went to Bangalore. Now he is a cardiologist in Orlando and they were there as our guests.

Dr. and Mrs. Roy Pearson had been at the hospital, he to give his services on three different occasions. He brought knee joints and hip joints and did replacements in the hospital. He and Mrs. Pearson had celebrated their twenty-fifth wedding anniversary in Bangalore. They were also in attendance.

Dr. and Mrs. Joe Pipkin, he a dentist, had been there many times. He had in fact donated the dental clinic to the hospital which is also located in the hospital. All of them are world witnesses and their presence as our guests was an unusual privilege.

Our son Dick and his wife Nancy were there from Austin, Texas. Millie Kohn, formerly a member of the staff of First Baptist Church, Dallas, and lifetime friend, together with her sister, Jo Littlejohn, were there. The Naylor privilege could not be overemphasized.

Roberta Damon of Virginia was the president and in charge. She made a very personal and warm expression of appreciation for Dr. Russell Dilday to which the more than six hundred present made enthusiastic response. Then there was the recognition of Rebekah, the first family to have three Distinguished Service Alumni.

Rebekah's unusual gift of speech was manifest in her response. The approbation of the alumni was a bit overwhelming.

Prior to the Convention there had been some controversy due to the fact that in an ecumenical, national meeting, two of our agency heads had signed an accord with the Catholics that actually did not compromise our Baptist position. The ecumenical note of it had left a great host of us uneasy. So this, too, became a matter of major address. We reaffirmed our basic doctrines, our differences with Catholics, and at the same time our desire to work with any who follow the Lord Jesus, who accept His saving grace, to join them in a witness anywhere in this world.

The Convention ended Thursday noon, and we returned immediately to Fort Worth. In retrospect, there was hope. It seemed to me that the prospect of healing was very real. Our own beloved seminary, to which I owe a lasting and immeasurable debt, appeared to be weathering the storm, and we would move on. There was a willingness to seek the leadership of God in selecting another president.

In Retrospect

IN 1995 WE HAVE ARRIVED AT THE SESQUICENTENNIAL YEAR OF THE SOUTHERN BAPTIST CONVENTION. WHEN WE GATHER IN ATLANTA IN JUNE 1995, THE CONVENTION will be 150 years of age. In the midst of that, I want to remember that I have been a Southern Baptist seventy-six plus years. That means that for more than half of the Convention's life, I have been a member of a church in cooperation with the Convention. What has God taught me in the privileges we have shared in this document?

Like every Christian pilgrimage, the dominant, emergent thing is hope. God has taught through our valleys and on our mountain tops that He has not deserted Southern Baptists, that He has the answer to our divisions, that there awaits a better day, if we will claim it. In some places I have found a disposition to despair as though we could not again be one people. Let me encourage you to look up and believe that God will lead us through.

When the Southern Baptist Convention was organized, the word "Convention" was not easily accepted. The idea of convention, no hierarchies, no dominant sources of power or authority, authority resident only in the fellowship of the body, was absolutely extraordinary. It remains that to this hour. We are a convention, finding its flesh and blood in conventions.

Our instruction is still the same. It is "into all the world." No people anywhere are exempt from our personal and corporate witness. The Bible also urges, "Forsake not the assembling of yourselves together." We need each other. There is a plus dimension given to us by God. His promises are equally constant and unchanging. He is with us always. It is still "'not by might, not by power, but by my Spirit,' saith the Lord of Hosts." That provides hope.

Our divisions, as they always do, multiply. It is a bit like shattered glass picked up at any point. It is an object in itself. Almost every meeting together of our Southern Baptist people finds a new organization emerging. We do not need new organizations. We need to be one people. I have tried to insist in all of this, that just to be a Southern Baptist is more than life itself can bring.

Let us be Convention-ers again, recover that sense of privilege in gathering. Let us sing with a sense of the overflow, "All Hail the Power of Jesus' Name." Let us go to the Convention. I am excited that God has given me the privilege of attendance. My church has chosen me as a messenger to the 1995 session of the Southern Baptist Convention. Remember—a messenger—not a delegate.